LANGUAGES AND COMMUNITIES IN EARLY MODERN EUROPE

D1574970

In this magisterial new study, Peter Burke explores the social and cultural history of the languages spoken or written in Europe between the invention of printing and the French Revolution, arguing that, from a linguistic point of view, 1450 to 1789 should be regarded as a distinct period.

One major theme of the book is the relation between languages and communities (regions, churches, occupations and genders, as well as nations) and the place of language as a way of identifying others, as well as a symbol of one's own identity. A second, linked theme is that of competition: between Latin and the vernaculars, between different vernaculars, dominant and subordinate, and finally between different varieties of the same vernacular, such as standard languages and dialects.

Written by one of Europe's leading cultural historians, this book replaces the history of the many languages of Europe in a large variety of contexts.

PETER BURKE is Professor of Cultural History and a Fellow of Emmanuel College, University of Cambridge. He has published over twenty books, which have been translated into over thirty languages.

The 2002 Wiles Lectures given at Queen's University, Belfast

LANGUAGES AND COMMUNITIES IN EARLY MODERN EUROPE

PETER BURKE

CAMBRIDGE
UNIVERSITY PRESS

PUBLISHED BY THE PRESS SYNDICATE OF THE UNIVERSITY OF CAMBRIDGE
The Pitt Building, Trumpington Street, Cambridge, United Kingdom

CAMBRIDGE UNIVERSITY PRESS
The Edinburgh Building, Cambridge, CB2 2RU, UK
40 West 20th Street, New York, NY 10011–4211, USA
477 Williamstown Road, Port Melbourne, VIC 3207, Australia
Ruiz de Alarcón 13, 28014 Madrid, Spain
Dock House, The Waterfront, Cape Town 8001, South Africa

http://www.cambridge.org

First published 2004

Printed in the United Kingdom at the University Press, Cambridge

Typeface Adobe Garamond 11/12.5 pt.   *System* LATEX 2$_\varepsilon$ [TB]

A catalogue record for this book is available from the British Library

Library of Congress Cataloguing in Publication data
Burke, Peter.
Languages and communities in early modern Europe / by Peter Burke.
p.   cm. – (The Wiles lectures given at the Queen's University, Belfast)
Includes bibliographical references and index.
ISBN 0 521 82896 1 – ISBN 0 521 53586 7 (pbk.)
1. Sociolinguistics – Europe – History.   I. Title.   II. Wiles lectures.
P40.45.E85B87   2004
306.44′094 – dc22   2004045499

ISBN 0 521 82896 1 hardback
ISBN 0 521 53586 7 paperback

PARA
MARIA LÚCIA

Contents

Acknowledgements

In the first place, my thanks are due to the Wiles Trust and the Department of History, Queen's University Belfast, for the invitation to deliver the Wiles Lectures for 2002 and for their hospitality during my time in Belfast. Peter Jupp in particular went out of his way to make me feel at home during that memorable week.

The Wiles Trust generously allow their lecturers to invite eight guests who participate in the often lively seminars that follow each of the public sessions. I am grateful to my eight interlocutors for pertinent questions, observations and references: to Robert Evans, Felipe Fernandez-Armesto, Angel Gurría Quintana, Steve Milner, Robert Muchembled, Jens Rahbeck Rasmussen, Herman Roodenburg and Robert St George. Ian Kershaw also made a memorable contribution to the discussions.

Other friends and colleagues have offered much-appreciated assistance. Mark Phillips suggested that I add the chapter on 'discovery'. Xavier Gil, György Gömöri, Richard Helgerson, Liesbeth van Houts, Simon Keynes, Berthold Kress, Metin Kunt, David Wallace, Kit Woolard and Ghil'ad Zuckermann all offered comments or references which I have tried to take into account. Xavier also gave me books about Catalan that were difficult to obtain in England and allowed me to read his unpublished essay: 'Political and Apolitical Uses of Language in Early Modern Spain'. Alessandra Mantovani sent me her edition of Pontano on language at the very moment I most needed it. Hanne Sanders sent me books about Skåne in the seventeenth century, while Harold Gustafsson allowed me to read and use an unpublished chapter of his on the same subject. Participants in my Cambridge seminars on the social history of language, including two colleagues from the neighbouring Faculty of Modern and Medieval Languages, Wendy Bennett and Virginia Cox, offered some stimulating ideas.

I am also grateful to the audiences who discussed chapters of this book presented as lectures in Båstad, Budapest, Canterbury, Dublin, Heidelberg,

Helsinki, London, Oxford, Santa Barbara and Vienna, as well as to my hosts on all these pleasant occasions.

Looking further back, it is impossible not to mention the late and much lamented Roy Porter, with whom I collaborated on three volumes of essays on language and who should have been around to comment on this one in his inimitable way. Still further back, I think of my father, a sometime professional translator, whose boast it was that he had been introduced at a party as 'the man who had forgotten twenty languages'. I suppose that I have been trying to emulate him all this time without realizing it.

Returning to the present and the future, I dedicate this book to my wife, Maria Lúcia, with whom I began the adventure of introducing a foreign language into everyday life.

Chronology 1450–1794

1461	first printed book in German
1468	first printed book in Czech
1471	first printed book in Italian
1474	first printed book in English
1474	first printed book in Catalan
c. 1476	first printed book in French
1477	first printed book in Flemish
1483	first printed book in Croat
1483	first printed book in Church Slavonic
c. 1483	first printed book in Spanish
1489	first printed book in Portuguese
1492	Nebrija, *Gramática castellana* (the first printed grammar of a vernacular)
1495	first printed book in Danish
1495	first printed book in Swedish
1499	first printed book in Breton
1501	first printed book in Provençal
1515	Castellesi, *De sermone latino*
1522	first printed book in Polish
1522–34	Luther's Bible
1525	Bembo, *Prose della vulgar lingua*
1525	first printed book in Latvian
1526	first printed book in post-classical Greek
1527	first printed book in Hungarian
1529	Amaseo, *De latinae linguae usu retinendo*
1529	Dante, *De vulgari eloquentia*, published
1529	Trissino, *Poetica*
1529	Tory, *Champfleury*
1530	Palsgrave, *Lesclaircissement de la langue francoyse*
1532	Welsh forbidden in court

1579–93	Kralice Bible
1579	Czech reaffirmed as the language of courts in Bohemia
1581	Fauchet, *Origine de la langue française*
1582	Stevin, *Weerdigheyt der duytsche tael*
1583	Accademia della Crusca founded
1584	Bohorič, *Arcticae Horulae* (Slovene grammar)
1584	Spieghel, *Nederduitsche Letterkunst*
1585	Morales, *Discurso sobre la lengua castellana*
1588	Geneva Bible
1588	Welsh Bible
1589	Rybinski, *De lingua polonica praestantia*
1590	Hungarian Bible
1592	Rhys, Welsh grammar
1596	Zizanij, *Gramatika slovenska*
1600	Cittadini, *Formazione della lingua toscana*
1604	Aldrete, *Del origen y principio de la lengua castellana*
1604	Kašić, *Institutiones linguae illyricae*
1606	Biffi, *Prissian da Milan*
1606	Nunes de Leão, *Origem da língua portuguesa*
1608	Estates of Bohemia declared Czech to be the official language
1611	Authorized Version
1612–23	*Vocabolario della Crusca*
1612	Beni, *Anticrusca*
1615	Carew, *On the Excellency of the English Tongue*
1617	Fruchtbringende Gesellschaft founded
1619	Smotrickii, *Grammatiki slavenskija syntagma*
1625	first printed book in Russian
1626	Banchieri, *Discorso della lingua Bolognese*
1635	foundation of Académie Française
1637	Dutch States' Bible
1638	St-Evremond, *Comédie des académistes*
1641	sermons in Castillian prohibited in Catalonia (after revolt)
1641	governor-general's edict that slaves could only wear hats and caps if they could speak Dutch
1642	Finnish Bible
1642	Rist, *Rettung der edlen Teutschen*
1643	Stiernhielm, *Gambla svea*
1644	Rehehusen, *Manuductio ad linguam lettonicam*
1646	Pontoppidan, *Grammatica danica*

1647	Vaugelas, *Remarques sur la langue française*
1649	first printed book in Sami
1649	*Lingua finnica institutio*
1651	Jonas, *Grammatica islandica*
1651	Dupleix, *Liberté de la langue française*
1653	Klein, *Grammatica Lituanica*
1659	Maunoir, Breton grammar
1660	Gösekenius, *Manuductio ad linguam Oesthonicam*
1662	'Partenio Tosco', *Eccellenza della lingua napoletana*
1663	Schottel, *Lob der Teutschen Haubtsprache*
1670	Balbín, *Dissertatio apologetica pro lingua slavonica praecipue bohemica* (written)
1674	Ray, *Collection of English Words*
1677	Rudbeck began lecturing in Swedish
1678	Karl XI ordered the former Danish provinces to use Swedish
1684	French used in court in Flanders
1685	French the administrative language of Alsace
1687	Thomasius announced lectures in German
1693	Callières, *Mots à la mode*
1694	*Dictionnaire de l'Académie Française*
1694	Sperling, *De danicae linguae antiqua gloria*
1696	Polish the sole administrative language of the Commonwealth
1696	Ludolf, *Grammatica russica*
1700	first printed book in Cornish
1707	first printed book in Manx
1708	reform of Russian alphabet
1713	Real Academia Española founded
1716	Egenolff, *Historie der Teutschen Sprache*
1726–39	Spanish Academy, *Diccionario de la lengua castellana*
1729	first printed book in Turkish
1734	chair in Italian eloquence founded at Turin
1735	Trediakovsky, speech in praise of Russian
1743	Richey, *Idioticon hamburgense*
1751	Ribinyi, *De cultura linguae hungaricae*
1755	Johnson, *A Dictionary of the English Language*
1755	Lomonosov, *Russian Grammar*
1757	Trediakovsky, *O pervenstve slovenskago yazyka pred teutonicheskim* (written)

1757	Portuguese made official language in Brazil
1767	Russian declared the language of instruction at Moscow University
1768	Charles III required Castilian in administration and education
1779	Galiani, *Del dialetto napoletano*
1783	Russian Academy founded
1784	German made official language in Habsburg Empire
1784	Rivarol, *Discours sur l'universalité de la langue française*
1786	Swedish Academy founded
1786	*Linguarum totius orbis vocabularia*
1789–94	Russian Academy's *Russian Dictionary*
1790	Joseph II revoked decree of 1784
1792	Dobrovský, *Geschichte der böhmischen sprache*
1793	Chair of Czech founded at Prague University
1793	J. Vargas y Ponce, *Declamación contra los abusos introducidos en el castellano*
1794	Gregoire, *Rapport*

Prologue: communities and domains

The principal aim of this book is to reflect on the changing relations between language and community, or, more exactly, between languages and communities in the plural, in Europe and other areas in which European languages were spoken, from the invention of printing to the French Revolution. This is not a general survey of the history of the languages of Europe in the early modern period so much as a series of linked essays (originally lectures) on a few major strands in that history.

Today, language is a topical subject. Indeed, the year 2001 was officially declared the 'European Year of Language'. There should be little need to remind anyone of the links between language and politics, or, better, the entanglement of language with politics at a time when phrases such as 'language rights' and 'identity politics' have recently entered our everyday speech. At a time of involvement, this book makes an attempt at detachment or distanciation, *reculer pour mieux sauter*.

Why should a cultural historian write about language? Why not leave the topic to the linguists? For one thing, because language is always a sensitive indicator – though not a simple reflection – of cultural change. In this respect, the history of linguistic borrowings (below, pp. 111ff.) is suggestive. What English borrowed from Italian in the sixteenth and seventeenth centuries, especially artistic terms such as *aria*, *chiaroscuro*, *fresco* and *piazza*, tells us something about both cultures, about Italian leadership in the arts and about English interest in catching up. In similar fashion, eighteenth-century French borrowings from English, notably political terms such as 'budget', 'club', 'jury', 'pamphlet' and 'vote', point to differences between the two political cultures and also to a movement of Anglophilia in France.

This book might be described as an essay in the 'cultural history of language', at a time when all history seems to be becoming cultural history. Some linguists speak of 'language culture' (especially in German,

Sprachkultur), to refer to a complex or system of attitudes to language and images of languages to be found in a given place and time.[1]

THE SOCIAL HISTORY OF LANGUAGE

The question a sociologist or a social historian wants to ask at this point is, of course, whose culture? A similar point may be made about studies of language consciousness, *Sprachbewusstsein*. Whose consciousness?

To sum up the last two hundred years of language studies in a simple formula, the famous historical turn of the nineteenth century has been followed by the structural and social turns of the mid-twentieth century, and more recently by the socio-historical turn of the 1980s and 1990s.

Nineteenth-century historians tended to focus on national unity and to write about the 'evolution' or the 'growth' of a given language as if it were a plant or animal, without concerning themselves over-much with social variation. By contrast, the advances in the social analysis of language made in the 1950s and 1960s were accompanied by a turning away from history. Individual sociolinguists or sociologists of language, including Robert Hall, Dell Hymes and Joshua Fishman, retained an interest in history. Fishman, for instance, was trained as a historian and has continued to draw on historical material.[2] Perhaps the best example to date of a serious attempt to combine a linguistic, a social and a historical analysis dates from this time, the Neapolitan Tullio De Mauro's *Linguistic History of United Italy*.[3] All the same, the thrust of the sociolinguistic approach was away from history, a trend that was due in part to the influence of structuralism and in part to the ethnographic emphasis on fieldwork in small communities.

More recently, a return to history has become visible, notably in studies of pidgins, creoles and mixed languages (p. 111).[4] More generally, one might even speak of the emergence, or invention, of a new field, which linguists have variously christened 'socio-historical linguistics', 'historical sociolinguistics' – something of a mouthful – or, more simply, 'historical

[1] Richard W. Bailey, *Images of English: a Cultural History of the Language* (Ann Arbor, 1991); Harald Weinrich, *Wege der Sprachkultur* (Stuttgart, 1985); Erich Strassner, *Deutsche Sprachkultur* (Tübingen, 1995). The term goes back to the linguists of the Prague Circle in the early 1930s.
[2] Joshua A. Fishman, *Language in Sociocultural Change* (New York, 1972), pp. xi–xii.
[3] Tullio De Mauro, *Storia linguistica dell'Italia unita* (1963: revised ed., Rome, 1991).
[4] Michael Richter, 'Towards a Methodology of Historical Sociolinguistics' (1985: repr. Richter, *Studies in Medieval Language and Culture*, Dublin, 1995), pp. 132–47; Peter Bakker and Maarten Mous (eds.), *Mixed Languages* (Amsterdam, 1994).

pragmatics' (a *Journal of Historical Pragmatics* was founded in the year 2000).[5]

My own preference, like that of some other historians and linguists, is for the 'social history of language'.[6] This phrase has the advantage of bringing the social functions of language into the open, leading on to a discussion of the place of language in expressing or constructing a variety of social relationships – dominance and subordination, friendship and fraternity, tolerance and prejudice, the maintenance and the subversion of a social order, and so on.

Whatever one calls this field, there is little doubt that it is growing fast. That the Regius Professor of Modern History at the University of Oxford should have devoted his inaugural lecture to the subject, in 1998, is an indicator of change.[7] Research groups in the field include one at the University College of Aberystwyth studying the social history of Welsh, another at the University of Helsinki working on 'Sociolinguistics and Language History', a third at the Free University of Berlin concerned with the 'Historical Anthropology of Language', and a fourth at the University of Lund focused on the 'History of the Modern Swedish Language in the Light of Social Change'. Work on the social history of language is also going on at the Vrije Universiteit in Brussels, at the Meertens Institute in Amsterdam, at the University of Campinas in Brazil, and doubtless in other countries as well.

The 'social history of language' may be a relatively new programme but, as is usually the case, the programme does not so much initiate the practice as follow it. An important contribution was made by an international community of linguists in classic studies published in the first half of the twentieth century, including Ferdinand Brunot on French, Christine Mohrmann and Josef Schrijnen on the Latin of the early Church, Peter Skautrup on Danish, Vladimir Vinogradov on Russian, and a French scholar who died young, Antoine Martel, on the conflict of languages in Ruthenia in the sixteenth and seventeenth centuries.[8]

[5] Suzanne Romaine, *Socio-historical Linguistics* (Cambridge, 1982); Klaus J. Mattheier, 'National-sprachentwicklung, Sprachenstandardisierung und historische Soziolinguistik', *Sociolinguistica* 2 (1988), pp. 1–9; Ernst H. Jahr (ed.), *Language Change: Advances in Historical Sociolinguistics* (Berlin, 1999).

[6] David Leith, *A Social History of English* (1983: second ed., London, 1997); Joey L. Dillard, *Toward a Social History of American English* (Berlin, 1985); Peter Burke and Roy Porter (eds.), *The Social History of Language* (Cambridge, 1987).

[7] Robert J. W. Evans, *The Language of History and the History of Language* (Oxford, 1998).

[8] Ferdinand Brunot, *Histoire de la langue française*, 12 vols. (Paris, 1905); Christine Mohrmann, *Die altchristliche Sondersprache in den Sermones des hl. Augustin* (Nijmegen, 1932); Josef Schrijnen,

Literary scholars have also been writing about the history of language for generations. Among them, the outstanding figure is surely the Russian Mikhail Bakhtin, whose study of Rabelais, begun in the 1930s but published only in 1965, led him to the study of what he called 'polyglossia' (the interaction between languages, such as Latin and Italian), and 'heteroglossia' (the interaction between different forms of the same language). Bakhtin criticized the linguists of his time for paying insufficient attention to social factors.[9]

Historians too have been making occasional contributions to language studies for some time. A major study published in 1975 by the French polymath Michel de Certeau, together with two historians, under the arresting and topical title, *Une politique de la langue*, was concerned with the relation between the French Revolution and the dialects of France, *les patois*.[10] This 'politics of language' approach has inspired a long series of later studies of the relations between the French language and the French Revolution (below, p. 165), revealing an interest that was doubtless inspired by contemporary language conflicts in France, Canada and elsewhere.[11]

Earlier studies by historians are not numerous but they include the work of some distinguished scholars, from Lucien Febvre to Américo Castro and Vivian Galbraith, and they deal with a range of topics, such as the language of the law, language and nationality, language and empire, and the language of diplomacy (the subject of two early articles, both in Swedish).[12]

Charakteristik des altchristlichen Latein (Nijmegen, 1932); Peter Skautrup, *Det danske sprogs historie*, 5 vols. (Copenhagen, 1944–70); Vladimir V. Vinogradov, *The History of the Russian Literary Language from the Seventeenth Century to the Nineteenth* (1949: condensed adaptation, Madison, 1969); Antoine Martel, *La langue polonaise dans les pays Ruthènes: Ukraine et Russie-Blanche, 1569–1667* (Lille, 1938).

[9] Mikhail M. Bakhtin ['V. S. Voloshinov'] *Marxism and the Philosophy of Language* (1929: English trans. New York, 1973); Bakhtin, *Rabelais and his World* (1965: English translation, Cambridge, MA, 1971); Erich Auerbach, *Literary Language and its Public* (1958: English translation, London, 1965); Paul Teyssier, *La langue de Gil Vicente* (Paris, 1959).

[10] Michel de Certeau, Jacques Revel and Dominique Julia, *Une Politique de la langue: la Révolution Française et les patois* (Paris, 1975).

[11] Jean-Yves Lartichaux, 'Linguistic Politics during the French Revolution', *Diogenes* 97 (1977), pp. 65–84; Patrice Higonnet, 'The Politics of Linguistic Terrorism', *Social History* 5 (1980), pp. 41–69; Martyn Lyons, 'Politics and Patois: the Linguistic Policy of the French Revolution', *Australian Journal of French Studies* (1981), pp. 264–81; Lorenzo Renzi, *La politica linguistica della rivoluzione francese* (Naples, 1981); Lynn Hunt, *Politics, Culture and Class in the French Revolution* (Berkeley, 1984), pp. 19–51; Henri Boyer and Philippe Gardy (eds.), *La question linguistique au sud au moment de la Révolution Française* (Montpellier, 1985) [special issue, no. 17, of *Lengas*]; Peter Flaherty, 'The Politics of Linguistic Uniformity during the French Revolution', *Historical Reflections* 14 (1987), pp. 311–28; David A. Bell, 'Lingua Populi, Lingua Dei: Language, Religion and the Origins of French Revolutionary Nationalism', *American Historical Review* 100 (1995), pp. 1403–37.

[12] T. Westrin, 'Några iakttagelser angående franskan såsom diplomatiens språk', *Historisk Tidskrift* 20 (1900), pp. 329–40; Lucien Febvre, 'Politique royale ou civilisation française? Remarques sur un

THE PROBLEM OF COMMUNITY

As the general title of the book suggests, the following pages will focus on the relation between languages and communities. 'Community' is at once an indispensable term and a dangerous one, whether we are practising history or sociology or simply living our everyday lives. In this respect, it is rather like the term 'identity', or indeed the word 'culture'. Sociolinguists would certainly find it difficult to do without the phrase 'speech community', or *Sprachgemeinschaft*, a term which came into use in German in the 1920s before spreading to English and other languages. The term is used to refer to the group – which may be as large as France or as small as a family – in which a particular language or variety of language is understood, a 'community of interpretation' as some literary critics call it.[13] The use of a particular variety of language expresses, maintains and even helps to create solidarity between the members of the group.

The danger of using the term 'community', again like 'culture', is that it seems to imply a homogeneity, a boundary and a consensus that are simply not to be found when one engages in research at ground level, whether this 'fieldwork' is historical, sociological or anthropological. So far as homogeneity is concerned, one of the main points to be made in this book concerns the variety of ways in which different social groups used the 'same' language. Again, the term 'community' seems to imply a sharp boundary between insiders and outsiders, whereas in practice the frontiers between languages are often vague, not so much lines as zones of bilingualism and language mixing. As for consensus, linguistic norms not infrequently hide conflicts and the dominance of one group over others.[14]

All the same, the term 'community' will recur again and again in this book. The point is not to deny linguistic, cultural or social conflicts, which will also recur in these pages, but to note that collective solidarities and identities are also a part of everyday life. To make the point in a linguistic

problème d'histoire linguistique', *Revue de synthèse historique* 38 (1924), pp. 37–53; Febvre, 'Langue et nationalité en France au 18e siècle', *Revue de synthèse historique* 42 (1926), pp. 19–40; Américo Castro, *La peculiaridad lingüística rioplatense y su sentido histórico* (Bucnos Aires, 1941); Vivian H. Galbraith, 'Language and Nationality in Medieval England', *Transactions of the Royal Historical Society* 23 (1941), pp. 113–28; Nils Ahnlund, 'Diplomatiens språk i Sverige', in his *Svenskt och Nordiskt* (Stockholm, 1943), pp. 114–22; George. E. Woodbine, 'The Language of English Law', *Speculum* 18 (1943), pp. 395–436.

[13] Karl Vossler, *Sprachgemeinschaft und Interessengemeinschaft* (Munich, 1924); Leonard Bloomfield, *Language* (New York, 1933), pp. 42–56; Joshua Fishman, *Sociolinguistics* (Rowley, MA, 1970), pp. 28–35.

[14] Louis-Jean Calvet, *Linguistique et colonialisme* (Paris, 1974); Calvet, *Language Wars and Linguistic Politics* (1987: English translation, Oxford, 1998); Ralph Grillo, *Dominant Languages: Language and Hierarchy in Britain and France* (Cambridge, 1989).

way, whenever we say 'we', we are expressing a sense of solidarity with some others, a sense of belonging to a community, whether it is small or large, temporary or permanent, harmonious or discordant. It might also be argued that solidarity and conflict are two sides of the same coin, and that conflicts between vernaculars encourage language loyalty and language consciousness.

If real communities are messy affairs, ideal ones – 'imagined communities', as Benedict Anderson has called them – have clear boundaries. Imagined communities, like other figments of the imagination, have real effects, and attempts to create communities by imposing a particular language or variety of language have important consequences, even if they are not always the consequences intended by the planners. Hence we have to examine the role of languages not only as expressions or reflections of a sense of community cohesion, but also as one of the means by which communities are constructed or reconstructed.[15]

The more distinctive the language, the more cohesive the community is likely to be, and vice versa. To speak of the English speech community in the singular has come to sound rather odd, and it is more useful to distinguish different communities and their 'Englishes'.[16]

It is also necessary to bear in mind the fact that individuals can and usually do belong to a number of different communities: local and national, religious, occupational and so on. Some of these communities are in competition, or even in conflict, for the loyalty of individual speakers – region versus nation, for instance. As socio-linguists have often pointed out, people use different forms or varieties of language, whether consciously or unconsciously, to express their solidarity with these different communities. This is a major reason for what is sometimes described as 'code-switching', the practice of shifting between languages or varieties of language.

Individual speakers may therefore be regarded as performing different 'acts of identity' according to the situation in which they find themselves.[17] In other words, a record of the language used by an individual on a particular occasion does not reveal his or her identity, let alone his or her national identity. It is no more than the record of the identity that came to the fore on that occasion.

[15] Benedict Anderson, *Imagined Communities* (1983: revised ed., 1991); Robert Le Page and Andrée Tabouret-Keller, *Acts of Identity* (Cambridge, 1985); Deborah Cameron, 'Demystifying Sociolinguistics: or why language does not reflect society', in John E. Joseph and Talbot J. Taylor (eds.), *Ideologies of Language* (London, 1990); Glyn Williams, *Sociolinguistics: a Sociological Critique* (London, 1992).

[16] Tom McArthur, *The English Languages* (Cambridge, 1998).

[17] Le Page and Tabourot-Keller, *Acts*.

Linguists often use the term 'diglossia' to describe the situation in which two or more languages or varieties of language are used by the same speakers in different 'speech domains', addressing different people or introducing different topics. One variety is typically more prestigious than the other, as in the case of classical and colloquial Arabic, with the high variety used for example to speak about religion, the lower about more mundane topics.[18] In the case of early modern Europe, examples include the use of French as a high variety by speakers of Occitan; Spanish by speakers of Catalan; German by speakers of Danish, and the general use of Latin for the discussion of scholarly topics. It is important to remember that the balance between languages or varieties is not a stable one and that it sometimes shifted in the course of the three centuries discussed below.

This pair of concepts, 'diglossia' and 'speech domain', will recur in the following pages. They are essential concepts in the approach followed here, concerned as it is with languages in the plural, with communities in the plural, and finally with a plurality of relations between the two.

THE COMPARATIVE APPROACH

The question, how many languages existed in early modern Europe, is at once obvious and deceptive. When is a language a language, and when is it a dialect? The classic answer takes the form of the epigram attributed to more than one famous linguist to the effect that a language is a dialect with an army, navy and air force. The political criterion is indeed an appropriate one in the case of the last two hundred or two hundred and fifty years, the age of what has been called the 'politicization of language', its increasingly close association with nations and nationalism (below, p. 166). It is much less applicable to early modern times.

In the early Middle Ages, the frontiers between Latin and the romance languages, or between different romance or Germanic or Slav languages, were still indefinite. Even in the early modern period, when print and other factors were contributing to the process of standardization, the frontiers between languages, like the frontiers between states, were less clear-cut than they became in the nineteenth and twentieth centuries.[19]

---

[18] Charles Ferguson, 'Diglossia', *Word* 15 (1959), pp. 325–40.
[19] Vaughan Cornish, *Borderlands of Language in Europe and their Relation to the Historic Frontiers of Christendom* (London, 1936); Michel Banniard, *Viva voce: communication écrite et communication orale du IVe au IXe siècle en occident latin* (Paris, 1992); Michael Richter, *Studies in Medieval Language and Culture* (Dublin, 1995).

Slovaks, for example, wrote in what we call 'Czech' and Norwegians wrote in what we call 'Danish'. It has been suggested that it might be more appropriate to refer to early modern 'Scandinavian' rather than to Danish, Swedish and Norwegian as separate languages.[20] A similar point might be made about the South Slav languages before the creation of 'Serbo-Croat' in the middle of the nineteenth century. Indeed, the sixteenth-century Polish chronicler Marcin Bielski treated all the Slavic languages as dialects of a single language.

It is hard to disagree with the French linguist Antoine Meillet when he declared it 'impossible' to say how many languages exist, or with the Norwegian linguist Einar Haugen when he admitted, in a classic essay on language and dialect, that 'there is no answer to these questions'.[21] If there is no precise or objective answer to the question, how many languages, it is surely better to offer a rough estimate than none at all. Five hundred years ago, from forty to seventy languages were spoken in Europe, forty according to a narrow definition and seventy according to a wider one (Appendix). It is worth noting that linguists today claim that there are from three thousand to five thousand languages in the world – a considerable margin of error or vagueness.

However counter-intuitive this may seem to Europeans, and in particular to anglophones, even seventy languages is a very small number compared to the eighty million people living in Europe in 1500 or the one hundred and eighty million living there in 1789. Today, the languages of Europe account for a mere 4 per cent of the world total, compared to 15 per cent in the Americas, 31 per cent in Africa and 50 per cent in Asia and the Pacific.[22] From the point of view of humanity, every language may be regarded a treasure, contributing something to the common stock of culture.[23] For a given region, however, this treasure is not necessarily an advantage, economically at any rate. Indeed, a case might be made for the existence of an inverse relationship in which poor regions are rich in languages and vice versa.

The historians who study the rise of the early modern West and, increasingly, of early modern China as well, might therefore be well advised to pay more attention to language. A relative lack of languages meant a relative

---

[20] Jahr, *Language Change*, p. 128.
[21] P. J. Antoine Meillet (1914) 'Le problème de la parenté des langues', repr. his *Linguistique historique et linguistique générale* (2 vols., Paris, 1921–38), vol. I, pp. 76–101, at 76; cf. Einar Haugen, 'Dialect, Language, and Nation' (1966: repr. *The Ecology of Language*, Stanford, 1972), pp. 237–54.
[22] David Crystal, *Language Death* (Cambridge, 2000).
[23] George Steiner, *After Babel* (Oxford, 1975).

lack of obstacles to communication. In 1600, China had a population of some one hundred and fifty million, larger than that of Europe at the time, but only one main written and spoken language, despite the presence of Cantonese and other languages in the South.

The overview presented here takes the form of an essay in comparative history. There is something of a paradox in offering a comparative history of language as a novelty, since pioneers in comparative history, notably Marc Bloch, learned this approach from linguists such as Antoine Meillet, who themselves stood in a tradition going back to the late eighteenth century, if not further.[24] Again, two Italian scholars, Riccardo Picchio and Aldo Scaglione, one of them a specialist on Slav languages and the other on German, have fruitfully extended the traditional Italian concept of language debate, *La questione della lingua*, to other parts of Europe.[25] More recently, the French linguist Daniel Baggioni, inspired by the historian Fernand Braudel to study change over the long term, has produced a comparative survey of European languages and nations over the last five hundred years.[26] All the same, a survey of the secondary literature reveals that studies of single languages predominate.

What follows is, I hope, a small step towards future surveys of the different tongues of Europe in interaction over the centuries, in other words (relatively new words) an 'ecology of language', placing language in its cultural and social environment, studying Latin in relation to the vernaculars, the vernaculars in relation to one another and the dialects of a given vernacular in relation to the standard language.[27] It is a reconnaissance of a large terrain, an attempt to produce a provisional map – including blank spaces where necessary – in the hope of encouraging further exploration.

THREE PROBLEMS

Such a history faces three major problems, which should be borne in mind throughout by the reader of this book, just as the author has tried to bear them in mind in the course of research and writing. They are the problem of periodization, the problem of evidence and the problem of explanation.

[24] L. Walker, 'A Note on Historical Linguistics and Marc Bloch's Comparative Method', *History and Theory* 19 (1980), pp. 154–64.

[25] Riccardo Picchio, 'Guidelines for a Comparative Study of the Language Question among the Slavs', in Picchio and Harvey Goldblatt (eds.), *Aspects of the Slavic Language Question*, 2 vols. (New Haven, 1984), vol. 1, pp. 1–42; Aldo Scaglione, 'The Rise of National Languages: East and West', in Scaglione (ed.), *The Emergence of National Languages* (Ravenna, 1984), pp. 9–49.

[26] Daniel Baggioni, *Langues et nations en Europe* (Paris, 1997).

[27] Einar Haugen, 'The Ecology of Language', repr. *Ecology*, pp. 325–39.

Every language has its own chronology. The use of Old Church Slavonic, for example, was at its height between 1100 and 1700. The Celtic languages went through their 'dark age' from around 1550 to around 1700. Norwegian scholars treat the years 1530–1814 as a discrete period in the history of their language, the time when it was dominated by Danish. In similar fashion, what is known as 'old Finnish' lasted from 1540 to 1820.[28] The problem then is to choose beginning and end dates for a book that attempts to deal with Europe as a whole.

In his recent study of languages and nations, Daniel Baggioni distinguished what he called three 'ecolinguistic' revolutions in European history, around the years 1500, 1800, and 2000.[29] My decision, not very different from his, is to begin in the middle of the fifteenth century with the printing press, since print had important consequences for written and even, in the long term, for spoken languages. The book ends in the later eighteenth century with the rise of national consciousness and language planning. In France, for instance, at the time of the Revolution, Henri Grégoire, a priest and a deputy to the National Assembly, advocated the teaching of French everywhere in France in order 'to melt the citizens into a national mass' (*fondre tous les citoyens dans une masse nationale*).[30]

Needless to say, a case might be made for other dates. For instance, 1492 is a date of obvious importance in the history of the languages of Europe as well as the New World. In the history of American English, 1776 is a significant date, like 1788 in that of the language of Australia, which has been described as 'English transported'.[31]

It is also important to note that major trends in the history of European languages had begun before Johann Gutenberg set up his press in Mainz, around the year 1450. For example, in some domains, such as the administration, Latin was being replaced by some vernaculars in the early fifteenth century (in the English chancery), in the fourteenth century, or even, in the case of the chancery of Castille, in the thirteenth century. In cases like these, the best thing is to transgress one's own boundaries.

The second major problem to be faced is the problem of evidence. This book is concerned with both written and spoken language. The evidence for the domain of writing and also for that of print is abundant enough. On the other hand, the problem of reconstructing the spoken language is

---

[28] Banfi, Emanuele (ed.), *La formazione dell' Europa linguistica* (Florence, 1993), pp. 164, 354; Didrik A. Seip, *Norwegische Sprachgeschichte* (Berlin, 1971); Aurélien Sauvageot, 'Le finnois de Finlande', in István Fodor and Claude Hagège (eds.), *Language Reform*, vol. III (Hamburg, 1984), pp. 173–90.
[29] Baggioni, *Langues*, pp. 47–50.   [30] Certeau, *Politique*.
[31] William S. Ramson (ed.), *English Transported* (Canberra, 1970).

an acute one. Essentially, historians have to use written evidence of speech while knowing that it cannot be fully trusted. Even historians of language in the twentieth century have had to grapple with this problem.[32]

In the age before the tape recorder, judicial records are the sources that give historians the opportunity to come closest to hearing the voices of ordinary people. The evidence of plays – including those of Shakespeare and Jonson, Lope de Vega and Molière, Holberg and Goldoni, who will all be called to give testimony in the following pages – is equally vivid, even if the representation of speech, especially in comedies, was probably stylized and stereotyped.[33]

Dictionaries of the period allow historians to avoid relying too exclusively on playwrights and satirists, since they offer valuable testimony to what the compilers and their circle considered to be low or high usage. For instance, Pierre Richelet's *Dictionnaire français* (1680) often comments that a particular term or phrase is 'bas', 'populaire', and so on, and Samuel Johnson's *Dictionary of the English Language* (1755) does the same.[34]

For a historian interested in language consciousness, to be discussed in chapter 1, there is also much to be learned from the descriptions of countries by foreign travellers, whose ears are sometimes well tuned to the distinctive qualities of local speech. For example, the Englishman Philip Skippon, making the Grand Tour of Italy in the 1660s together with his Cambridge tutor, John Ray, set down his (or their) observations on local customs, including speech habits. Skippon noted, for instance, how people laughed and talked during Mass, or during meetings of the Great Council in Venice, while at a play the audience 'stamped and whistled and called to one another' and those sitting on the stage 'would often interrupt the actors and discourse with them'. He recorded the most popular swear-words and the differences in regional accents. In Milan, for instance, he noted that 'the people . . . leave out the last vowels of words', and in Bologna that 'the vulgar speak Italian very corruptly, cutting their terminating vowels off and huddling their words together'.[35]

Even advertisements in the newspapers have been used effectively by historians of language. Descriptions of runaway servants in the colonial American press noted their speech habits, such as 'plain', 'slow', or 'broad

---

[32] Johannes Fabian, *Language and Colonial Power* (Cambridge, 1986).

[33] For a balanced discussion of the problem, focusing on Molière, see Roger Lathuillère, *La préciosité* (Geneva, 1966), pp. 143–57.

[34] Cf. Ferdinand Brunot, *Langue française*, vol. IV, 1660–1715, pp. 161–79.

[35] Philip Skippon, 'An Account of a Journey', in Awnsley and John Churchill (eds.), *A Collection of Voyages* (6 vols., London, 1732), vol. VI, pp. 489, 502, 510, 520, 534, 582.

Yorkshire' as a help to identifying them. In similar fashion, the description of a runaway apprentice in the *Belfast Newsletter* for 1756 as someone who 'speaks the Scotch tongue' has been employed to argue that this accent had become unusual enough in Northern Ireland by this time to serve as a clue to an individual's identity.[36]

The third major problem is the problem of explanation. Explanations of linguistic change, like other historical explanations, may be divided into two main categories, internal and external. Both have their value. In this book, concerned as it is with cultural history, external factors will be privileged. Problems remain, notably the relative importance of structure and agency and the contrast between actor- or speaker-oriented accounts and system-oriented ones.

On one side, the system side, we find both the nineteenth-century linguists who treated language as an organism in evolution and the more recent structuralists, as well as post-structuralists such as Jacques Derrida, who follows the philosopher Martin Heidegger in claiming that although humans act as if they control language, language is actually in control of them.[37]

On the action side, by contrast, we find the argument that 'it is speakers not languages which innovate' in a process of everyday 'speech acts'.[38] Individuals can play a role in language change, and a number of important individuals will recur in these pages: Pietro Bembo in the case of Italian, Claude de Vaugelas in that of French, Martin Luther in that of German, Shakespeare in that of English and so on.[39] Conscious collective action can also be identified in the early modern period. If it is too early to speak of 'language planning', it is not too soon to refer to language 'campaigns', like the battles for purification to be discussed in chapter 6.

All the same, as in other kinds of history, the unintended consequences of conscious actions also need to be taken into consideration. For example, the emigration of the southern Netherlanders northwards for religious and political reasons at the end of the sixteenth century, when Spanish armies suppressed the revolt of Antwerp and Ghent against King Philip II, made

---

[36] Allen W. Read, 'The Assimilation of the Speech of British Immigrants in Colonial America', *Journal of English and Germanic Philology* 37 (1938), pp. 70–9; Philip Robinson, 'The Scots Language in Seventeenth-Century Ulster', *Ulster Folklife* 35 (1989), pp. 86–99, at p. 98.

[37] Jacques Derrida, *Dissemination* (1972: English translation, Chicago, 1982), especially chapter 1.

[38] James Milroy, *Linguistic Variation and Change* (London, 1992), p. 169; cf. Milroy, 'Toward a Speaker-Based Account of Language Change', in Jahr, *Language Change*, pp. 21–36.

[39] Bruno Migliorini, 'The Contribution of the Individual to Language' (1952: repr. in *Saggi Linguistici*, Florence, 1956), pp. 318–30.

a considerable impact on the language of the north, especially Amsterdam (below, p. 39).

In short, neither structural explanations nor explanations in terms of action seem sufficient by themselves. Is a synthesis between them possible? A way towards a possible synthesis is shown by a recurrent problem in the history of language, as in cultural history in general, the problem of reception, in this case the difficulty of explaining why some speech acts were successful while others were not. Some of Shakespeare's neologisms have passed into ordinary language, but others are only remembered by professional students of the plays. The individual proposes but the community disposes, in the sense of accepting some innovations into the repertoire and turning them into current usage, while resisting others or allowing them to fall by the wayside. The road to the modern vernaculars is strewn with forgotten neologisms. In other words, speech communities as well as individuals have played an active role in the history of language.

STORIES

Despite its thematic organization, this book also attempts to tell a story. A survey of the use of Latin and the communities that it fostered (chapter 2) is followed by a discussion of the so-called 'rise of the vernaculars', partly at the expense of Latin (chapter 3). As the vernaculars expanded into new domains, it became more important to standardize them (chapter 4). Interaction between rival vernaculars led to exchanges, or language 'mixing' (chapter 5). The mixing process provoked some hostile reactions, which took the form of movements of language purification (chapter 6). These 'puritan' movements became still stronger following the 'nationalization' of language from the late eighteenth century onwards (epilogue).

All the same, the story to be told in these pages is not a simple linear one, still less a story of progress. If this book has a single theme, it is the constant conflict between centripetal and centrifugal forces, convergence and divergence, assimilation and resistance, discipline and freedom, unity and diversity. As Antoine Meillet observed almost a century ago, in the history of language 'deux tendances antagonistes sont en jeu, l'une vers la differentiation, l'autre vers l'unification'.[40] We see divergence with the breakup of the Church and invasion of the domain of print by some vernaculars, but

---

[40] Antoine Meillet, 'Différenciation et unification dans les langues' (1911: repr. in his *Linguistique historique*), pp. 110–29, at p. 110.

we see convergence too, as print helped standardize the vernaculars, and the Spanish, Portuguese, Dutch, British and other empires expanded.

It may well be the case that some periods are more favourable to unification, just as some periods are favourable to large empires, as the French historian Fernand Braudel argued in his famous study *The Mediterranean* (1949). Looking at the early modern period, it often seems that the centralizing, standardizing forces are winning, for both political and technological reasons (the rise of printed matter and the centralizing state). We seem to be in a similar situation today, in an age of globalization. All the same, we should not underestimate the strength of decentralizing forces, the power of resistance, or the resilience of linguistic and cultural traditions.

CHAPTER I

'Speak, that I may see thee': the discovery of language in early modern Europe

In the prologue, the point of view expressed was that of scholars today, whether linguists or historians. Language was a topic on which a number of early modern Europeans also expressed their opinions, sometimes forcefully. A study of languages and communities cannot afford to neglect such opinions.[1] The following account is not intended as a history of linguistics, emphasizing the achievement of individual scholars, but rather as a map of attitudes to language, or changes in attitude, as revealed in commonplaces, or in ideas that gradually became commonplace at this time. Indeed, we might describe the early modern period as the age of what I shall call the 'discovery of language'.

THE LATER MIDDLE AGES

The point of this dramatic expression is not to suggest that medieval people were unconcerned with the languages that they were speaking and writing. In thirteenth-century Spain, for example, the standardization of the language associated with King Alfonso the Wise (below, p. 63) implied knowledge of the alternatives to that standard. The fourteenth and fifteenth centuries, in particular, were a time of increasing linguistic awareness, not only in the Italy of the early Renaissance but also in England, France and Central Europe.[2]

In Italy, for instance, Dante contributed to the debate on the vernacular in his *De vulgari eloquentia*, written around the year 1305. In England, Geoffrey Chaucer's *Canterbury Tales*, written in the late fourteenth century,

---

[1] For a survey, see Emma Martinell Gifre and Mar Cruz Piñol (eds.), *La consciencia linguistica en Europa* (Barcelona, 1996); for a case-study, Claudio Marazzini, *Storia e coscienza della lingua in Italia dall'umanesimo al romanticismo* (Turin, 1989).

[2] Vivian H. Galbraith, 'Language and Nationality in Medieval England', *Transactions of the Royal Historical Society* 23 (1941), pp. 113–28; Anna Daube, *Der Aufstieg der Muttersprache im deutschen Denken des 15 und 16 Jahrhunderts* (Frankfurt, 1949); Serge Lusignan, *Parler vulgairement: les intellectuels et la langue française aux 13e et 14e siècles* (Montreal and Paris, 1986).

reveal the social position of each pilgrim through his or her language, with the Reeve and the Miller, for example, speaking in 'churl's terms', in other words, lower-class English.[3] In early fifteenth-century Bohemia, the religious reformer Jan Hus was worried by the influence of German on Czech and tried to defend his native language (below, p. 150).

The fear of what we now call 'language death' was expressed on a number of occasions in the Middle Ages. In 1295, Edward I of England claimed that the King of France planned to invade England and 'wipe out the English language'. At the end of the fourteenth century, according to the chronicler Adam of Usk, the King of England considered 'a decree for the destruction of the Welsh language' (*decretum destructionis lingue wallicae*). In similar fashion, a Polish chronicler recorded the story that the knights of the Teutonic Order intended 'to exterminate the Polish language'. Again, speeches in the English parliament in the fourteenth century – ironically enough, delivered or at least recorded in French – claimed that the French wanted 'to annihilate the whole nation and the English language' (*aneantir tote la nation et la langue Engleys*).[4]

DISCOVERING LANGUAGE

All the same, from the middle of the fifteenth century onwards, more people were becoming conscious of varieties of language and some people were becoming more sharply aware of these matters than before, even if they did not agree how to use key terms like 'language', 'dialect' or 'idiom'. Some scholars have gone so far as to speak of a 'crisis' of language at the end of the Middle Ages.[5] However, 'discovery' seems a more appropriate word than 'crisis', since the change to be described in the following pages was gradual rather than sudden, not a moment but a process.

At a philosophical level, the revival of the classics at the Renaissance inspired a return to the ancient debate over the relation between words and things expressed in Plato's dialogue *Cratylus* and Aristotle's treatise

---

[3] Christopher Cannon, *The Making of Chaucer's English: a Study of Words* (Cambridge, 1998), p. 149.

[4] Robert Bartlett, *The Making of Europe* (1993: second ed., Harmondsworth, 1994), p. 202; Adam quoted in Peter R. Roberts, 'The Welsh Language, English Law and Tudor Legislation', *Transactions Cymmrodorion* (1989), pp. 19–75, at p. 21n; the Annals of Cracow, quoted in Bartlett, p. 203; speeches quoted in Susan Crane, 'Social Aspects of Bilingualism in the Thirteenth Century', in Michael Prestwich, R. H. Britnell and Robin Frame (eds.), *Thirteenth-Century England* (Woodbridge, 1989), pp. 103–15, at p. 113.

[5] Gianfranco Folena, 'Espansione e crisi dell'italiano quattrocentesco' (1953: repr. Folena, *Il linguaggio del caos: studi sul plurilinguismo rinascimentale*, Turin, 1991), pp. 3–17.

On Interpretation.[6] At a more pragmatic level, language consciousness was encouraged by the fact that increasing numbers of people were studying Greek and Hebrew as well as different European vernaculars (below, p. 114). Interest in the history of languages and in linguistic diversity becomes more visible around the year 1500, including the discussion of some ideas that in a more formal dress we would now describe as forming part of 'sociolinguistics'.

For example, the functions of language in general and of certain languages, such as Latin, in particular became an object of critical attention on the part of religious and social reformers. In sixteenth-century Italy, two unorthodox thinkers from the lower classes condemned the use of Latin in the ecclesiastical and legal domains. Giambattista Gelli, a shoemaker who achieved fame by publishing dialogues, put into the mouth of one of his speakers the idea that the point of the Latin liturgy was to keep the faith secret from the laity, to exclude them from the community of the Church. Menocchio the miller, a forgotten figure until he was brought back to life by the historian Carlo Ginzburg, declared that speaking Latin in court was 'a betrayal of the poor', since it prevented ordinary people from following the proceedings.[7]

Similar ideas were expressed in seventeenth-century England, especially during the civil wars, when the use of Latin in the universities and French in the law courts was denounced by radicals such as the clergyman William Dell, the shoemaker Samuel How, author of *The Sufficiency of the Spirits Teaching* (1639) and the Digger leader Gerrard Winstanley. The main point of these critiques was that the use of foreign languages allowed professionals to mystify and so to dominate ordinary people.[8]

DEFECIT AND ABUNDANCE

Much more widespread was the concern with the riches or poverty (what linguists now call the 'defecit') of particular languages. One might even speak of the 'anxiety of defecit'.[9] As in the later Middle Ages, there were

---

[6] Marie-Lucie Demonet, *Les voix du signe. Nature et origine du langage à la Renaissance (1480–1580)* (Paris, 1992).

[7] Giambattista Gelli, *Capricci del bottaio* (Florence, 1546), the fifth dialogue; Carlo Ginzburg, *Cheese and Worms* (1976: English translation, London, 1980), p. 9.

[8] Christopher Hill, *Puritanism and Revolution* (London, 1958), p. 73; Hill, *The World Turned Upside Down* (London, 1972), pp. 269–76; Peter Burke, 'William Dell, the Universities, and the Radical Tradition', in Geoff Eley and William Hunt (eds.), *Reviving the English Revolution* (London, 1988), pp. 181–9.

[9] I owe the term 'anxiety of defecit' to Richard Helgerson.

comments on the poverty of the vernaculars by comparison with Latin. In the case of Polish, a native speaker referred in 1566 to the 'poverty' of the language (*niedostatek*), while the poet Szymon Szymonowić expressed his regret for what he called 'the acute lack of words among us' (*u nas brak wielki w slowiech*).[10] Even Joachim Du Bellay, in his famous apologia for French, the *Deffense et illustration de la langue françoyse* (1549), admitted that 'our language is not as copious and rich as Greek and Latin' (*nostre langue n'est si copieuse et riche que la Grecque et le Latin*), and limited himself to arguing (in book 1, chapter 4) that it was not as poor as many people think.

Comments of this kind have been described as instances of the 'humility topos'.[11] That they also had some empirical justification is suggested by the frequent use of Latin words and phrases in some European languages whenever abstractions were needed, a practice which was common until the later seventeenth century (below, p. 131).

On the other side, however, references to linguistic abundance or copiousness became more and more frequent. Thus the printer Sebastian Franck claimed in 1541 that no language had 'so many varieties and formulae for speaking' as German (*so vil varietet und Formulas zu reden*); the humanist Claudio Tolomei described Italian in his dialogue *Il Cesano* (1546) as 'richer' than Greek or Latin. The merchant Richard Eden declared in 1562 that English was no longer 'indigent' because it had been 'enriched and amplified' by translations like the ones he had himself undertaken.[12] Hendrik Spieghel claimed in 1584 that Dutch was 'richer' than other languages. In his *Discurso sobre la lengua castellana* (1585), Ambrosio Morales called Spanish 'equal to all the good languages in abundance, propriety, variety and beauty' (*igual con todas las buenas en propriedad, variedad y lindeza*).[13] Christian Gueintz, a German superintendent of schools, declared in 1641 that 'The perfection of the German language is so great that virtually nothing can be discovered that cannot be named in this language' (*Die Völligkeit der Deutschen Sprache ist so gros dass auch fast nichts kan gefunden werden welches man in dieser sprache nicht nennen könnte*).[14] Comments of this kind form part of what might be called 'the topos of pride', a topos that turned into a literary genre (below, p. 65).

[10] Claude Backvis, *Quelques remarques sur le bilinguisme latino-polonais dans la Pologne du xvie siècle* (Brussels, 1958), p. 12n.

[11] Andrzej Borowski, 'General Theory of Translation in Old Polish Literary Culture', in Giovanna Brogi Bercoff et al. (eds.), *Traduzione e rielaborazione nelle letterature di Polonia, Ucraina e Russia* (Alessandria, 1999), pp. 23–38, at p. 27.

[12] Eden quoted in Richard F. Jones, *Triumph of the English Language* (Stanford, 1953) p. 92.

[13] José Francisco Pastor (ed.), *Las apologías de la lengua castellana en el siglo de oro* (Madrid, 1929), p. 78.

[14] Gueintz quoted in Erich Strassner, *Deutsche Sprachkultur* (Tübingen, 1995), p. 67.

The sense of abundance was encouraged by the introduction of many new words into the European vernaculars, a process that gave rise to a lively debate in which words were often compared to immigrants seeking citizenship. Thus Du Bellay declared in his *Deffense* that new words 'seront en notre langue comme étrangers dans un cité'. The comparison of foreign words to 'free denizens' who have been or are trying to be 'naturalized' was also made by two English poets, George Peele, who approved of the process, and Samuel Daniel, who regretted it.[15] There was a general European debate about the mixture of languages and the need to purify them, a debate to be discussed in detail below (pp. 111ff., pp. 141ff.).

The remainder of this chapter focuses on two themes that will receive less emphasis later in the book than those of abundance, mixture or purity: in the first place, views of the history of different languages, a history that was studied systematically in this period; in the second place, attitudes to linguistic diversity, a topic on which individuals commented unsystematically from time to time.

1. THE HISTORY OF LANGUAGE

As change becomes more rapid there is usually more awareness of change, in language as in other domains of culture. Giorgio Vasari's history of Italian art, for example, was written in the middle of the sixteenth century, following the major changes that the author was the first to describe as the 'Renaissance'.

In the case of language, the schoolmaster Richard Mulcaster (writing in 1582) described 'this present period of our English tongue' as 'the very height thereof', while in 1635 Juan de Robles declared that Spanish was 'in the state that Latin was at the time of Cicero' (*Está hoy nuestro lengua en el estado que la Latina estuvo en tiempo de Cicerón*).[16] The Académie Française made the same point about French two generations later in the preface to the first edition of its famous dictionary (1694). This increasingly acute sense of change was encouraged by and in its turn encouraged the publication of histories of different languages.

It was the so-called 'dead' languages, Latin, Hebrew, and to a lesser extent Greek, that attracted most historical interest, at least at first. The idea of a 'dead' language itself goes back to the debates among Italian humanists at this time. In Sperone Speroni's *Dialogo della lingua* (1542), one speaker

---

[15] Peele and Daniel quoted in Paula Blank, *Broken English: Dialects and the Politics of Language in Renaissance Writings* (London, 1996), p. 20.

[16] Quoted in Jones, *Triumph*, p. 165 and Weinrich, *Wege*, p. 179.

remarked that Latin was not a spoken language but 'simply paper and ink' (*carta solamente ed inchiostro*), while in Benedetto Varchi's *L'Ercolano* (1570), languages were classified into 'living', 'half-alive' (*mezze vive*) and 'dead'.[17]

In the middle of the fifteenth century, the humanist Lorenzo Valla had already discussed the relation between the rise and fall of Latin and the rise and fall of the Roman Empire, while his colleagues Leonardo Bruni and Flavio Biondo debated the question of the language spoken by the ancient Romans, whether it was Latin or Italian.[18] Following the model of the Roman scholar Varro's history of Latin (a text that had survived in fragmentary form), Cardinal Adriano Castellesi wrote a treatise on Latin, *De sermone latino* (1515), dividing the history of the language into four periods, 'most ancient', 'ancient', 'perfect' and 'imperfect', a division followed by later writers such as Angelo Rocca in his *Osservazioni intorno alla bellezza della lingua Latina* (1590). In 1538, the French scholar Guillaume Postel published a study of the origins of Hebrew.[19] For a history of Greek, on the other hand, it was necessary to wait until the middle of the seventeenth century, when another French scholar, Claude de Saumaise, published his study of the language in the late classical or Hellenistic period.[20]

Valla's remarks about language and empire were adapted to the case of contemporary Castilian by the Spanish humanist Antonio Nebrija. Nebrija's *Gramática castellana* (1492) included the famous phrase in the dedication to Queen Isabella that 'language was always the companion of empire' (*Siempre la lengua fue compañera del imperio*). The author argued that Hebrew, Greek and Latin had all had their day, and that the time of Spanish had now come.[21]

Histories of the vernaculars followed the model of histories of Latin. In the sixteenth century, the Benedictine Joachim Perion and the lawyers Etienne Pasquier and Claude Fauchet all wrote on the history of French.[22] The Florentine scholar Vincenzio Borghini's work on the history of Italian

---

17 Sperone Speroni, *Dialogo della lingua* (1542: ed. Helene Harth, Munich, 1975), p. 92; Benedetto Varchi, *L'Ercolano* (Venice, 1570), pp. 93–4.
18 Cecil Grayson, *A Renaissance Controversy, Latin or Italian* (Oxford, 1959); Mirko Tavoni, *Latino, grammatica, volgare* (Padua, 1984).
19 Guillaume Postel, *Origines hebraicae linguae* (Paris, 1538). Cf. Arno Borst's encyclopaedic work, *Der Turmbau von Babel*, 4 vols. in 6 (Stuttgart, 1957–63), pp. 1128–31; Demonet, *Les voix du signe*, pp. 337ff.
20 Claude de Saumaise, *Hellenistica* (Leiden, 1643).
21 On Nebrija, Francisco Rico, *Nebrija frente a los barbaros* (Salamanca, 1978); Miguel Angel Esparza Torres, *Las ideas lingüísticas de Antonio de Nebrija* (Münster, 1995).
22 Joachim Perion, *De linguae gallicae origine* (Paris, 1554); Etienne Pasquier, *Recherches de la France* (Paris, 1566); Claude Fauchet, *Origine de la langue française* (Paris, 1581).

remained in manuscript, but in the year 1600 a Sienese, Celso Cittadini, published an account of what he called 'the formation of the Tuscan language'.[23] Two studies of the history of English were published five years later, one by the famous scholar William Camden (in his *Remains*) and the other by the Catholic Richard Verstegan.[24] At much the same time, Bernardo de Aldrete, a canon of Córdoba, wrote on the history of Spanish and Duarte Nunes de Leão on Portuguese.[25] For a history of German, on the other hand, it would be necessary to wait until Johann Augustin Egenolff's *Historie der Teutschen Sprache* (1716), in which the author lamented that German scholars had fallen behind their European colleagues. For histories of Slavonic languages, readers had to wait even longer.

The interest in the roots of languages (as well as of individual words) is revealed by the common use of the term 'origin' in the titles of books on the history of Hebrew, French, German, Italian, Spanish, Portuguese and so on. A favourite topic, and a controversial one, was the original language of humanity, the language of Adam, or if not of Adam, at least the language of Japhet (son of Noah), who was believed to have migrated to Europe after the Flood.[26]

It had often been argued, from the time of St Jerome onwards, that this original language was Hebrew, a theory that gained support when words in some American Indian languages seemed to suggest Hebrew origins.[27] Other scholars supported the claims of Chaldean or Scythian (sometimes identified with Gothic, German or Celtic). The Frenchman Jean Picard argued the case for French, Johannes Goropius of Antwerp for Flemish, Olof Rudbeck of Uppsala and others for Swedish, while the French Jesuit Joachim Bouvet and the English architect John Webb argued the case for Chinese.[28]

[23] Mario Pozzi, 'Il pensiero linguistico di Vincenzo Borghini', *Giornale Storico della Letteratura Italiana* 88 (1971), pp. 216–94; Vincenzio Borghini, *Scritti inediti e rari*, ed. John R. Woodhouse (Bologna, 1971); Celso Cittadini, *Formazione della lingua toscana* (Florence, 1600); cf. Claudio Marazzini, *Storia e coscienza della lingua in Italia dall'Umanesimo al Romanticismo* (Turin, 1989), pp. 39–45; Michael T. Wood, 'Bernardo Aldrete and Celso Cittadini', *Hispanic Review* 61 (1993), pp. 65–85.
[24] William Camden, *Remains Concerning Britain* (London, 1605); Richard Verstegan, *Restitution of Decayed Intelligence* (sine loco, 1605).
[25] Bernardo de Aldrete, *Del origen, y principio de la lengua castellana* (1604: facsimile ed., Madrid, 1972); cf. Ward, 'Aldrete', and Kathryn A. Woolard, 'Bernardo de Aldrete and the Morisco Problem', *Comparative Studies in Society and History* 44 (2002), pp. 446–80; Duarte Nunes de Leão, *Origem de língua portuguesa* (1606: in Maria Leonor Carvalhão Buescu (ed.), *Ortografia e Origem da Língua Portuguesa*, Lisbon, 1983).
[26] Hans Aarsleff 'The Rise and Decline of Adam and his *Ursprache* in Seventeenth-Century Thought', in Allison P. Coudert (ed.), *The Language of Adam* (Wiesbaden, 1999), pp. 277–95.
[27] Edward G. Gray, *New World Babel: Languages and Nations in Early America* (Princeton, 1999), p. 240.
[28] On the debate, Claude Gilbert Dubois, *Mythe et langage au 16e siècle* (Bordeaux, 1970), pp. 83–92. On Goropius and Rudbeck, Johan Nordström, *De Yverborenes Ö* (Stockholm, 1934), pp. 111–15, 134–54;

In similar fashion, a controversy developed about the nature of 'primordial Castilian', which some thought had been created at Babel and brought to Spain by Tubal (grandson of Noah), while Aldrete argued that it had gradually developed out of Latin at the time that Spain was a province of the Roman Empire. Returning to the analogy used by Valla and Nebrija, but thinking of the New World, Aldrete declared that conquered peoples have to adapt or 'accommodate' themselves to the language of the conquerors and that 'languages are like empires, that rise to a peak and then fall again, without being able to recover' (*las lenguas son como los imperios, que suben a la cumber, de la cual como van caiendo, no se vuelven a recobrar*).[29] Again, in his history of Portuguese, Nunes de Leão noted that 'just as conquerors of countries and provinces give them their laws, so they give them their language' (*assim como os vencedores de terras e províncias lhes dão leis em que vivam, assim lhes dão língua que falem*), citing the case of Portuguese in Ethiopia and India.[30]

The analogy or connection between language and empire had become a topos. A speaker in Claudio Tolomei's dialogue on Tuscan had already regretted the lack of a Tuscan empire that would allow the language would spread in the way that Latin had done. The topos was particularly common, as well as appropriate, in the case of Spanish, and a number of writers echoed one another in describing the language as following the flag, accompanying the banners of the armies. Giovanni Botero, an Italian writer on politics with a global vision, added the examples of the Arabs, Aztecs and Incas. As the French Jesuit Dominique Bouhours put it a century later, 'Les langues ont leur naissance, leur progress, leur perfection et même leur decadence, comme les empires'.[31]

This imperial topos was linked to the ancient idea that everything on earth goes through a sequence of stages, from beginning to end, or from childhood to old age. 'Ont les langues comme toutes choses humaines', wrote the French scholar Louis Le Roy, 'commencement, progres, perfection, corruption, fin'. The Swedish poet-scholar Georg Stiernhielm concurred: 'Together with people, languages appear, change, differentiate

George J. Metcalf, 'The Indo-European Hypothesis in the Sixteenth and Seventeenth Centuries', in Dell Hymes (ed.), *Studies in the History of Linguistics* (Bloomington, 1974), pp. 241–4, 249–51; Daniel Droixhe, *La linguistique et l'appel de l'histoire* (1600–1800) (Geneva and Paris, 1978), pp. 53–60, 118–26.

[29] Aldrete, *Origen*, p. 185.   [30] Nunes de Leão, *Origem*, pp. 189–329, at p. 195.

[31] Guillermo L. Guitarte, 'La dimension imperial del español en la obra de Aldrete', in Antonio Quilis and Hans-Juergen Niederehe (eds.), *The History of Linguistics in Spain* (Amsterdam and Philadelphia, 1986), pp. 129–81; Dominique Bouhours, *Entretiens d'Ariste et d'Eugène* (1671: new ed., Paris, 1962), p. 67.

themselves, grow up, become mature and die' (*Cum hominibus oriuntur, mutantur, differuntur, adolescunt, exolescunt, occidunt linguae*). Stiernhielm also made the point that over time some dialects develop into languages, while some languages fragment into dialects.[32]

Some writers told the story of change in terms of the improvement or refinement of the language. The poet John Dryden, for instance, believed that English was improving in his day. However, a more common explanation for linguistic change was in terms of corruption. Unlike Dryden, Jonathan Swift believed that English had been in decline since the middle of the seventeenth century (more exactly, since 1642). Earthly languages were viewed as corruptions of the original language of paradise. More recent changes were described as the corruption of an originally pure language by the influx of foreign words (below, pp. 141ff.). Cardinal Castellesi, for instance, described the fourth and last period in the history of Latin, the period after Cicero, as 'imperfect and corrupt'. An English writer on language, Edward Brerewood, summarizing earlier sixteenth-century writers on the topic, suggested that Spanish, Italian and French 'are but the Latin depraved and corrupted by the inundation of the Goths and Vandals'.[33] Nunes de Leão made the same point about Portuguese, while the printer Jan Malecki argued that Polish was a corruption of Czech.[34]

Historians of language, such as Borghini or Stiernhielm, took a particular interest in rustic speech – in one case in Tuscany, in the other in Dalarna – on the grounds that, as Borghini remarked, 'since the peasants converse less with foreigners' (*perché i contadini conversano manco con forestieri*), they must have preserved archaic or pure forms of language, just as they preserved old customs in general. The Icelandic scholar Arngrímur Jónsson also explained the purity of his native language by his country's isolation.[35] The German polymath Gottfried Wilhelm Leibniz, a major figure in the history of linguistics as well as in philosophy, mathematics and sinology, made the point in a general way in a letter to a Swedish correspondent: 'Swedish is to us in some manner what Icelandic is to you, for the more remote the regions, the better they preserve ancient languages' (*Le suédois*

[32] Louis Le Roy, *Vicissitudes* (Paris, 1575), book 2: Georg Stiernhielm (ed.), *Evangelia ab Ulfila* (Stockholm, 1671), folio C.3, recto.

[33] Edward Brerewood, *Enquiries Touching the Diversity of Language* (London, 1614), preface.

[34] Nunes de Leão, *Origem*, pp. 217, 219, 314; Irena Mamcarz, 'Alcuni aspetti della questione della lingua in Polonia nel '500', in Riccardo Picchio (ed.), *Studi sulla questione della lingua presso gli slavi* (Rome, 1972), pp. 279–326, at p. 295.

[35] Borghini, *Scritti*, pp. 139–42; Stiernhielm, *Evangelia*, folio B.3, recto; Jónsson discussed in Pierre Halleux, 'Le purisme islandais', *Etudes Germaniques* 20 (1965), pp. 417–27, at p. 418.

nous est en quelque façon ce que l'islandois est à votre égard. Car plus les pays sont reculés, et mieux conservent ils les anciennes langues).[36]

The comparative approach

The comparative approach to language advocated and pursued by Leibniz was a major feature of early modern scholarship. Changes in language were linked to the corruption of customs in the ambitious comparative histories by Louis Le Roy, the *Vicissitudes* (1575), and by Claude Duret, the *Thresor* (1613). Le Roy took as his theme 'the variety of things in the universe', and especially the rise and fall of civilizations (discussing the vicissitudes of languages in book 2), while Duret's book concentrated on languages and their 'decadences, mutations, changes, conversions and ruins'.[37] In similar fashion, the English clergyman John Wilkins, in his scheme for a 'universal language', declared that 'every change is a gradual corruption'.[38] More optimistic, Borghini described Italian as increasingly polished from Dante's time onwards, while Bouhours suggested that the polishing of language and the polishing of manners occurred together, as in the case of French from the fifteenth century onwards.[39]

Comparative studies also led to increasing interest in the division of languages into 'families' and the analysis of their 'affinities' or descent. Thus Guillaume Postel, who taught oriental languages in Paris, and Theodor Bibliander, professor of Hebrew at Zürich, were among the first to demonstrate a series of similarities between Semitic languages, including Hebrew and Arabic (though these languages had already been compared in more general terms in the eleventh century, if not before). The Dutchman Abraham Mylius discussed the history of the Germanic languages in his *Lingua belgica* (1612).[40] A Slovene grammar of 1584 by the schoolmaster Adam Bohorič claimed to be introducing the reader at the same time to Russian, Ruthenian, Polish, 'Bohemian' (Czech), 'Lusatian' (Sorb), Croat and Dalmatian, in other words to what is now known as the Slavonic or Slavic family of languages.

Again, the histories of Italian, Spanish, Portuguese and French discussed earlier dealt with the romance languages as a family of idioms that

[36] Leibniz to Sparfvenfelt, 1695, quoted in Sigfrid von der Schulenburg, *Leibniz als Sprachforscher* (Frankfurt, 1973), p. 206.

[37] Dubois, *Mythe*, pp. 115–16.

[38] John Wilkins, *Essay toward a Real Character and a Philosophical Language* (London, 1668), p. 8.

[39] Borghini, *Scritti*, p. 184; Bouhours, *Entretiens*, pp. 73–5.

[40] George J. Metcalf, 'Abraham Mylius on Historical Linguistics', *Publications of the Modern Language Association* 68 (1953), pp. 535–54.

all descended from Latin. Tuscan, Castilian and Provençal were 'sisters', according to Borghini. Latin was the 'mother' of French, Spanish and Italian, according to Bouhours. In similar fashion, according to Stiernhielm, German and Swedish were 'two legitimate sisters born of the first primeval Japhetic-Scythian mother'.[41] Some scholars took the family analogy seriously as a hypothesis for research. The English scholar George Hickes was a student of what he called the 'northern' or, as we would say, the Germanic languages, writing on Anglo-Saxon and Gothic and editing a grammar of Icelandic. Leibniz took a keen interest in the Celtic languages, including Cornish, while the Welsh antiquarian Edward Llwyd made a comparative analysis of Celtic vocabulary, following a tour in search of manuscripts which lasted from 1697 to 1701 and took him to Wales, Scotland, Ireland and even Brittany (where he was suspected of being a spy).[42]

Still more ambitious, combining a historical with a comparative and a structural analysis, the British Indologist Sir William Jones claimed that the Greek, Latin, Persian, Germanic and Celtic languages belonged to the 'family' of Sanskrit (it was only in the nineteenth century that the Slavonic languages would be added to this 'Indo-European' group). Outside the Indo-European orbit, the Hungarian scholar János Sajnovics noticed the affinity between Sami and Hungarian when he was in northern Norway in 1769 as part of an expedition of astronomers, while at the very end of the eighteenth century, Sámuel Gyarmathi demonstrated the links between Hungarian and Finnish that earlier scholars, including Leibniz, had already suspected.[43]

2. LINGUISTIC DIVERSITY

The interest in the changes in one language in different periods was linked to a concern with the diversity of languages or varieties of language spoken in different places or by different kinds of people. In an age of expansion, in which Europeans discovered, explored, conquered and colonized so many parts of the world, they were forced to become much more aware

---

[41] Borghini, *Scritti*, p. 177; Bouhours, *Entretiens*, p. 45; Stiernhielm, quoted in Einar Haugen, *The Scandinavian Languages: an Introduction to their History* (London, 1976), p. 422.

[42] Edward Llwyd, *Archaeologia Britannica* (London, 1707), preface.

[43] Hans Aarsleff, 'Sir William Jones and the New Philology', in *The Study of Language in England, 1780–1860* (Princeton, 1967), pp. 115–61; Miklós Zsirai, 'Sámuel Gyarmathi, Hungarian Pioneer of Comparative Linguistics' (1951: repr. Thomas Sebeok (ed.), *Portraits of Linguists*, 2 vols., Bloomington, 1966), vol. 1, pp. 58–70; Daniel Droixhe, 'Leibniz et le finno-ougrien', in Tullio De Mauro and Lia Formigari (eds.), *Leibniz, Humboldt and the Origins of Comparativism* (Amsterdam and Philadelphia, 1990), pp. 3–29.

of the number and variety of human languages. Antonio Pigafetta, for instance, in his account of Magellan's famous voyage round the world (1519–22), recorded some words from a number of exotic languages, from the Moluccas to the giants of Patagonia.[44] Jacques Cartier, or a companion on his expedition to New France in the 1530s, compiled a vocabulary of the Mohawk and Iroquois languages. Jean de Léry did the same for Tupí in the course of his stay in Brazil. Missionaries in the New World and elsewhere studied the local languages (below, p. 92), and in 1629 a Spanish Carmelite, Vázquez de Espinosa, commented on the American Babel, 'the confusion and diversity of languages in the Indies'.

In short, the number of languages known to Europeans increased steadily between Columbus's landfall in 1492 and 1786, the year of the publication in St Petersburg of the first volume of a dictionary of all the languages of the world, *Linguarum totius orbis vocabularia*, commissioned by Catherine the Great, a ruler of a multilingual empire, who had begun by attempting to discover how many languages were spoken in her extensive domains.[45]

This topic, fascinating as it is, will not be discussed further here. Following the main theme of the book, the relation between languages and communities, this section is primarily concerned with the rise of an interest which we would describe today as 'sociolinguistic'. One of the many reasons for the growing interest in the diversity of languages was the belief that they revealed the nature of the speakers. Ben Jonson made the essential point in epigrammatic form when he declared (following Socrates) that 'Language most shows a man: speak that I may see thee. No glass renders a man's form or likeness as true as his speech'.[46] Like other playwrights of the period, Jonson exploited this diversity for comic effect, as we shall see.

The discussion of the merits and defects of different languages was linked to the international debate on national character, as well as to the competition between vernaculars (to be discussed below, pp. 70ff.). Thus the Italian humanist Giovanni Pontano declared that 'Boastful speech delights the Spaniards, colourful and complicated language the Greeks; the conversation of the Romans was grave, that of the Spartans brief and rough, of the Athenians fulsome and stilted, of the Carthaginians and Africans shrewd and dry' (*Magniloquentia delectat Hispanos, fucatus et compositus sermo Graecos, Romanorum gravis fuit oratio, Lacedaemoniorum brevis et*

---

[44] Maria Leonor Carvalhão Buescu, *O estudo das línguas exóticas no século xvi* (Lisbon, 1983), pp. 46–9.

[45] Mary R. Key, *Catherine the Great's Linguistic Contribution* (Carbondale and Edmonton, 1980).

[46] Ben Jonson, *Timber or Discoveries* (1641: ed. Ralph S. Walker, Syracuse, 1953), pp. 45–6. Cf. Nunes de Leão, *Ortografia* (Lisbon, 1576), the dedication.

horrida, Atheniensium multa et studiosa, et Carthaginensium Afrorumque callida et safra).[47]

The French lawyer Etienne Pasquier described 'the arrogant Spaniard' as 'creating a proud and ceremonious vernacular', while 'the Italians, having degenerated from ancient Roman virtue' produced 'a soft and effeminate' one.[48] A once-celebrated comparison and contrast between the Spaniards and the French declared that 'The French generally speak much and loudly, while the Spaniards always speak little and low' (*Los franceses ordinariamente hablan mucho y alto, y los españoles siempre hablan poco y bajo*).[49] Bouhours treated the gravity of Spanish and what he called the 'coarseness' of German as symptoms of national character.[50]

A few writers argued for linguistic relativism. One speaker in the dialogue by Speroni mentioned earlier declared: 'I am convinced that all languages, including Arabic and Indian as well as Latin and Greek, have the same merit' (*Io ho per fermo, che le lingue d'ogni paese, così l'Arabica e l'Indiana, come la Romana e l'Ateniense, siano d'un medesimo valore*).[51]

A point more frequently made in the period is that every language has its own distinctive qualities.[52] As the Tuscan humanist Leonardo Bruni put it, 'Every language has its own perfection' (*Ciascuna lingua ha sua perfezione*). The German humanist Aventinus (Johann Thurmair) agreed, writing that 'each language has its own use and its special quality' (*ein ietliche sprach hat ir aigne breuch und besunder aigenschaft*).[53] In Poland, Jan Seklucjan argued that 'There are many properties in a given language which it is difficult to express in another language with an equally important word'.[54]

In France, the scholar-printer Etienne Dolet and the poets Joachim Du Bellay and Jacques Peletier du Mans made similar points: 'chacune langue a ses propriétés'; 'chaque langue a je ne sçay quoy propre seulement à elle'; 'les mots et manières de parler sont particuliers aux nations'. Nunes de Leão made a list of Portuguese words and phrases that he considered to be

---

[47] Giovanni Pontano, *De sermone*, ed. Alessandra Mantovani (Rome, 2002), p. 78.

[48] Quoted in Donald Kelley, *Foundations of Modern Historical Thought* (New York, 1970), pp. 279–80.

[49] Carlos García, *La oposición y conjunction de los dos grandes luminares de la tierra, o la antipatia de franceses y españoles* (1617: ed. Michel Bareau, Edmonton, 1979).

[50] Bouhours, *Entretiens*, p. 41.   [51] Speroni, *Dialogo*, p. 116.

[52] Edward Stankiewicz, 'The "Genius" of Language in Sixteenth Century Linguistics', in Horst Geckeler et al. (eds.), *Logos Semantikos* (Berlin, 1981), vol. 1, pp. 177–89.

[53] Quoted in Monika Rössing-Hager, 'Küchenlatein und Sprachpurismus im frühen 16. Jht', in Nikolaus Henkel and Nigel F. Palmer (eds.), *Latein und Volksprache im deutschen Mittelalter, 1100–1500* (Tübingen, 1992), pp. 360–86, at p. 361.

[54] Quoted in Maria R. Mayenowa, 'Aspects of the Language Question in Poland', in Riccardo Picchio and Harvey Goldblatt (eds.), *Aspects*, vol. 1, pp. 337–76, at p. 345.

untranslatable, among them the example – still quoted today – of *saudade* (more or less 'yearning' or 'nostalgia').[55]

Particular languages had their own images, masculine or feminine. For example, the idea that the Germanic languages were especially manly was a commonplace. In his essay-oration *On the Excellency of the English Tongue*, the English scholar-poet Richard Carew described what he called 'Dutch' (probably German) as 'manlike'. The Welsh writer James Howell described both German and English as masculine languages. John Dryden noted the 'masculine vigour' of English and contrasted it with French. The poet Friedrich Gottlieb Klopstock described German as *männlich*. Other languages might also be described in this way on occasion: Montaigne, for instance, called Gascon 'un langage masle et militaire', while the historian João de Barros made a similar case for Portuguese, claiming that French and Italian 'seem more like women's talk than a serious language for men' (*A francesa como a italiana mais pareçem fala para mulheres que grave para homems*).[56]

Italian was often regarded as a feminine language. Pasquier's remark about it as 'soft and effeminate' has already been quoted.[57] Klopstock described Italian as soft and voluptuous.[58] Voltaire agreed, describing Italian as a language that, thanks to the frequency of vowels, suits 'la musique efféminée', while the French journalist Antoine Rivarol declared Italian to be 'presque insupportable dans une bouche virile'.[59]

There is a famous anecdote about the linguistic abilities of Charles V which tells us little about the emperor but a good deal about early modern views of languages. In the earliest known version, the story claimed that the emperor 'used to say, that he spoke Spanish to his God, Italian to courtiers, French to his ladies and German to his horse'. In variants of the story, he speaks German to his enemies or to his soldiers, French to his friends, Italian to ladies, and English to the birds. In the early version of the story, French is presented as a female language, but in a later version, the female language is Italian.

---

[55] Etienne Dolet, *La manière de bien traduire* (1540: repr. Paris, 1830), p. 15; Joachim Du Bellay, *Deffense et illustration de la langue française* (1549: ed. Jean-Charles Monferras, Geneva, 2001), book 1, chapter 5; Jacques Peletier du Mans, *L'art poétique* (1555: ed. André Boulanger, Paris, 1930), p. 110; Nunes de Leão, *Origem*, pp. 303–4.

[56] João de Barros, *Diálogo* (1540: ed. Luciana Stegnano Picchio, Modena, 1959), pp. 78–9.

[57] Bouhours, *Entretiens*, p. 41.

[58] Quoted in Joshua Fishman, *Language in Sociocultural Change* (New York, 1972), p. 65.

[59] Voltaire quoted in Gianfranco Folena, *L'italiano in Europa: Esperienze linguistiche del Settecento* (Turin, 1983), p. 223; Antoine Rivarol, *De l'universalité de la langue française* (1786: ed. T. Suran, Paris, 1930), p. 197.

This story not only illustrates the tradition of the *blason*, the genre in which one group – more or less playfully – insults others, but also introduces the idea of what linguists now call a 'speech domain' (above, p. 7). A similar point was made in less picturesque fashion by the seventeenth-century Scottish lawyer Sir George Mackenzie, when he declared that 'the English is fit for haranguing, the French for complimenting, but the Scots for pleading'.[60]

There is nothing like conflict for encouraging consciousness. The growing awareness of diversity within a given language was linked to campaigns for standardization and debates about the standard, to what is known in Italian as 'the language question' (*la questione della lingua*), to be discussed in chapter 4 below. Standard languages were defined by the standardizers in contrast to dialects and jargons, but writers who consciously chose dialect, in seventeenth-century Italy for example, often did so in deliberate opposition to the literary norm. From this point of view, each form of language needed the other.

Sociolects

The point on which I should most like to insist in this chapter is that 'sociolects', the distinctive languages of particular social groups, were already attracting attention at this time. 'In every language', wrote the Spaniard Martin Viziana, 'there are three ways of speaking (*maneras de hablar*), those of the scholars, the nobles and the common people'. Another Spaniard, the scholarly friar Luis de León, distinguished the language of what he called 'the wise and the dignified' (*los sabios y los graves*) from that of 'the humble and simple' (*los humildes y simples*). In similar fashion, Bernardo de Aldrete noted the diversity of Spanish *modos de hablar*, varying between the city and the country as well as according to the region.[61]

The linguistic hierarchy reflected or sustained the social hierarchy. In his history of Portuguese, Nunes de Leão provided a list of terms that 'polite people (*os polidos*) should not use', such as 'dance' (*dança*) for 'business' or *dissingular* instead of the correct *dissimular* ('hide'), associating these banned words with 'plebeians and simple people' (*os plebeus ou idiotas*).[62]

---

[60] Harald Weinrich, 'Sprachanekdoten um Karl V' (1980: repr. *Wege der Sprachkultur* (Stuttgart, 1985), pp. 181–92); Mackenzie quoted in Peter Giles, 'Dialect in Literature', in *The Scottish Tongue* (London, 1924), pp. 91–123, at p. 113.

[61] Martin Viziana, *Libro de alabanças de las lenguas castellana y valenciana* (Valencia, 1574), folio B.ii, verso; Luis de León quoted in Amado Alonso, *Castellano, español, idioma nacional* (Buenos Aires, 1938), p. 87; Aldrete, *Origen*, p. 192.

[62] Nunes de Leão, *Origem*, pp. 295–6.

In France, the famous *Remarques* (1647) by Claude de Vaugelas (discussed below, p. 99) were concerned with distinguishing what the author called *la façon de parler* and *la façon d'escrire* of the court and the upper classes from that of the rest of the country.

Particular interest was taken in the language of peasants, not because linguists admired its purity but because urban readers found it exotic. For example, a number of poems and dialogues in Italian dialects were described on their title-pages as written in 'rustic language' (*lingua rustica, lingua villanesca*), including a dialogue written by Galileo in which two peasants from the Padua area discussed the appearance of a new star. Plays, such as those written by Angelo Ruzzante in northern Italy, or by Gil Vicente in Portugal, showed peasants speaking differently from the other characters, using the archaic word *samica* ('certainly') in Portuguese, for instance.[63] The difference between rustics and town-dwellers was one of accent as well as vocabulary, as more than one observer noted. The English schoolmaster John Palsgrave claimed that French peasants did not stress their words.[64] James Howell, travelling in France in the mid-seventeenth century, noted a rather different characteristic of peasant speech, 'a whining kind of querulous tone', which he explained in terms of 'the pitiful subjection they are brought unto'.

The language of other social groups was also studied and imitated. For example, the sixteenth-century Venetian playwright Andrea Calmo wrote a sonnet in what he called *lingua nicolota*, in other words the speech of the fishermen who lived near the church of San Niccolò in Venice. In similar fashion, the goldsmith Alessandro Caravia wrote a mock-epic poem, *La verra antiga* (1550) in what he called *lengua brava*, the language of tough guys, in this case the rival communities of fishermen and boat-builders, who engaged in regular fist-fights on the bridges of Venice. The title of the poem may be translated as 'the ancient war', the dialect form *verra* replacing the normal Italian *guerra*.

An object of special interest was the jargon or 'cant' of the community of beggars and thieves, with its overtones of secrecy and the exotic. This jargon was sometimes employed by poets, like the Pole Sebastian Klonowicz in *Worek Judaszów* ('Judas's Bag', 1600). Already in the fifteenth century the French poet François Villon had written six *ballades* in thieves' jargon, while the Italian poet Luigi Pulci made a glossary of its Italian equivalent, and a vocabulary of *Rotwelsch* or beggar's German was compiled in 1479. A

---

[63] Paul Teyssier, *La langue de Gil Vicente* (Paris, 1959), pp. 76–171, at pp. 84–5.
[64] Gabriele Stein, *John Palsgrave as Renaissance Linguist* (Oxford, 1997), pp. 379–81.

number of vocabularies of this jargon in different languages were printed in the sixteenth and seventeenth centuries, including the Italian *Nuovo modo de intendere la lingua zerga* (1545), the Dutch *Fielten Vocabulaer* (1563), the English *Caveat for Common Cursitors* (1566) and the French *Jargon de l'argot réformé* (1628).[65]

The language of the bourgeoisie also attracted the attention of satirists because of the place of language in strategies for social mobility, or at least in attempts at passing for noble. In the 1950s the socialite Nancy Mitford and the linguist Alan Ross, by distinguishing upper-class usage from the rest ('U' from 'non-U'), had made the English middle class anxious about their language. Over four hundred years earlier, however, the satirist Pietro Aretino had written a dialogue set in a Roman brothel, in which one of the whores is mocked for her linguistic affectations, calling a window a *balcone* instead of the common *finestra*, a door *uscio* instead of *porta*, a face *viso* instead of *faccia* and so on.[66]

In France, what was called *la façon de parler en bourgeois* was already stigmatized in 1616.[67] Vaugelas, one of the most influential writers on French, criticized some of the Parisians of his day for pronouncing *commencer* as if it were *quemencer* and *bureau* as if it were *burreau*.[68] Antoine Furetière, later the compiler of a famous French dictionary, published a novel in 1666 with the title *Le roman bourgeois*. In this satire on the Parisians of his day, Furetière introduces us to a young *abbé* who spoke in an affected way because he thought it made him appear to be of higher status, or more literally 'affected to speak in a slightly oily manner, so that his language would be more dainty' (*affectoit de parler un peu gras, pour avoir le langage plus mignard*).[69]

Fashions in language, from the 'jargon' of the younger courtiers to *façons de parler bourgeoises*, were also stigmatized by the diplomat François de Callières in his book *Des mots à la mode* (1692). Among these bad bourgeois habits were referring to the fruit course as *dessert*, soup as *soupe* (rather than *potage*), and a chambermaid as *une fille de chambre* (rather than *femme de chambre*). By this time even the word *courtois* was banned from high society: the right adjective to use was *honnête*.[70]

---

[65] Peter Burke, 'Introduction', in Burke and Roy Porter (eds.), *Languages and Jargons* (Cambridge, 1995), pp. 5, 18.

[66] Pietro Aretino, *Sei Giornate*, ed. Giovanni Aquilecchia (Bari, 1975), p. 82.

[67] Le Savatier (1616) quoted in Ferdinand Brunot, *Langue française*, vol. III, 1600–60, p. 165n.

[68] Claude de Vaugelas, *Remarques sur la langue française* (Paris, 1647), p. 425.

[69] Antoine Furetière, *Le roman bourgeois* (1666), repr. in Antoine Adam (ed.), *Romanciers du 17e siècle* (Paris, 1968), p. 906.

[70] François de Callières, *Des mots à la mode* (Paris 1692), pp. 43, 65.

In Germany in the seventeenth and eighteenth centuries, people with social aspirations liked to use French words and phrases (below, p. 139, pp. 150ff.). The writer Johann Christoph Gottsched gave an explanation of the affected, Frenchified language of the upper classes in his time that is reminiscent of the social theory of the late Pierre Bourdieu: 'One has to distinguish oneself from the mob even in the way one speaks' (*Man muss sich von der Canaille auch en parlant distinguiren*).[71] The ideas of an earlier sociologist, Thorstein Veblen, are also apposite at this point. Like the long fingernails of Chinese mandarins, speaking a foreign language in public is a sign of belonging to what Veblen called a 'leisure class', a group that has the time to devote to pursuits that are not necessary for survival.[72]

Language and religion

The social groups identifiable by their language included religious groups. Latin was sometimes unkindly described in late medieval France as *clerquois*, the jargon or dialect of the clergy.[73] In his *Confessions*, Jean-Jacques Rousseau described the drawl of the nuns he had known as *le ton lent et traînant des religieuses*. The language of French Protestants, impregnated as it was with phrases from the translation of the Old Testament, was sometimes described as 'the dialect of the Promised Land' (*le patois de Canaan*: below, p. 105). Eighteenth-century German Pietists were supposed to speak in a 'whimpering', 'whining' or 'sighing' manner, as well as employing distinctive turns of phrase, such as 'the fullness of the heart' (*Fülle des Herzens*). In the Dutch Republic, where the Pietist movement was also strong, its supporters could be identified by their regular use of diminutives, a habit that remains audible in the Netherlands to this day.[74]

In England, the speech habits of the Quakers made them distinctive, including their use of terms such as 'steeple-house' (to describe a church), or 'meeting' (to describe their religious services), their practice of saying 'thou' to everyone, even to their social superiors, and the important function of silence in their worship. Puritans were also recognizable, like their predecessors the Lollards, because they used a distinctive vocabulary, in

---

[71] Quoted in Blackall, *German*, p. 94; cf. Pierre Bourdieu, *Distinction* (1979: English translation, London, 1984).

[72] Thorstein Veblen, *The Theory of the Leisure Class* (New York, 1899). Cf. Robert A. Hall, Jr, 'Thorstein Veblen and Linguistic Theory', *American Speech* 35 (1960), pp. 124–30.

[73] Ferdinand Brunot, *Langue française*, vol. II, p. 15.

[74] August Langer, *Der Wortschatz des deutschen Pietismus* (Tübingen, 1954); J. M. Bulloch, 'The Delight of the Doric in the Diminutive', in William A. Craigie et al., *The Scottish Tongue* (1924), pp. 127–51, at p. 132.

which terms such as 'backsliding', 'godly', 'idol', 'saint' and 'zeal' were frequent (hence Ben Jonson's creation of a comic puritan named 'Zeal-of-the-Land-Busy' in his *Bartholomew Fair*). One of their opponents, Robert Sanderson, referred to 'That uncouth affected garb of speech, or canting language' of 'the godly party'.[75] The godly also appear to have spoken with distinctive accents, for a character in a play by Ben Jonson, Aurelia in *The Case is Altered* (1609), uses the phrase, 'learn to speak i' the nose and turn puritan'.[76]

It was to peculiarities of this kind that the diarist Samuel Pepys referred when he recorded a visit to his old Cambridge college, Magdalene, on 25 February 1660. On meeting some of the fellows, Pepys remarked that 'there was nothing at all left of the old preciseness in their discourse' (the Puritans were nicknamed 'precisians'). Whether Pepys is referring to formality or some other feature of Magdalene speech, the point is that the fellows realized that Charles II was soon to return to England and so they no longer wished to sound distinctive.

Language and gender

An awareness of the links between language and gender was not uncommonly expressed in this period, though the texts usually take the form of men criticizing the language of women by saying that they talk too much, cannot spell, know no grammar, or speak in an affected manner. The affected accents and 'clipped pronunciation' of some middle-class women had already been the target of a satirist in the fourth century, St Jerome. In the early sixteenth century, Erasmus, in some respects a new Jerome, wrote a treatise on pronunciation, in which he placed the blame for the disappearance of diphthongs on women, who thought it ladylike 'to open their mouths and move their lips as little as possible when forming their words'.[77]

More specifically, Erasmus and the printer Geoffroy Tory both commented on the peculiarities of the pronunciation of the ladies of Paris in

[75] Richard Bauman, *Let Your Words be Few: Symbolism of Speech and Silence among the Quakers* (Cambridge, 1983); Hugh Ormsby-Lennon, 'From Shibboleth to Apocalypse: Quaker Speechways during the Puritan Revolution', in Burke and Porter, *Language, Self*, pp. 72–112; Marinus van Beek, *An Enquiry into Puritan Vocabulary* (Groningen, 1969); Sanderson quoted in Samuel Johnson's *Dictionary* (London, 1755), sub voce 'cant'.

[76] Patricia Fumerton, 'Homely Accents: Ben Jonson Speaking Low', in Fumerton and Simon Hunt (eds.), *Renaissance Culture and the Everyday* (Philadelphia, 1999), pp. 92–111.

[77] Quoted in John N. D. Kelly, *Jerome: his life, writings and controversies* (London, 1975), p. 42; Erasmus, 'On Pronunciation' (1528: English translation in *Works*, vol. 26, Toronto, 1985), p. 403.

from Greek and the model situation was that of ancient Greece with its Ionic, Doric, Attic and other varieties of speech. The growing interest in regional dialects in the early modern period may be linked to the rediscovery of ancient Greece. One sign of this interest is the increasing use of the word 'dialect', in Latin in the early sixteenth century, for instance, in French from 1563 at the latest and in English from 1577. Luther, for example, remarked – in the mixed language he employed in his table-talk – that 'Germany has dialects of many kinds' (*Deutschland hat mancherley Dialectos*).

In an age of increasing linguistic standardization (below, p. 89), discussions by townspeople expressed the same contempt for rural dialect as for the 'boors' who spoke it. French definitions of *patois* were pejorative, notably that of Antoine Furetière in his famous *Dictionary* (1690), 'corrupt and crude language, such as that of the lower orders' (*langage corrompu et grossier, tel que celui du menu peuple*). The Englishman Randle Cotgrave had already glossed the term *patois* in his French-English *Dictionary* (1611) as 'gibridge' (gibberish), 'clownish language' or 'rusticall speech'. Alexander Gill, distinguishing northern, southern, eastern and western forms of English, simply remarked that the western is 'the most barbarous'. The statutes of the Deutsche Gesellschaft proscribed what were called 'provincial forms of speech' (*Provinzial-Redensarten*).[84]

The playwrights, who anticipated the scholars in their interest in dialects (as in other sociolects), encouraged contemptuous or patronizing attitudes to these provincial forms by employing them for comic effect. In the Italian *commedia dell'arte*, for instance, Pantalone, the heavy father, speaks Venetian and Graziano, the pedant, Bolognese, while Capitano, the boastful and cowardly soldier, speaks Neapolitan, sometimes laced with Spanish.[85] Shakespeare's *Henry V* includes a stage Welshman, Fluellen, a stage Scot, Jamy, and a stage Irishman, Macmorris, all identified by their speech. Jonson's *Bartholomew Fair* mocks the accents of the north ('northern') and the west ('puppy'). Stage west-countrymen in particular became a staple of English comedy in the seventeenth and eighteenth centuries.

All the same, there is evidence of more positive attitudes to dialect in this period, especially towards its end. In Italy, for instance, the literature in support of vernacular languages (below, p. 65) included texts praising Milanese (1606), Bolognese (1622) and Neapolitan (1662). A number of

---

[84] Alexander Gill, *Logonomia anglica* (1619: ed. and trans. Bror Danielsson and Arvid Gabrielson, Stockholm, 1972); the Deutsche Gesellschaft quoted in Blackall, *German*, p. 107.

[85] Ivano Paccagnella, *Il fasto delle lingue: plurilinguismo letterario nel '500* (Rome, 1984).

literary texts in the standard language were translated into various dialects. In the case of the catechism of the Jesuit Roberto Bellarmino, which was translated into the dialect of Turin in 1738, Sicily in 1744, and Friuli in 1745, the motive was obviously to reach ordinary people by speaking their language, part of the Jesuit missionary policy of accommodation to local customs. The Jesuits in Sardinia used Sardinian on the grounds that, as one of them put it – in Spanish – in 1561, 'the ordinary language of Sardinia is Sarda just as that of Italy is Italian' (*la lengua ordinaria de Cerdeña es la sarda como de Italia la italiana*).[86]

More difficult to interpret are the translations of literary classics such as Ludovico Ariosto's *Orlando Furioso*, Giambattista Guarini's *Pastor Fido* and Torquato Tasso's *Gerusalemme Liberata*, into Bergamask, for instance, or Neapolitan. Today, it is not easy to say whether these translations were made out of playfulness or to show off the ingenuity of the translators or whether they also expressed, as is likely to have been the case, a reaction against standardization and a sense of regional identity, all the stronger because the peninsula was not politically united. As in ancient Greece, there was a link between local dialects and local autonomy.

It is worth noting that the Italian fashion for dialect in print did not please everyone. A translation of the *Liberata* into Bolognese published in 1628 was left unfinished, the colophon informing readers that the municipal government had forbidden it to be continued, 'since the idiom was somewhat ridiculous' (*l'idioma sendo un poco ridicolo*).[87]

After 1650, on the other hand, dialect was rediscovered, or at least revalued. A number of scholars compiled and published dictionaries of dialect, usually from their own region. Once again, the Italians were in the vanguard of the movement with dictionaries of Bolognese (1660) and Venetian (1671), though in 1674 the Cambridge don John Ray published his *Collection of English Words*, a glossary of dialect terms that was doubtless inspired by his botanical researches (given the variety of local names for plants) but became much more ambitious in the course of its compilation.[88] Since it was with Ray that Philip Skippon (above, p. 11) travelled to Italy,

---

[86] Quoted in Raimondo Turtas, 'La questione linguistica nei college gesuitici nella Sardegna nella seconda metà del Cinquecento', *Quaderni sardi di storia* 2 (1981), 55–86, at 61n.

[87] Contrast Benedetto Croce, 'La letteratura dialettale riflessa', *Uomini e cose della vecchia Italia*, vol. 1 (Bari, 1926), pp. 222–34, emphasizing playfulness, with W. Theodor Elwert (1939) 'Die mundartlichen Kunstdichtung Italiens und ihr Verhältnis zur Literatur in der Hochsprache' (1939: repr. *Aufsätze zur italienischen Lyrik*, Wiesbaden 1967, pp. 156–91), emphasizing politics.

[88] Jo Gladstone, '"New World of English Words": John Ray, FRS, the Dialect Protagonist, in the Context of his Times', in Peter Burke and Roy Porter (eds.), *Language, Self and Society* (Cambridge, 1991), pp. 115–53.

we may surmise that his fascinating observations on spoken Italian owed something to his tutor.

In the German-speaking world, Leibniz took a great interest in dialect, as in other forms of language, and encouraged the researches of others into the subject, though it was only in the eighteenth century that dictionaries were published for the dialect of Hamburg, for instance, of Bremen and of Bavaria. A Swedish dialect dictionary came out in 1766, and in France, studies of the *patois* of the Limousin, Lorraine and Marseilles appeared in the 1770s and 1780s.[89]

The high point of the investigation of dialect in this period comes at its end, with the questionnaire designed by Henri Grégoire to produce a map of dialect in France, paying particular attention to the contexts and occasions of its use. Ironically enough, this language survey was carried out not to support dialect but to destroy it.

Playwrights as witnesses

As we have already seen in the cases of Shakespeare, Jonson and Molière, playwrights exploited sociolects for comic effect, representing marginal communities as funny foreigners who do not know how to speak. In sixteenth-century Spain and Portugal, for instance, comic Jews, Gypsies, Basques, Moors and Blacks all made their appearance on the stage. The Gypsies, for instance, replace 'o' by 'u' and 's' by 'z', as in the sentence 'give us alms for the love of God', *Dadnuz limuzna pur la amur de Diuz*. The Jews say *guai*! instead of 'Alas!' and pronounce the dipthong *ou* as *oi* ('oiro' for *ouro*, 'poico' for *pouco* and so on).[90] As for the language of the Africans, what the Spaniards called *guineo* and the Portuguese, *língua de preto* is represented by the use of 'me' instead of 'I' (*mi vem lá*), and by the use of R in the place of D or L, from *Rios* ('God') to *diabro*. The similarities between the structure of this 'Black Portuguese' and what used to be called 'Black English' (now known as African-American English or AAE) suggest that the evidence of these plays is fairly trustworthy (below, p. 126).[91]

---

[89] Sigrid von der Schulenberg, 'Leibnizens Gedanken zur Erforschung der deutschen Mundarten', *Abhandlungen des Preussischen Akademie der Wissenschaften* (1937), pp. 3–37; Droixhe, *La linguistique*, pp. 334–45.

[90] Gil Vicente, 'Farça das ciganas', and 'Farça de Ines Pereira', in *Obras* (3 vols., Coimbra, 1912–14), vol. 2, pp. 318–46, and vol. 3, pp. 238–43. Cf. Teyssier, *Gil Vicente*, pp. 211, 220.

[91] Edmund de Chasca, 'The Phonology of the Speech of the Negroes in Early Spanish Drama', *Hispanic Review* 14 (1946), pp. 322–39; Teyssier, *Gil Vicente*, pp. 227–54; Elvezio Canonico-de Rochemonteix, *El poliglotismo en el teatro de Lope de Vega* (Kassel, 1991).

Alternatively, a playwright might exploit the comic vein to comment on language, like Molière and Somaize in their satires on the *précieuses*. The problem of circularity, of trying to assess the reliability of the satires yet depending on them for virtually all our information, is a serious one. All the same, the texts and the interest taken in them together reveal a widespread awareness of social variations in language.

In the Dutch Republic, the Amsterdam poet Gerbrand Bredero's most successful play was *The Spanish Brabanter* (1617). The protagonist, a gentleman who wears Spanish dress and is given the Spanish name Jerolimo, is also an enthusiast for the dialect of Brabant, especially the form of the language used in Antwerp, 'splendid' (*heerloyck*) and full of 'perfection' (*perfeccy*) and 'correctness' (*correccy*). His servant, on the other hands, speaks broad Amsterdam and mocks the language of his master, turning 'Brabanters' into 'Brabbelaars', in other words speakers of gibberish.

In this way, Bredero is able to strike at least two targets. His social target is the emigrant from the southern Netherlands, who fails to recognize that Amsterdam has overtaken Antwerp. His linguistic target, on the other hand, is the humanist writer Hendrik Spieghel, whose book in praise of the vernacular of the Netherlands (*Nederduitsche* or 'Low German', as he called it), recommended the adoption of the dialect of Brabant as the standard. Bredero was thus expressing the reaction of the Hollanders against the linguistic hegemony of the south.[92]

In the eighteenth century, the playwright Ludvig Holberg, sometimes described as the Danish Molière (he came from Bergen in Norway but wrote in Danish) had a sharp ear for sociolects. In his *Erasmus Montanus* (1731), for instance, Holberg portrayed the son of a prosperous peasant who comes back from university mixing his spoken and written Danish with Latin words and phrases, something that was not uncommon at this time, or at least a generation earlier (below, p. 131). Holberg also made fun of pretentious people, who were replacing traditional Danish words with foreign ones like *Lakei* (lackey) for 'servant', or *Spillemand* (from the German *Spielman*) for 'musician'.

At about the same time, Carlo Goldoni was noting the peculiarities of the speech of Venice and the Veneto. For example, he tried in his *Baruffe chioggiote*, as he remarks in the preface, to reproduce the unusual vocabulary (*termini particolari*) and the accent (*maniera di pronunziare*) of the lower classes of the small town of Chioggia.

[92] Andries A. Verdenius, *Bredero's Dialectkunst als Hollandse Reaktie tegen zuidnederlandse taalhegemonie* (Groningen, 1933).

The importance of accent

An awareness that different communities spoke with different accents is in no way new. After all, what gave St Peter away when he denied being a follower of Christ was his Galilean accent. 'Your speech betrays you', he was told (*loquela tua manifestum te facit*: Matthew, 26.73). All the same, it is possible to document a growing preoccupation with accent in this period, a growing stigmatization of departures from the new linguistic standards in pronunciation as in vocabulary and syntax.

That the English were not the only people to worry about their accents may be demonstrated from some French and Italian examples. In France, the printer Henri Estienne (like his colleague Tory, whose remarks on women's accents were quoted above), mocked affected pronunciation, especially those who said 'chouse' for 'chose', 'j'ouse' for 'j'ose', 'troas moas' for 'trois mois' and 'la guarre' for 'la guerre'.[93] In Spain, a French visitor noted that the villagers of Castille said *guevo* instead of *huevo*, 'egg', *guente* for *fuente*, 'stream', and *cablito* for *cabrito*, 'little goat'.

As for Italy, in Speroni's dialogue on language, the Greek humanist Janos Lascaris remarks on what he calls 'certain unpleasant accents' (*certi accenti . . . noiosi*) associated with the common people, or, as he puts it, *gente vile*. The rules drawn up for the seminary established in Milan in 1590 specified that the teachers should correct 'the mispronunciations which the pupils brought with them from their places of origin' (*vitiosas quasdam inflexiones vocis . . . quas a patria secum extulerunt*).[94] Again, a seventeenth-century account of the regions of Italy – written by a Bolognese – claimed that the Genoese spoke with the tip of the tongue on the teeth, that the Florentines swallowed their words, that the mouths of the Venetians were full of vowels, and that the Milanese placed the stress on the last syllable instead of the last but one (*alcuni parlano con le labra, e con la punta della lingua sù i denti, come i Genovesi: Alcuni ingorgano, come i Fiorentini: Altri sono nel parlar tardi, e hanno le voci piene di vocali, come gli Venetiani . . . I Milanesi . . . parlano con una certa fiacchezza e pongono molti accenti nell'ultimo di molte parole*).[95]

In England, perhaps predictably, social discrimination on the basis of accent can be traced from the time that the term 'accent' came into use in

[93] Henri Estienne, *Deux dialogues du nouveau langage françois* (1578: ed. Pauline M. Smith, Geneva, 1980).
[94] Quoted in Adriano Prosperi, *Tribunali di Coscienza* (Turin, 1996), p. 314n.
[95] Camillo Baldi, *Lettera missiva* (Bologna, 1622), pp. 26, 30. On Milan, cf. the testimony of Skippon (above, p. 11).

the later sixteenth century, if not before. In 1562, for instance, the inspectors of Merchant Taylor's school in London complained that the teachers, 'being northern men born', had failed to teach the boys 'to pronounce their words as well as they ought'.[96] George Puttenham, an Elizabethan writer on the art of poetry, noted what he called the 'strange accents' of the 'inferior sort'.[97] When a student from Wales went up to St John's College Cambridge in 1598, it is recorded that 'such as had giggling spleens would laugh at him for his Welsh tone'.[98] Again, an account of Suffolk in the early seventeenth century noted the 'disgrace of a broad or rude accent'.[99]

Some individuals of high status still spoke in a manner that diverged from the standard. Sir Walter Raleigh, although a leading courtier, 'spake broad Devonshire', according to the seventeenth-century biographer John Aubrey (it may well be a sign of changing standards that Aubrey drew attention to this point). In the eighteenth century, at a time when spoken English was increasingly standardized (below, p. 108), accents that diverged from the norm were stigmatized even more sharply than before. In his *Accidence of the English Tongue* (1724), the grammarian Hugh Jones referred to the 'odious tones' of dialect. The Irish actor and elocution teacher Thomas Sheridan emphasized the need to avoid 'rusticity of accent', arguing that what he called 'the court pronunciation' was 'a sort of proof that a person has kept good company'.[100]

These ideas or prejudices were not confined to theorists. In the 1760s, an English clergyman, confiding to his diary the bad impression made on him by the bishop of Lincoln, declared 'his humble education and mean extraction' to have been revealed by his 'want of behaviour and manners', including in this category his 'Yorkshire dialect'.[101] If parents were spending money on elocution lessons for their children, a good accent must have appeared to be a social advantage.

The use of accent as a social shibboleth in Britain in the nineteenth and twentieth centuries has become notorious, thanks to a succession of gifted novelists from Charles Dickens to Evelyn Waugh and beyond, the successors as social observers of the playwrights discussed earlier in this

---

[96] Quoted in Adam Fox, *Oral and Literate Culture in England, 1500–1700* (Oxford, 2000), p. 59.
[97] George Puttenham, *The Arte of English Poesie* (1588: ed. Gladys D. Willcock and Alice Walker, Cambridge, 1936), p. 144.
[98] Quoted in Geraint H. Jenkins (ed.), *The Welsh Language before the Industrial Revolution* (Cardiff, 1997), p. 301.
[99] Quoted in Fox, *Oral and Literate Culture*, p. 101.
[100] Thomas Sheridan, *A Course of Lectures on Elocution* (London, 1762), pp. 29–38.
[101] William Cole, *The Blecheley Diary* (London, 1931), p. 35.

chapter.[102] I hope to have shown that this phenomenon is neither as new nor as peculiarly English as is often thought to be the case. Using the 'received pronunciation' has been a strategy for maintaining or claiming high status over the centuries.

An alternative strategy in the early modern period was to show off a knowledge of Latin. The uses of Latin in the construction of communities will be discussed in the following chapter.

[102] Kenneth C. Phillipps, *Language and Class in Victorian England* (London, 1984); Lynda Mugglestone, *'Talking Proper': The Rise of Accent as Social Symbol* (Oxford, 1995).

CHAPTER 2

Latin: a language in search of a community

In the last chapter, we saw how some people objected to the employment of Latin in church and in the courts because it excluded the majority of the population from the community of interpretation.[1] Here, by contrast, the focus will be on inclusion, on the community or communities whose cohesion was expressed, encouraged or constructed by the use of that language.[2]

A discussion of Latin provides a good opportunity for noting continuities between the early modern period and the Middle Ages, before turning to the changes. In medieval and early modern times alike, Latin offers a classic example of 'diglossia' (above, p. 7), in the sense that it was considered appropriate to use that language in some situations and domains. Rules become more visible when they are broken, so that one of the traditional conventions for the use of Latin is revealed when the sixteenth-century Polish Cardinal Stanislas Hosius chided a colleague, bishop Jakub Uchański, for writing to him about theology in the vernacular.[3]

The case of Latin also allows us to return to some of the problems that, as we have seen (above, p. 5), the concept 'community' brings in its train, since by the ninth century, if not before, Latin had turned into a language without native speakers. For this reason, post-classical Latin has been called

---

[1] Stanley Fish, *Is there a text in this class? The Authority of Interpretive Communities* (Cambridge, MA, 1980).

[2] General surveys include Jozef Ijsewijn, 'Neolatin: a Historical Survey', *Helios* 14 no. 2 (1987), pp. 93–107; Bo Lindberg, *De lärdes modersmål* (Göteborg, 1984) and Lindberg, *Europa och Latinet* (Stockholm, 1993); Françoise Waquet, *Latin: the Empire of a Sign* (1998: English translation London, 2001). Cf. Peter Burke, '*Heu Domine adsunt Turcae*: a Sketch for a Social History of Post-medieval Latin', in Burke and Roy Porter (eds.), *Language, Self and Society* (Cambridge, 1991), pp. 23–50.

[3] Claude Backvis, *Quelques remarques sur le bilinguisme latino-polonais dans la Pologne du xvie siècle* (Brussels, 1958), p. 8n.

a language 'without a people' or 'without a speech community' (*Eine Sprache ohne Sprachgemeinschaft*).[4]

I should prefer to call Latin a language in search of a community. This expression may sound as odd as Pirandello's characters in search of an author, but it makes the point that the search was ultimately successful. Post-classical Latin, like the vernaculars, exemplifies the uses of language in binding together a group. In this case, the people who were bound together formed a 'community of ideas' or an 'imagined community' that was international in scope. In the early modern period, Latin both expressed and contributed to the cohesion of two international communities in particular, the Catholic Church and the Republic of Letters.

Before turning to these two communities, it may be useful to say something about four other groups which used Latin and may have been bonded by Latin: lawyers, officials, diplomats and travellers.

Latin was employed by lawyers and notaries in many parts of Europe in the early modern period and even later. In the case of lawyers, the importance of Latin corresponded to the importance of Roman law in many parts of Europe. As for notaries, at the end of the Middle Ages, the University of Bologna, for instance, offered special courses in Latin for their benefit.[5] Kilometres of documents in the archives of major Italian cities attest the importance of the language, especially for the formal parts of documents.

Even the record of the interrogation of a suspect in the vernacular normally included Latin formulae for what might be called the 'stage directions'. For example, the painter Paolo Veronese was summoned before the Inquisition in Venice in 1573 on suspicion of heresy. The record of his interrogation begins: *Constitutus in sancto offitio coram sacro tribunali* ('arraigned before the Holy Tribunal of the Holy Office'), while each section opens with the formula *interrogatus respondit* ('on being questioned, he replied'). If the suspect was shown a book or the instruments of torture, this would also be recorded in Latin.

In the second place, Latin was a language of justice and administration in early modern Europe, although it was becoming less important in this respect than it had been in medieval times. For example, in the joint

[4] Ludwig Bieler, 'Das Mittellatein als Sprachproblem', *Lexis* 2 (1949), pp. 98–104, at p. 104; cf. Christine Mohrmann, 'Le dualisme de la latinité médiévale' (1952: repr. Mohrmann, *Latin vulgaire, Latin des chrétiens, Latin médiéval*, Paris, 1955, pp. 37–54), and Banfi, *Formazione*, p. 9.
[5] Helene Wieruszowski, '*Ars dictaminis* in the time of Dante' (1943: repr. in her *Politics and Culture in Medieval Spain and Italy*, Rome, 1971), pp. 359–77, at p. 362.

Polish-Lithuanian Commonwealth founded in 1569, many municipal and court records were kept in Latin.

It was in the Habsburg Empire in particular that Latin remained important in the bureaucratic domain. In the seventeenth century, the officials of the imperial chamber or *Hofkammer* in Vienna, concerned with the financial affairs of the empire, corresponded in Latin with their opposite numbers in Bratislava (otherwise known as Pressburg or Pozsony). The proceedings or *Acta* of the imperial Diet or *Reichstag* were recorded in Latin, while in the Hungarian Diet Latin was, at least in principle, the language of debate, as well as that of the documents emanating from the Diet, notably the complaints or petitions (*gravamina*). In that multilingual empire, a dead language had the advantage of being politically neutral as well as a *lingua franca* that allowed speakers of German, Hungarian, Czech, Croat and other languages to communicate on equal terms, provided they enjoyed the benefits of a classical education.[6]

In the third place, Latin was the principal language of diplomacy. Queen Elizabeth's denunciation of the Polish ambassador for his 'insolent audacity' (*insolentem audaciam*) is a vivid reminder of this traditional diplomatic practice. The queen was fluent enough in the language to lose her temper in Latin. Elizabeth may have been unusual among the rulers of the period in this respect – the humanist Roger Ascham had been in charge of her education – but some of her royal colleagues also knew the language tolerably well, including her father Henry VIII, her sister Mary, Mary's husband Philip of Spain, Isabella of Castille (who studied Latin when she was an adult), Margaret of Austria and Stefan Bathory, King of Poland.

Latin is a conspicuous absence from the list of languages attributed to the emperor Charles V, but an English ambassador testified that although 'The Emperor hath no pleasure to speak Latin', he was able to understand it. Ministers were sometimes fluent in the language, Cardinal Wolsey for instance, or Axel Oxenstierna, while ambassadors needed to be at least competent in Latin.[7] This situation made relations between Western Europe

---

[6] Jean Béranger, 'Latin et langues vernaculaires dans la Hongrie du 17e siècle', *Revue Historique* 242 (1969), pp. 5–28; Béranger (ed.), *Les 'Gravamina': remonstrances des diètes de Hongrie de 1655 à 1681* (Paris, 1973); Robert J. W. Evans, *The Making of the Habsburg Monarchy, 1550–1700: an Interpretation* (Oxford, 1979), pp. 20–4, 259.

[7] Garrett Mattingly, *Renaissance Diplomacy* (London, 1955), pp. 38–9; Joycelyne G. Russell, *Diplomats at Work: Three Renaissance Studies* (Stroud, 1992), pp. 1, 8–10, 12, 19–20; Janet M. Green, 'Queen Elizabeth I's Latin reply to the Polish Ambassador', *Sixteenth–Century Journal* 31 (2000), pp. 987–1006; on Stefan Bathory, Norman Davies, *God's Playground: a History of Poland*, vol. 1 (Oxford, 1981), p. 478.

and Muscovy or the Ottoman Empire more difficult, since Latin was not a normal part of elite culture in either state. Dmitri Gerasimov, the Muscovite ambassador to pope Clement VII, was unusual in his command of the language.

One of the advantages of Latin in the diplomatic domain was that it was relatively well known by members of the elite, another that it was prestigious, a third that it was neutral compared to the vernaculars that were competing for cultural hegemony at this time, notably Italian, Spanish and French. The Swedish chancellor, Oxenstierna, spoke Latin rather than French to Cromwell's envoy, Bulstrode Whitelocke (so he explained) partly because Latin was 'more honourable', but also because 'at present that language was not peculiar to any people'.[8]

Latin retained its importance in international relations for most of the seventeenth century, at the peace congresses of Münster and Nijmegen, for instance, and even beyond, despite the legend that French became the language of diplomacy in the reign of Louis XIV (below, p. 86). Even in the eighteenth century, Latin continued to be used as a written language, for example to draw up international treaties. It was only slowly that French became what it was to remain until the first half of the twentieth century, the diplomatic language *par excellence*.[9]

Travellers too often had recourse to Latin as a *lingua franca*. At one end of Europe, Elizabethan Englishmen sometimes used the language in their dealings with the Irish, while a Spaniard who landed in Ireland after the wreck of the Armada probably owed his life to his ability to communicate with the inhabitants in Latin.[10] Towards the other end of Europe, Poland and Hungary were frequently described as places where some knowledge of Latin was unusually widespread. Daniel Defoe expressed his surprise that 'a man who can speak Latin may travel from one end of Poland to another as familiarly as if he was born in the country. Bless us! What would a gentleman do that was to travel through England and could speak nothing but Latin'.[11]

As for Hungary, a Flemish Capuchin went so far as to claim in 1633 that 'peasants and shepherds' there 'speak Latin more fluently than many priests do elsewhere'. This remark may have been more of a critique

[8] Bulstrode Whitelocke, *A Journal of the Swedish Embassy* (2 vols., London, 1855), vol. 1, p. 300. Cf. Nils Ahnlund, *Svenskt och Nordiskt* (Stockholm, 1943), p. 115.
[9] Ferdinand Brunot, *Langue française*, vol. v, pp. 387–422, esp. pp. 392–5, 402, 407–8; Lucien Bély, *Espions et ambassadeurs* (Paris, 1990), pp. 450–55.
[10] Patricia Palmer, *Language and Conquest in Early Modern Ireland* (Cambridge, 2001), pp. 70, 83.
[11] Defoe quoted in Davies, *God's Playground*, pp. 236–7.

of the secular clergy than an encomium to shepherds, but the more detailed testimony of the English traveller Edward Browne deserves to be taken seriously. Browne noted in 1668 that in Hungary and Transylvania, 'coachmen, watermen and mean persons' could all make themselves understood in Latin. Soldiers, another nomadic group, also knew some Latin, while a Hungarian scholar has noted that 'the criminal law suits of the eighteenth century often bear evidence to the fact that ordinary people spoke Latin'.[12]

We should not, of course, imagine coachmen and ostlers declining and conjugating the language without errors in a country in which noblemen frequently made mistakes (below, p. 57). It is more likely that in this part of the world spoken Latin had become a pidgin. As in the case of more recent pidgins, inflections probably disappeared while verbs were reduced to their infinitives, so that it would have been sufficient to enter a Hungarian tavern and utter the phrase 'vinum bibere' in order to be served. 'Travellers' Latin', as we might call it, was Latin without the frills and indeed without most of the resources of the language.

Even outside Europe a knowledge of Latin had its value, as the eighteenth-century Englishman John Barrow found in Brazil, when he found himself able to use it to communicate with a friar in Rio de Janeiro.[13] This was one of the advantages of Latin being the official language of the Catholic Church, taught in schools and seminaries not only in Brazil (beginning with the school at Piratininga founded in the later sixteenth century by the Jesuit José de Anchieta), but also in Mexico and Peru.

Latin schools were founded in Mexico City, Michoacán, and most famous of all, in Tlatelolco, where the college of Santa Cruz opened in 1536. At this college, Indian boys learned Latin (in Nahuatl) and also some Spanish. In 1584, some of the pupils were fluent enough to make speeches in both Latin and Spanish. A story told by a missionary concerns the surprise of a priest who had just arrived from Spain when an Indian student spoke to him in Latin.

By the end of the century, the college of Tlatelolco had ceased to exist, but Latin continued as the medium of instruction in the universities of Mexico and Lima, both of them founded in the middle of the sixteenth century. Indeed, at the inauguration of the University of Mexico in 1553, a Latin oration was delivered by Francisco Cervantes de Salazar, the professor

---

[12] Further examples in Burke, 'Heu domine', pp. 35–7; István G. Tóth, 'Beyond Literacy: Latin as a Spoken Language', in his *Literacy and Written Culture in Early Modern Europe* (1996: English translation, Budapest, 2000), pp. 130–45, at pp. 135, 137, 140.
[13] Gilberto Freyre, *The Masters and the Slaves* (1933: English translation, New York, 1946), p. 375.

of rhetoric and later rector. The *Commentaries* of Cervantes, including three dialogues about Mexico, were used as a Latin textbook.

In Japan, Latin was introduced by Jesuit missionaries alongside Christianity. In the later sixteenth century, the Jesuit colleges founded at Azuchi and Arima taught the boys Latin from locally-printed editions of classical texts, including Cicero. However, Latin did not survive the outlawing of Christianity and the 'closing' of the country in 1639. In the Dutch colony of Batavia, in what is now Indonesia, Latin went through a similar rise and fall. Founded by the Governor-General in 1642 for both Dutch and *mestizo* boys, the Latin school was closed in 1670.[14]

LATIN IN THE CHURCH

The function of Latin as the language of the Church is well known. All the same, an exact description of its place in practice is not easy. Research is still needed for the contours to be fully mapped, and what follows should be regarded as no more than a rough approximation.

In the first place, Latin was generally the language of the Catholic liturgy – the Mass, baptisms, weddings, funerals and the daily round of prayer in the monasteries.[15] This was the case for some sixteen hundred years, from the 360s, more or less, to the 1960s (before the 360s, Greek had been in use).[16] The dominance of Latin in this domain was challenged in the early sixteenth century but it was re-affirmed in a decree of the Council of Trent on 5 September 1562 and survived until 7 March 1965.

In the case of certain minorities, liturgies in other languages were permitted. The so-called 'Uniates' in the Ukraine and the Balkans were allowed, from 1596 onwards, to use what is now called Old Church Slavonic in their liturgy, like their neighbours in the Eastern Church in Muscovy. Greek was also used for liturgical purposes in the Balkans in the seventeenth and eighteenth centuries. Syriac, Arabic and Georgian were in use in parts of the Catholic world in the seventeenth century, while Pope Paul V permitted the use of mandarin for the Mass in China (apparently this decree was not implemented).[17]

---

[14] Shirley Heath, *Telling Tongues: Language Policy in Mexico, Colony to Nation* (New York, 1972), pp. 28–9, 228; Kees Groeneboer, *Gateway to the West: the Dutch Language in Colonial Indonesia, 1600–1950: a history of language policy* (1993: English translation, Amsterdam, 1998), p. 45.

[15] Giovanni Michele Hanssens, 'Lingua liturgica', in *Enciclopedia Cattolica* (Vatican City, 1951), vol. VII, columns 1377–82.

[16] Gustave Bardy, *La question des langues dans l'Eglise ancienne* (Paris, 1948).

[17] Alphonsus Raes, *Introductio in liturgiam orientalem* (Rome, 1947), pp. 220–5; Hanssens, 'Lingua'.

The use of Latin for the liturgy over so wide an area with such diverse vernaculars helped create a sense of distance from everyday life and a sense of universality. It also encouraged a sense of tradition, which might be defined as membership of a community that includes the dead as well as the living.

The Protestant Reformation obviously led to a drastic reduction in the territory of Latin. The positive side of the change will be discussed in the next chapter, but the negative side, the loss of the sense of universality and continuity, deserves to be remembered here. This loss is exactly what some of the reformers wanted. Using the everyday vernacular was a way of desacralizing religious services, of reducing the gap between the religious domain and ordinary life. Other reformers, like Thomas Cranmer, arch-bishop of Canterbury, favoured the vernacular for practical reasons, but adopted a form of vernacular that would as far as possible rival Latin in its dignity thanks to the use of archaic forms.

Latin was also the language of the clergy, at least when carrying out their official duties, the *lingua sacerdotum*, as John of Salisbury had called it in the twelfth century. It was the language of the *respublica clericorum*, the 'commonwealth of clerks', as a twentieth-century linguist has described it.[18] One might call it, somewhat less kindly, the jargon of the clergy, and as we have seen (above, p. 32), it was indeed sometimes described in late medieval France as *clerquois*.

From the clergy's point of view, in the Middle Ages at least, there were two cultures, that of the clergy, the *literati* who knew Latin, and that of the laity, *vulgus* or *illiterati*, who did not (the adjective *illiteratus* usually meant 'ignorant of Latin' rather than 'illiterate' in the modern sense). In that sense, Latin, like other languages and dialects, created a community by including some people and excluding others. In practice, this 'folk model' was never completely accurate and it was working less and less well as time went by. A growing group of laity were learning Latin, including a few women, among them learned ladies of the Renaissance, such as Isotta Nogarola and Laura Cereta in Italy, Caritas Pirckheimer in Germany, Beatriz Galindo, nicknamed 'La Latina', in Spain, and Mildred Cooke in England.[19] In the Venetian convent of Santa Maria delle Vergini, it was customary for the election of an abbess to be marked by a Latin oration by one of the nuns.[20]

---

[18] Mohrmann, 'dualisme', p. 43; Benedict Anderson, *Imagined Communities* (1983: revised ed., London, 1991).

[19] Jane Stevenson, 'Women and Latin in Renaissance Europe', *Bulletin of the Society for Renaissance Studies* 19, no. 2 (2002), pp. 10–16.

[20] Mary Laven, *Virgins of Venice* (2002: second ed., London, 2003), p. 76.

On the other side, the visitations conducted by some Italian bishops in the fifteenth century give a strong impression that a substantial proportion of the parish clergy did not know the language. This point was drawn to the attention of the pope in 1513 by some would-be reformers, but nothing was done to remedy the situation.[21] In Palermo, for instance, the problem was apparently much the same in the middle of the sixteenth century.[22] It is likely that the Italian clergy were not alone in their ignorance. Awareness of this problem was one reason for the foundation of seminaries from the later sixteenth century onwards, institutions in which future parish priests were able to learn the Latin they needed.

In the case of meetings of the clergy – church councils, synods of dioceses, and so on – it is often difficult to discover what language was spoken. Sermons raise a similar problem. It may seem counter-intuitive to suggest that sermons could have been preached in Latin to audiences including ordinary people, but speakers of romance languages at least might well have understood simple Latin, especially if it alternated with passages in the vernacular. 'Macaronic' sermons of this kind were not uncommon in Italy and France at the end of the Middle Ages (below, p. 133).

Well or ill understood, Latin left traces on the culture, including the vernacular of ordinary people, as was shown both fully and vividly in a recent study of 'the Latin of those who do not know it' by the linguist Gian Luigi Beccaria. Beccaria points out that in Italy, 'the dialects are full of liturgical Latin' even today, while some of the examples he quotes go back to early modern times. In the Venetian of Chioggia, for instance, an authoritarian person is nicknamed *potente de sede*, and someone full of himself *un egosum*, phrases derived respectively from the Magnificat, *Deposuit potentes de sede*, and from St John's Gospel 11.25, *Ego sum resurrectio et vita*.

Some of the Italian examples are simple borrowings, like *introibo* for 'preamble' or *confiteor* for 'apology'. Others seem to be cases of mishearing or misunderstanding, like *visibilio* in the sense of 'confusion', derived from the phrase in the Credo, *visibilium omnium et invisibilium*. Examples of popular Latin of this kind are not confined to Italy. In a sixteenth-century Portuguese play, a black woman is represented as saying *sato biceto nomen tuu!* (*sanctificetur nomen tuum*).[23] Yet other examples express playfulness, irony and mockery, including the mockery of liturgical Latin itself,

[21] Denys Hay, *The Church in Italy in the Fifteenth Century* (Cambridge, 1977), pp. 49–57.
[22] Mari D'Agostino, *La Piazza e l'altare: momenti della politica linguistica della chiesa siciliana* (Palermo, 1988), pp. 27, 43.
[23] António Ribeiro Chiado, *Auto das regateiras*, ed. Giulia Lanciani (Rome, 1970), p. 56.

'uncrowning' it as Bakhtin would say, stripping it of its dignity. A woman regarded as too pious, for instance, was known in the sixteenth century as *una magnificatte*, while shouting was described as 'singing Vespers', *cantare il vespro*.[24]

This semi-comprehension of Latin does not mean that no one felt excluded, that no one was excluded or that no one rebelled against the dominance of Latin in the Church. It was often said that Latin was employed by the clergy precisely in order to keep the laity at a distance, to keep them in ignorance. In fifteenth-century Bohemia, the reformer Jan Hus challenged the use of Latin in the Church, as other heretics, such as the Waldensians, had done before him. In similar fashion, in 1524, the radical Protestant Thomas Münzer declared it intolerable 'that people ascribe a power to Latin words, as the magicians do' (*das man den Lateinischen worten wil eine kraft zuschreiben, wie die zaubrer thun*). Menocchio the miller and Gelli the shoemaker (quoted above, p. 17) were not alone in their complaints.[25] Heretics demanded the right to read the Bible in the vernacular and, conversely, those who wanted to read the Bible for themselves were labelled heretics.

The supporters of Latin in church were not all Catholics, and the opponents of that language were not all Protestants. On one side, Martin Luther, for instance, took up a moderate position, advocating the retention of a Latin liturgy for its educational value, and the creation of a vernacular liturgy for those who lacked Latin.[26] On the other side, the Venetian hermits Paolo Giustiniani and Vincenzo Quirini wrote a letter to the pope in 1513 recommending a vernacular liturgy, while three years later Erasmus made his famous appeal – in Latin, since he was addressing the learned – for the translation of the Bible into the vernacular so that ploughmen, weavers, and 'the lowliest women' would be able to read it. As late as the 1560s, at the last sessions of the Council of Trent, some cardinals and bishops continued to argue – in Latin, since that was the language of the Council – in favour of a Bible and a liturgy in the vernacular.[27]

Generally speaking, however, Catholics accepted the arguments of people like the Roman humanist Angelo Colocci, who defended the use of Latin in the liturgy and the law alike 'because they lose their force without brevity

[24] Gian Luigi Beccaria, *Sicuterat: il Latino di chi non lo sa* (1999: second ed., Milan, 2001), pp. 14–17, 77, 89, 99, 100, 105, 110.
[25] Quoted in Strassner, *Sprachkultur*, p. 55.
[26] Herman Schmidt, *Liturgie et langue vulgaire: le problème de la langue liturgique chez les premiers Réformateurs et au Concile de Trente* (Rome, 1950), p. 50.
[27] Leopold Lentner, *Volksprache und Sakralsprache: Geschichte einer Lebensfrage bis zum Ende des Konzil von Trient* (Vienna, 1964), ch. 5; Vittorio Coletti, 'Il volgare al Concilio di Trento' (repr. *Parole del pulpito: chiesa e movimenti religiosi tra latino e volgare*, Casale, 1983), pp. 189–211.

and majesty'. The idea that Latin was a more dignified language and therefore more appropriate in the religious domain was widespread at the time.
At the Council of Trent, some of the participants argued that Latin kept the
sacraments sacred, and others that it was necessary to follow the 'ancient rite'
(*ritus antiquus*).[28] The arguments of the reformers in favour of a vernacular
liturgy were rejected. Fears were also expressed that divergent translations
from Latin into different languages would lead to a fragmentation of the
Church into what we might describe as different 'communities of interpretation'. In any case, the vernacular was associated with Protestantism by this
time. It was finally agreed by participants in the Council that the liturgy
should remain in Latin, with explanations in the vernacular provided in
sermons for those who needed them.[29]

There were, of course, other religious languages current in early modern
Europe. The Jews used Hebrew, the Muslims in Spain and the Ottoman
Empire used Arabic, while in Eastern Christendom, the language of the
Church was not Latin but Slavonic. Church Slavonic was close enough to
the local vernaculars to be generally intelligible but distant enough to sound
distinct and dignified. It was understood, as a monk from Kiev, Zakhariya
Kopystens'ky, remarked with pride in 1623, from the Adriatic to the Arctic,
and so, like Latin, encouraged the sense of belonging to a trans-national or
supranational religious community.

In Europe, then, we see a contraction of the empire of ecclesiastical Latin,
the result of the Reformation. In the New World, to redress the balance, the
empire of Latin expanded, as Catholic missionaries taught that language to
some of the Amerindians. Latin also expanded eastwards, as the following
section will show.

LATIN IN THE REPUBLIC OF LETTERS

In Eastern Christendom, Church Slavonic was the language of the learned
in the sixteenth and seventeenth centuries, as well as the language of the
liturgy. As the German scholar Heinrich Ludolf observed in his Russian
grammar (1696), 'Russian is for speaking and Slavonic is for writing'
(*loquendum est Russice et scribendum est Slavonice*). We might therefore
describe Church Slavonic as the functional equivalent of Latin, especially
in the Romance-speaking parts of Europe. Although this language was
not used for official documents, the 'chancery language' (*prikazni jazik*) of
Muscovy took the form of a Russian influenced by Church Slavonic, just
as official English or French was influenced by Latin.

---

[28] D'Agostino, *La Piazza*, p. 29.   [29] Schmidt, *Liturgie*, pp. 110–11, 174–5.

In the West, in Protestant and Catholic countries alike, Latin was the language of 'the learned communitie' as the English schoolmaster Richard Mulcaster called it, or to quote a Swedish scholar, 'the mother tongue of the learned' (*lingua eruditorum vernacula*).[30] The fact that scholars from Lisbon to Cracow could correspond in Latin gave them a sense of belonging to an international community that they described as the 'Republic of Letters', or 'Commonwealth of Learning' (*Respublica Litterarum*). On the other hand, the use of Latin virtually excluded Orthodox Europe from this Republic, at least in the sixteenth century, since a fluent Latinist like the diplomat Dmitri Gerasimov, who frequented learned circles in Renaissance Rome, or Prince Kurbsky, who owned a number of Latin books, were rare birds in Russia.

The foundation of new universities in the early modern period enlarged the network of centres of Latin. In the sixteenth century, new universities included Dillingen, Dublin, Franeker, Geneva, Helmstedt, Jena, Königsberg, Leiden, Olomouc and Wilno (Vilnius). In the seventeenth century, Åbo, Altdorf, Cagliari, Giessen, Innsbruck, Kassa, Lund, Lwów (L'viv), Nijmegen and Utrecht. In the eighteenth century, Bonn, Breslau (now Wrocław), Dijon, Erlangen, Göttingen, Moscow, Pau, Rennes, St Petersburg and Stuttgart.

As the examples of Koenigsberg, Wilno, Lwów (like Wilno, originally a Jesuit college), Moscow and St Petersburg show, the practice of writing and speaking Latin gradually spread eastwards. In Lithuania, for instance, Augustin Rotundus, burgomaster of Wilno, composed a Latin chronicle in 1576 and translated the laws of Lithuania into Latin. He claimed that the Lithuanians were attracted to Latin as an alternative to Polish at a time when they were ruled by the Poles. Latin schools, including the Slavo-Greco-Latin Academy, were opened in Moscow, and the inventory of the library of the Zaikonopassky monastery there reveals the presence of 414 Latin books in 1689.[31]

In the eighteenth century, the proceedings of the Academy of Sciences of St Petersburg were published in Latin, rather than the German proposed by some expatriate scholars. Latin was taught in the Academy's school at this time.[32] In the Balkans too there was a rise of interest in Latin culture. The Bulgarian monk Christophor Žefarović knew Latin well enough to translate poetry.

---

[30] Richard Mulcaster, *The First Part of the Elementarie* (1582: facsimile repr., Menston, 1970), p. 257; Lindberg, *lärdes modersmål*.
[31] Antoine Martel, *La langue polonaise dans les pays ruthènes, Ukraine et Russie Blanche, 1569–1667* (Lille, 1938), pp. 52–3, 70, 279, 305.
[32] Riccardo Picchio and Harvey Goldblatt (eds.), *Aspects*, vol. 1, p. 18.

In Western and Central Europe (including Bohemia, Poland and Hungary) Latin had long been taught in schools, especially 'grammar schools', and it was often the means as well as the object of instruction. Latin grammars were written in Latin. The boys were supposed to speak Latin in class and even in the playground, and a spy, known as a 'wolf' (*lupus*) was supposed to inform the teacher if anyone lapsed into the vernacular. The point of this insistence was that spoken as well as written Latin was of practical importance in that society, given the need to make speeches and deliver sermons. Spoken Latin was taught by reading plays aloud (notably the plays of the Roman playwright Terence), as well as by modern dialogues written for the purpose, by Erasmus, for instance, and also by the French Protestant schoolmaster Mathurin Cordier, whose *Colloquia* appeared in 1563 and went through numerous editions.

Latin remained virtually the only language of instruction in the universities, officially at least, thus allowing them to function as a pan-European system in which students could move from country to country with relative ease, a custom known as *peregrinatio academica*. The right of Masters of Arts 'to teach everywhere', the *ius ubique docendi*, reinforced the opportunities provided by Latin. It is only recently, with the rise of English as an academic *lingua franca*, that the mobility of European students and teachers has been able to return to something like early modern levels.[33] The statutes of the colleges of Oxford and Cambridge not infrequently required the students to speak Latin at meals or more generally in public places, such as the college hall or chapel.[34]

Treatises in Latin helped to create what have been described as 'textual communities'.[35] The sheer number of books published in Latin in early modern Europe (including Britain) deserves to be remembered. At the annual Frankfurt fairs, for instance, the majority of books for sale were books in Latin until quite late in the seventeenth century (67 per cent in 1650, declining to 38 per cent in 1700).[36] Educated men who spoke different vernaculars often corresponded in Latin, as John Wesley and the German Pietist Peter Böhler did as late as the eighteenth century. In this respect, the

[33] Hilde de Ridder-Symoens (ed.), *A History of the University in Europe*, vol. I (Cambridge, 1992), pp. 280–304; vol. II (1996), pp. 416–48.
[34] For Brasenose, Jesus and Worcester College, Oxford, Robert J. W. Evans, *The Language of History and the History of Language* (Oxford, 1998), p. 20.
[35] Brian Stock, *The Implications of Literacy: Written Language and Models of Interpretation in the Eleventh and Twelfth Centuries* (Princeton, 1983).
[36] James W. Binns, *Intellectual Culture in Elizabethan and Jacobean England* (Oxford, 1990); Timothy Blanning, *The Culture of Power and the Power of Culture: Old Regime Europe 1660–1789* (Oxford, 2002), p. 145.

continuity between the Middle Ages and early modern times was important indeed.

What was new in this period was the challenge to Latin, the debate over its place in the world of scholarship. Several humanists wrote against the employment of the vernacular in the domain of learning, as Romolo Amaseo did in his oration at Bologna 'On retaining the use of Latin', *De linguae latinae usu retinendo* (1529). Similar points to Amaseo's were made by the character 'Ercole Strozzi' and the character of 'Lazzaro Bonamico' in the famous dialogues on language written by Pietro Bembo and Sperone Speroni.[37]

Writers now had to choose which language to employ. Erasmus and Luther represent two strategies and indeed two conceptions of community, which might be described as the horizontal and the vertical.[38] Erasmus chose geographical breadth. A native speaker of a small language, he chose Latin in order to broadcast his message to the Republic of Letters, in other words to learned readers in most countries of Europe, from Portugal to Poland and from England to Hungary. Luther, who also wrote in Latin for the learned public, devoted more effort to the vernacular in order to achieve social depth, to reach out to ordinary people, or, as he used to say, 'the common man' (*der gemeine Mann*) in the German-speaking world.

As scholars increasingly followed Luther's example and wrote in their own vernaculars, translations became necessary. They included translations from the vernacular into Latin, a demonstration, if one were needed, of the continuing importance of Latin in European intellectual life. Well over a thousand such translations were made between 1500 and 1800, reaching their height in the first half of the seventeenth century (at least 367 such texts were published between 1600 and 1649, in other words more than seven a year). About forty per cent of the texts translated were religious, while about twelve per cent might be described as works of what was known in the period as 'natural philosophy', ranging from mathematics to medicine and magic.[39]

For example, Galileo Galilei began his scholarly career with a book published in Latin, the 'Starry Messenger' (*Sidereus nuncius*). He switched to Italian later in order to widen his domestic audience. His change of strategy – from Erasmian to Lutheran, one might say – provoked a protest

---

[37] Pietro Bembo, *Prose della vulgar lingua* (1525: in *Prose e rime*, ed. Carlo Dionisotti, Turin, 1960, pp. 71–309); Sperone Speroni, *Dialogo della lingua* (1542: ed. Helene Harth, Munich, 1975).
[38] Lindberg, *lärdes modersmål*, p. 149.
[39] Ann Blair, 'La persistance du Latin comme langue de science à la fin de la Renaissance', in Roger Chartier and Pietro Corsi (eds.), *Sciences et langues en Europe* (Paris, 1996), pp. 21–42.

from one of his German admirers, Mark Welser, who could no longer understand the words of the master. Although a number of foreigners understood Italian at this time, as we shall see (below, pp. 113ff.), it was necessary for Galileo to be translated into Latin, by the German professor Matthias Bernegger and the Swiss lawyer Elio Diodati, so that his ideas could continue to circulate widely beyond Italy.

In similar fashion, René Descartes, who published his *Meditations* in Latin, switched to French for his *Discourse on Method*, for his study of the passions and for other works directed towards a socially diverse public. Thanks to translators such as the Protestant clergymen Etienne de Courcelles and Henri Desmarets, these works too continued to circulate in the language of the learned. At the end of the seventeenth century, Newton took a similar decision, shifting from his Latin *Principia* to his English *Optics*, which was then translated into Latin by his disciple Samuel Clarke.[40]

For the Erasmian solution to work, Latin needed to be learned early. It generally was learned early, even if Montaigne, who claimed in his *Essays* (book 1, chapter 25) that it was actually his first language, is an admittedly extreme case: 'I was over six before I could understand more French or the dialect of Périgord than I did Arabic' (*J'avois plus de six ans avant que j'entendisse non plus de françois ou de perigordin que d'arabesque*). Erasmus himself, who spent much of his life outside his native Netherlands, is virtually never recorded speaking Dutch, except on his deathbed (his last words were *lieve Godt*, 'dear God').

There remains the question, what kind of Latin did people know and use in this period? We need to speak and to think of 'Latins' in the plural, just as linguists have recently been speaking and writing about different 'Englishes'.[41] One might begin with the problem of divergent pronunciations. The English, for instance, pronounced their Latin so differently from other people that foreigners had difficulty understanding what they were saying.

Written Latin also came in numerous varieties. The main distinction was the one between the neoclassical Latin of the humanists and the medieval Latin of the Church. However, Church Latin was far from monolithic. It ranged from the simplicity of the liturgy or the Vulgate to the complexity of the prose of St Bernard. In any case, some of the sixteenth-century clergy wrote like humanists.

[40] Peter Burke, 'Translations into Latin in Early Modern Europe', in Peter Burke and Ronnie Hsia (eds.), *The Cultural History of Translation in Early Modern Europe* (forthcoming).
[41] Tom McArthur, *The English Languages* (Cambridge, 1998).

By contrast, the Latin of notaries was generally mixed with vernacular terms, and it was described at the time as 'Coarse Latin, the friend of the laity' (*Latinum grossum pro laicis amicum*).[42] Scholastic Latin in the universities, which would be known later as 'the jargon of the schools', was different again, influenced as it was by philosophers' Greek.[43] The Latin of the majority of learned publications in early modern Europe was not so much classical as a hybrid of ancient and medieval Latin, together with some neologisms.[44] To these varieties should be added the many individual mistakes committed by people who had not learned Latin properly, like the Hungarian nobleman who wrote *malum propria*, more or less 'with his own apple', when he meant to write *manu propria*, 'with his own hand'.[45]

These varieties were either confused or deliberately conflated by the humanists in their general condemnation of what they described as 'kitchen Latin' or 'dog Latin' and viewed as part of the barbarism of what they called the 'Dark Ages'.[46] The humanists focused on a negative characteristic of these different Latins, the fact of not being classical. All they noticed in medieval Latin was what white teachers used to notice in Black English, a kind of defecit. They were the first linguistic purists – or, more exactly, the first since Hellenistic times (below, p. 156).

For their part, the humanists tried to follow ancient models in writing and even in speaking Latin. The term 'models' needs to be used in the plural, since there was room for differences and debates. Many humanists followed the example of Cicero, imitating his complex sentences and even his mannerisms, such as ending a sentence with the stock phrase *esse videatur*. In the later sixteenth century, however, there was a movement, associated with the Netherlander Justus Lipsius in particular, to follow a later classical model, based on two writers of the so-called 'silver age', the philosopher Seneca and the historian Tacitus. The new model, described as 'Attic' rather than 'Asiatic' (terms originally applied to varieties of ancient Greek), was defined in terms of simplicity – less ornament, fewer words – and also a looser structure, with relatively frequent parentheses.[47]

---

[42] Philippe Wolff, *Western Languages AD 100–1500* (London, 1971), p. 201.
[43] Peter Burke, 'The Jargon of the Schools', in Burke and Roy Porter (eds.), *Languages and Jargons* (Cambridge, 1995), pp. 22–41.
[44] Waquet, *Latin*, pp. 124–9.
[45] Tóth, 'Beyond Literacy', p. 132; on a more recent period, Waquet, *Latin*, pp. 119–71.
[46] Paul Lehmann, 'Mittelalter und Küchenlatin' (1928: repr. in his *Erforschung des Mittelalters*, 5 vols., Leipzig, 1941), pp. 46–62, at p. 57; Rudolf Pfeiffer, 'Küchenlatein' (1931: repr. in his *Ausgewählte Schriften*, Munich, 1960), pp. 183–7.
[47] Morris W. Croll, 'Juste Lipse et le mouvement anticicéronien' (1914: repr. in his *Style, Rhetoric and Rhythm*, Princeton, 1966), pp. 7–44; Croll, 'Attic Prose in the Seventeenth Century', repr. ibid., pp. 51–106.

The great paradox of humanist Latin was that the so-called 'revival' of the classical language meant replacing a living language with a 'dead' one. Or, to use a more appropriate metaphor, it meant replacing a fluid language with one that was fixed. Erasmus saw the problem more clearly than most of his colleagues. In his dialogue the *Ciceronianus* (1528), he raised the awkward question, how a modern follower of Cicero would refer to institutions and objects that had not existed in Cicero's day.[48] After all, writers and speakers alike might want to refer to Muslims, or to canon, or the pope. The alternatives were to coin neologisms, such as *mahometani* or *bombardae*, or to adopt classical terms that had originally had a different meaning, such as *pontifex maximus*.[49] One solution sounded inelegant, but the other was potentially misleading, translating vague similarities into identity.

However, more was at stake in this debate than utility or lucidity. Latin was not only a means of communication but also a symbol, indeed a shibboleth.[50] Like italic handwriting, ciceronian Latin was a sign of participation in the humanist movement. Fluent Latin was a badge of membership in the community known as the *Respublica Litterarum*, the 'Republic of Letters' or 'Commonwealth of Learning' (*litterae*, literally 'letters' meant learning as well as literature). This Latin phrase appeared in the early fifteenth century, became more common at the time of Erasmus, and remained in use until the eighteenth century.[51] In this republic, the citizens in the full sense of the term were the scholars, while the second-class citizens were the boys who had attended grammar schools.

The history of Latin might be summed up in the language of the Swiss historian Jacob Burckhardt, who distinguished 'three powers', the State, the Church, and Culture.[52] Latin was first the language of the state, more precisely of the Roman Empire. Then it became the language of the Church, in this sense replacing the Roman Empire, as the political theorist Thomas Hobbes maliciously noted in his *Leviathan* (1651), 'the ghost of the Roman Empire sitting crowned upon the grave thereof'. Finally, Latin became the language of culture, at least of high culture.

However, from the middle of the seventeenth century onwards Latin began to lose this position. A slow decline is discernible after 1650, and a more rapid one after 1750 (of the 180 vernacular texts that were published in

[48] Erasmus, *Ciceronianus* (1528: English translation, *Collected Works* 28, Toronto, 1986), pp. 323–68.
[49] Burke, 'Translations'.
[50] Waquet, *Latin*, pp. 173–229: Ian Buruma, 'The Road to Babel', *New York Review of Books* (31 May 2001), pp. 23–6.
[51] Marc Fumaroli, *L'âge de l'éloquence* (Geneva, 1980): Waquet, *Latin*.
[52] Jacob Burckhardt, *Reflections on History* (1906: English translation, London, 1943).

Latin translation in the eighteenth century, only fifty appeared between 1750 and 1799). The geography as well as the chronology of decline is significant. Speakers of small vernaculars often clung on to Latin as a defence against encroachments from larger vernaculars. In Denmark and Hungary, for instance, Latin was a means of defence against German, in Finland against Swedish.[53]

Elsewhere, Latin was becoming increasingly associated with pedantry, an association linked to cultural changes, such as an increasing interest in literature on the part of the nobility in France and elsewhere. A study of the French book trade in the seventeenth century shows a dramatic shift from learned folios in Latin in the first half of the century to works in octavo format in the vernacular after 1650.[54] A vestige of Latin survived to the end of our period and beyond in the custom of referring to topics considered obscene in Latin, even in a book written in the vernacular, such as Pierre Bayle's famous historical dictionary, in order to limit the readership of such passages to educated men.

The seventeenth century was a time of many attempts to create universal languages that would allow people from all parts of the world to communicate without misunderstanding. Among the published projects were the merchant Francis Lodwick's *Groundwork* (1652), the schoolmaster George Dalgarno's *Ars Signorum* (1661), and, the most famous, the *Essay towards a Real Character and a Philosophical Language* (1668) by John Wilkins, a bishop who was also a natural philosopher and a Fellow of the Royal Society.

These projects, which interested philosophers of the calibre of Bacon, Descartes and Leibniz, were in part attempts to eliminate ambiguities of terminology, so as to describe more accurately the new discoveries in natural philosophy. The ideal was to construct a 'philosophical' or, as we would say, a 'scientific' language. One of the models for this language was the Chinese system of writing in ideograms or 'characters'. Bacon, for instance, was aware that the Chinese and the Japanese could communicate by means of these characters, despite the mutual unintelligibility of their languages, and he, like his follower Wilkins, regarded the characters as 'real' rather than nominal, expressing ideas without the mediation of a spoken language. Another stimulus to the development of a universal language was the expansion of the mission field, making the missionaries more and

---

[53] Iiro Kajanto, 'The Position of Latin in Eighteenth-Century Finland', in Pierre Tuynman et al. (eds.), *Acta Conventus Neo-Latini Amstelodamensis* (Munich, 1979), pp. 93–106.
[54] Henri-Jean Martin, *Print, Power and People in 17th-Century France* (1969: English translation, London, 1993), pp. 528–9, 544–6, 566–7.

more conscious of the number, variety and complexity of non-European languages.

However, these schemes for universal languages were also reactions to the decline of Latin as a medium for international communication. As Umberto Eco has suggested, it may be no accident that Lodwick, Dalgarno and Wilkins were all British. As Protestants, they may have been hostile to Latin because of its associations with the Catholic Church (above, p. 48). They were also speakers of a language that few people in Europe could understand (below, p. 115). Hence, the new philosophical languages were intended as substitutes for Latin. In similar fashion, later utopians would pin their hopes on Esperanto.[55]

An alternative response to the decline of Latin was for educated Europeans to adopt a single vernacular as an international language. The shift towards French in the late seventeenth century was part of the so-called 'rise of the vernaculars', to be discussed in the following chapter.

[55] Vivian Salmon, *The Works of Francis Lodwick* (London, 1972), esp. pp. 43–51; James Knowlson, *Universal Language Schemes in England and France, 1600–1800* (Toronto, 1975); Mary M. Slaughter, *Universal Languages and Scientific Taxonomy in the Seventeenth Century* (Cambridge, 1982); Umberto Eco, *The Search for the Perfect Language* (1993: English translation, Oxford, 1995), especially pp. 209–316.

CHAPTER 3

Vernaculars in competition

It has often been argued that the early modern period was one of the 'emergence', the 'rise' or the 'triumph' of the national vernaculars, at the expense of cosmopolitan Latin on the one hand and local dialects on the other.[1] To the extent that this happened, the phenomenon was important for the creation of new 'speech communities' and eventually new trans-regional or super-regional loyalties. By 1750, the European linguistic system was very different from the medieval system, which had been divided between a living but non-classical Latin and regional dialects which were spoken rather than written.

However, the simple statement that the vernaculars of Europe 'rose' is a rather crude one. The short comparative survey which follows will attempt to offer some at least of the necessary distinctions, nuances and qualifications, as well as reflecting on the place in the history of different European vernaculars of the Renaissance, the Reformation, Absolutism (or at least the centralizing state), European expansion and the Enlightenment.

THE WHIG INTERPRETATION AND ITS PROBLEMS

The story of the rise of the vernaculars is one that has often been told in a triumphalist manner, notably in the cases of French and English, with a stress on their victory over Latin or their 'emancipation' in the course of the Renaissance and Reformation. We might call this version a 'Whig' history of language and compare it to the traditional but much-criticized story of the rise of the middle class.[2]

---

[1] Richard F. Jones, *The Triumph of the English Language* (Stanford, 1953); Aldo Scaglione (ed.), *The Emergence of National Languages* (Ravenna, 1984); Fredi Chiappelli (ed.), *The Fairest Flower: the Emergence of Linguistic National Consciousness in Renaissance Europe* (Florence, 1985).

[2] Jack Hexter, 'The Myth of the Middle Class in Tudor England' (1950: repr. in *Reappraisals in History*, London, 1961), pp. 71–116.

The British medievalist George Coulton and the Russian theorist Mikhail Bakhtin expressed the fundamental idea with characteristic vividness when they wrote of a 'revolt' of the vernaculars against Latin and their subsequent 'victory'.[3] Ferdinand Brunot had written still earlier about what he called 'the emancipation', 'campaign', and 'the victory' of French in the sixteenth century and of its 'new conquests' in science, philosophy and elsewhere in the seventeenth.[4] Again, Richard Jones's famous study of early modern English bears the title *The Triumph of the English Language*.[5] A history of early Italian prose emphasizes 'The gradual rise and expansion of the Italian literary language at the expense of its Latin rival'.[6] A study of medieval Catalan speaks of its 'constant race with Aragonese for victory over Latin' and its need 'to attack the sovereignty of Latin in one field after another'.[7]

There is, of course, something to be said for this traditional view. For example, Italian, French, Spanish, English, German and Czech came to be used more frequently in the domains of law and administration from the fourteenth century onwards.

The same languages, together with others such as Flemish and Portuguese, were becoming increasingly important in the domain of literature, boosted by the appearance of printed books in one vernacular after another following 1460. The expansion of the vernaculars into these domains was linked to the rise of lay literacy and so to the decline of the clerical quasi-monopoly of knowledge. It was also linked to attempts to reform or codify the vernaculars to make them more suitable for their new functions.

In short, the 'Whig' argument is not exactly false. All the same, it is in need of considerable refinement. The criteria for 'victory' or 'emancipation' need to be spelled out in order to respond to some serious problems, five in particular:

1. In the first place, the persistence of Latin, emphasized in the previous chapter, together with its spread eastwards, is a reminder not to exaggerate the victory of any vernacular. In his history of French, Ferdinand Brunot was somewhat hasty in his dismissal of what he called the 'obstacles' to

---

[3] George G. Coulton, *Europe's Apprenticeship: a Survey of Medieval Latin with Examples* (London, 1940), p. 84; Mikhail Bakhtin, *Rabelais and his World* (1965: English translation, Cambridge, MA, 1968), pp. 465, 473.
[4] Ferdinand Brunot, *Langue française*, vol. II, pp. 2, 4, 31, and vol. III, pp. 713–5.
[5] Jones, *Triumph*.
[6] Paul Kristeller, 'The Origin and Development of the Language of Italian Prose', in his *Renaissance Thought*, vol. II (New York, 1965), pp. 119–41, at p. 120.
[7] Helene Wieruszowski, 'The Rise of the Catalan Language in the Thirteenth Century' (1944: repr. in her *Politics and Culture in Medieval Spain and Italy*, Rome, 1971), pp. 107–18, at pp. 107, 111.

the rise of French (including the use of Latin) as 'résistances sans intérêt'.[8] Today, by contrast, there is considerable interest in the history of post-medieval Latin. The study of 'Neo-Latin', as it is often called, is supported by associations of scholars that organize international conferences and publish regular bulletins. Thanks to these scholars, the continuing importance of Latin culture in the sixteenth and seventeenth centuries has become abundantly clear.

2. In the second place, there is the problem of assuming harmony or consensus, ignoring the variety of and the conflicts between early modern 'Englishes', for instance, or different forms of German or Italian.[9] There was often what might be called a 'struggle for the standard', to be discussed in more detail in chapter 4.

3. In the third place, to speak of the rise or 'emergence' of the vernaculars in the sixteenth century runs the risk of forgetting the importance of the earlier rise of some European vernaculars, in other words their use in the domain of writing, including what we now call 'literature'. This was the case for French, Saxon and Irish in the ninth century or thereabouts, for Spanish and Slovene in the tenth century, Italian around the year 1000, Provençal around 1100, Dutch and Icelandic in the twelfth century, Hungarian and Danish in the thirteenth, Catalan and Polish in the fourteenth.[10] As for administration, the French royal chancery switched to the vernacular soon after 1200. It was also in the thirteenth century that King Alfonso X, known as *El Sabio* ('the Wise', or 'the Learned') made Spanish the language of government.

4. In the fourth place, there is the danger of projecting back into the early modern period the close associations between language and nation that only became common at the end of the eighteenth century. Linguistic pluralism was commonplace in early modern Europe, as it had been in the Middle Ages, and this at official as well as unofficial levels.[11]

In the empire of Charles V, for instance, official letters were regularly written in Latin, French and Italian, as well as in Spanish and German. In some parts of Europe, such as Switzerland in the sixteenth century, a single family might write letters in five languages (in Romansh as well

[8] Brunot, *Langue française*, vol. ii, pp. 6–7, 31.
[9] Paula Blank, *Broken English: Dialects and the Politics of Language in Renaissance Writings* (London, 1996).
[10] Banfi, *Formazione*, p. 11.
[11] János Bak, 'Linguistic Pluralism in Medieval Hungary', in Marc A. Meyer, *The Culture of Christendom* (London, 1993), pp. 269–79.

as Latin, German, French and Italian (below, p. 117).[12] Linguistic pluralism was particularly common in East-Central Europe, where speakers
of Hungarian and Slovak, Czech and German, or Croat and Italian
lived close together. In the Grand Duchy of Lithuania, at least five
spoken vernaculars coexisted: Lithuanian, Polish, German, Ruthenian
and Latvian.

5. Finally, the term 'rise', although more neutral than 'triumph' or 'emancipation', does suffer from the disadvantage of ambiguity. It may refer to
an increase in prestige, in the number of speakers, or in the number of
functions. There is also the implication that the trend is irresistible. This
implication is a misleading one, at least on occasion. After all, in the case
of French one might just as reasonably speak of the Renaissance as the
age of the collapse of what had once been a French linguistic empire,
extending in the late Middle Ages to England, Spain, Italy, Germany,
Hungary and Cyprus.[13] There was also a German linguistic empire at
this time, in Central Europe and the Baltic world, but it declined much
more slowly, as we shall see.

For these reasons, what follows is intended to offer a few qualifications
to the Whig or orthodox account, adopting a comparative approach and
distinguishing between the history of different vernaculars and between
different linguistic domains.

A comparative approach to the history of the enlargement of the vocabulary of different vernaculars would be particularly useful. Unfortunately,
the statistical work that has been carried out on French and in still more
detail on English has not yet been emulated for other languages.[14]

In the case of English, the contribution of a number of individuals to
the resources of the language has also been studied. We know, for instance,
that Thomas More coined the terms 'absurdity', 'exaggerate' and 'frivolous',
while Thomas Elyot was responsible for 'accommodate', 'frugality' and
'modesty'. As for Shakespeare, he coined some seventeen hundred neologisms, derived in the main from Latin, and about two-thirds of these, from
'antipathy' to 'vast', were accepted into the language. It has been calculated
that more than thirty-eight thousand words entered English between 1450
and 1750, with the high point of word-coining occurring in the twenty

---

[12] Christian S. Stang, *Die west-russische Kanzleisprache des Grossfürstentums Litauen* (Oslo, 1935);
Randolph C. Head, 'A Plurilingual Family in the Sixteenth Century', *Sixteenth-Century Journal*
26 (1995), pp. 577–93.

[13] Brunot, *Langue française*, vol. 1, pp. 376–417.

[14] Pierre Guiraud, *Les mots étrangers* (Paris, 1965); Richard Wermser, *Statistische Studien zur Entwicklung
des englischen Wortschatzes* (Bern, 1976); cf. Charles L. Barber, *Early Modern English* (Cambridge,
1976).

years between 1590 and 1609, when some six thousand terms were added to the language.[15]

THE RENAISSANCE AND THE PRAISES OF THE VERNACULAR

Another important change in this period was the rise in the status of the vernacular, or more exactly of some vernaculars. Like orations and treatises on the dignity and excellence of humanity, the praises of the vernacular were a Renaissance genre. Humanists such as Romolo Amaseo, Carlo Sigonio and Uberto Foglietta entered the debate to argue for the excellence of Latin, as we have seen (above, p. 55), and others to praise Hebrew. In Eastern Christendom, at the end of the sixteenth century, Ivan Vyšenskyi called Church Slavonic 'the most fruitful of all languages and God's favourite', while Latin was the language of the devil.[16]

However, these scholars were outnumbered by the supporters of the vernaculars. The printing of Dante's treatise on the eloquence of the vernacular in 1529 seems to have set off a chain reaction, beginning in the 1540s.

Select printed defences of the vernacular, 1529–1663

1529	Dante, *De vulgari eloquentia*
1540	J. de Barros, *Louvor de nossa linguagem*
1542	S. Speroni, *Dialogo della lingua*
1549	J. Du Bellay, *Deffense et illustration de la langue française*
1574	M. Viziana, *Alabanças de las lenguas . . . castellana y valenciana*
1579	H. Estienne, *Precellence de la langue française*
1586	S. Stevin, *Weerdigheyt der duytsche tael*
1589	J. Rybinski, *De lingua polonica praestantia et utilitate*
1615	R. Carew, *On the Excellency of the English Tongue*
1617	M. Opitz, *De contemptu linguae teutonicae*
1642	J. Rist, *Rettung der edlen Teutschen*
1663	J. G. Schottel, *Lob der Teutschen Haubtsprache*

---

[15] Bryan A. Garner, 'Shakespeare's Latinate Neologisms', *Shakespeare Studies* 15 (1982), pp. 149–70; Terttu Nevaainen, 'Lexis and Semantics', in Lass, *History of the English Language* vol. III, pp. 332–458, at p. 341.

[16] Quoted in Antoine Martel, *La langue polonaise dans les pays Ruthènes: Ukraine et Russie Blanche, 1569–1667* (Lille, 1938), pp. 72–3, and Bohdan Strumins'kyi, 'The Language Question in the Ukrainian Lands before the Nineteenth Century', in Picchio and Goldblatt, *Aspects*, vol. 2, pp. 9–47, at pp. 16–17.

pot, and that, when the pot began to boil, he made the English language out of the scum'.[24]

On the positive side, the point was to show that one's own language was as good as Latin, Greek or Italian, if not better. For example, the Spaniard Pedro Mexia declared that 'Castilian does not need to concede the advantage to any other language' (*la lengua castellana no tien... porque reconozca ventaja a otra ninguna*).[25] Not to be outdone, Du Bellay claimed that French had as much grace as Latin and Greek, while Estienne argued that it was 'more capable of eloquence or capable of greater eloquence than the others' (*plus capable d'eloquence, ou capable de plus grand eloquence que les autres*). The idea that French is distinguished by its clarity goes back to the middle of the seventeenth century, when Vaugelas declared that it is 'plus ennemi des equivoques et de toute sorte d'obscurité' than any other language.[26] A few years later, Bouhours argued that 'notre langue est capable de toutes choses', contrasting it unfavourably with Italian and Spanish, the only rivals he considered to be worth discussing at all.[27]

For his part, Martin Luther claimed in his table talk that 'the German language is the most perfect of all' (*Germanica autem lingua omnium est perfectissima*: no. 4018). The sixteenth-century translator Johann Fischart agreed, arguing in his vivid way that 'our language is a language too and can name a sack as well as the Latin *saccus*' (*Unser sprach ist auch ein sprach und kan so wohl ein Sack nennen, als die Latinen saccus*).[28] The poet Martin Opitz declared that German possessed the majesty of Spanish, the decorum of Italian and the charm of French.[29] Turning eastwards, we find that the printer Hieronim Wietor claimed in 1542 that Polish was not inferior to any language, while Marcin Siennik declared, in the preface to a herbal published in 1568, that 'The Polish language . . . can refer to everything without the help of neighbours'.[30]

As for English, Thomas More had already claimed in the book he wrote against the reformer William Tyndale that the language was not 'barren' but 'plenteous enough'. The schoolmaster Richard Mulcaster declared that

---

[24] Ludvig Holberg, *Memoirs*, ed. and trans. Stewart E. Fraser (Leiden, 1970), p. 220. A slightly less picturesque version was recorded by Johann Schottel: 'Denn als in einem Topfe . . . alle Sprachen gekocht worden, ware der Schaum davon die Englische Sprache geworden': quoted in Sigfrid von der Schulenburg, *Leibniz als Sprachforscher* (Frankfurt, 1973), p. 134n.

[25] José Francisco Pastor (ed.), *Las apologías de la lengua castellana en el siglo de oro* (Madrid, 1929), p. 34.

[26] Brunot, *Langue française*, vol. III, pp. 46–56.   [27] Bouhours, *Entretiens*, p. 46.

[28] Quoted in Walter E. Spengler, *Johann Fischart* (Göppingen, 1969), p. 258.

[29] Martin Opitz, *Aristarchus* (1617: in his *Gesammelte Werke*, Stuttgart, 1968, 53–75), p. 64.

[30] Claude Backvis, *Quelques remarques sur le bilinguisme latino-polonais dans la Pologne du xvie siècle* (Brussels, 1958), pp. 19–21. Cf. the texts collected in Witold Taszycki, *Obrońcy języka polskiego* (Wrocław, 1953).

'I do not think that any language . . . is better able to utter all arguments' than English, and that it was 'not any whit behind either the subtle Greek . . . or the stately Latin'. His colleague Alexander Gill agreed, claiming that no language is 'more graceful, elegant, apt or offers more possibilities for the expression of every thought' (*aut cultior, aut ornatior, aut ad omnia animi sensa explicanda aptior aut facundior*).[31]

In the eighteenth century, the claim was extended to still more languages. In a treatise on the primacy of the Slavonic language over the Teutonic, Vasili Trediakovsky described Slavonic as the oldest European language. The writer Mikhaylo Lomonosov declared in the dedication to his *Russian Grammar* that 'Russian is not inferior to any of the languages of Europe', possessing as it did 'the grandeur of Spanish, the vitality of French, the firmness of German, the tenderness of Latin, and besides these the richness and forceful conciseness of expression of Greek and Latin'. In similar fashion, Catherine the Great remarked to princess Dashkova that Russian united 'the strength, the richness and the energy of the German with the sweetness of the Italian'. According to the Hungarian János Ribinyi, 'Italian is pleasant, French is beautiful, German earnest: but all these qualities are so united in Hungarian that it is difficult to say wherein its superiority consists'.[32]

From an Olympian or comparative point of view, the texts undermine one another, since it is obviously impossible for every language to be the noblest, the richest or the oldest in Europe, or even in the world. The original language spoken by Adam was identified as Flemish by the Antwerp humanist Johannes Goropius and as Swedish by the seventeenth-century polymath Olaf Rudbeck of Uppsala, while some eighteenth-century welsh men thought it was Welsh.[33] These claims might be described as a form of collective narcissism, an extreme case of the still common belief that one's own language, like one's nation, region, city or family – not to mention football team – is the best. Yet the way in which these treatises should be read remains a problem, less simple than it may appear.

---

[31] Richard Mulcaster, *The First Part of the Elementarie* (1582: facsimile repr., Menston, 1970); Alexander Gill, *Logonomia anglica* (1619: ed. and trans. Bror Danielsson and Arvid Gabrielson, Stockholm, 1972).

[32] Lomonosov quoted in Christopher D. Buck, 'The Russian Language Question in the Imperial Academy of Sciences', in Picchio and Goldblatt, *Aspects*, vol. 2, pp. 187–233, at p. 218; cf. Antoine Martel, *Michel Lomonosov et la langue littéraire russe* (Paris, 1933), p. 20; Catherine quoted in Hans Rogger, *National Consciousness in Eighteenth-Century Russia* (Cambridge, MA, 1960), p. 113; Ribinyi quoted in Joshua A. Fishman, *Language in Sociocultural Change* (New York, 1972), p. 65.

[33] Arno Borst, *Der Turmbau von Babel* (4 vols. in 6, Stuttgart, 1957–63), pp. 1215–19, 1339–41: Jenkins, *Welsh Language*, pp. 378–9.

Like the treatises on the dignity of humanity, they may be rhetorical exercises by writers equally capable of arguing the opposite case. They may be expressions of confidence, but they may also be signs of an inferiority complex relative to Latin, Italian, or, from the seventeenth century onwards, French.

COMPETITION

The treatises or orations discussed above give a vivid impression of conflict, the 'linguistic battle' or the 'war of languages'.[34] It may be even more illuminating to speak of linguistic competition, of the struggle for the centre and of attempts to marginalize rivals.[35] As Henri Estienne put it in his defence of French, 'our language had two competitors (*competiteurs*), Italian and Spanish'.[36] In the seventeenth and eighteenth centuries, German speakers, including Leibniz, sometimes express a fear that their language is lagging behind Italian, French and English.[37]

Remember the number of vernaculars in early modern Europe, between forty and seventy (above, p. 8). If there were winners in this competition, there obviously had to be losers. If the 'rise' of a language is a meaningful expression, the movement must take place at the expense of another. There were 'master languages', as one Briton called them in 1650, and there were 'subordinate languages'.[38] There were contests for territory and even sometimes for survival. The process that the French linguist Louis-Jean Calvet calls *glottophagie*, the big fish swallowing the smaller, was already noticeable at this time.[39]

At the extreme, there are recorded cases of language extinction, or, in the current phrase, 'language death'.[40] Gothic, for instance, was still spoken in the Crimea in the middle of the fifteenth century, when it was heard and recorded by a visiting Venetian merchant, but it seems to have disappeared soon after this time.[41] Around the year 1600, Curonian became extinct,

---

[34] Ricardo García Carcel, 'La lengua e la batalla lingüística', in his *Historia de Cataluña: siglos xvi–xvii* (Barcelona, 1985), pp. 81–112, at p. 81; Louis-Jean Calvet, *Language Wars and Linguistic Politics* (1987: English translation, Oxford, 1998).

[35] Ronald Wardhaugh, *Languages in Competition* (Oxford, 1987).

[36] Henri Estienne, *La précellence du langage françois* (1579: ed. Edmond Huguet, Paris, 1896), p. 14.

[37] Jürgen Schiewe, *Die Macht der Sprache: Eine Geschichte der Sprachlichkeit von der Antike bis zur Gegenwart* (Munich, 1998), p. 70.

[38] Richard Flecknoe, *A Relation of Ten Years' Travels* (London, no date, but c. 1650), p. 106. The master languages, according to Flecknoe, were French, Spanish and (somewhat optimistically) English.

[39] Calvet, *Language Wars*.

[40] Daniel Nettle and Suzanne Romaine, *Vanishing Voices* (London, 2000); David Crystal, *Language Death* (Cambridge, 2000).

[41] Macdonald Stearns, *Crimean Gothic: Analysis and Etymology of the Corpus* (Saratoga, CA, 1978), pp. 6–7.

replaced by its neighbours Lithuanian and Latvian.[42] In the late seventeenth century, it was the turn of Old Prussian. On the title-page of a catechism in that language someone wrote around the year 1700 that 'This old Prussian language has now quite completely vanished for ever' (*Diese alte Preusnische Sprache ist nunmehr gantz und gar vergangen worden*), adding that an old man who lived on the Courland Spit and still knew the language had died in 1677. Around the middle of the eighteenth century Polabian disappeared, a Slavonic language spoken along the Elbe.[43]

Further west, a relatively well-documented case of language extinction is that of Cornish. In 1542, it was reported that in Cornwall 'there be many men and women the which cannot speak one word of English but all Cornish'.[44] By 1600, however, Cornish speakers had diminished to some twenty thousand, and a hundred years later, to about five thousand. Dolly Pentreath of Mousehole, who died in 1777, has sometimes been described as the last native speaker of the language.

However, an unqualified story of the 'fall' of certain languages would be as gross a simplification as that of the 'rise' of others. As a social historian of Welsh puts it, 'a simple linear geographical and chronological perspective of the steady retreat of the Welsh language must be modified by considerations of language maintenance, class and occupation' (and, it should be added, by considerations of linguistic domain as well).[45]

LINGUISTIC DOMAINS

Much more common than language extinction was the disappearance of certain languages from certain public domains such as courts and schools, in other words a kind of linguistic retirement into private life.[46]

For example, Galician is said to have 'disappeared' from written sources in the early sixteenth century (though it is attested in private letters a hundred years later) and did not make its reappearance until after the year 1800.[47] Frisian too was in decline in the domain of writing. The last official document in that language dates from 1573, and Dutch was becoming the language of the church, the towns, and the elites.[48]

---

[42] William B. Lockwood, *A Panorama of the Indo-European Languages* (London, 1972), p. 138.

[43] William R. Schmalstieg, *An Old Prussian Grammar* (University Park, MD, 1974), p. 3; Banfi, *Formazione*, p. 153.

[44] Quoted Lockwood, *Panorama*, p. 53.   [45] Jenkins, *Welsh Language*, p. 53.

[46] Crystal, *Language Death*, pp. 22, 83.

[47] Glanville Price (ed.), *Encyclopaedia of the Languages of Europe* (Oxford, 1998), p. 185, contrast Fernando Bouza, *Corre manuscrito: una historia cultural del siglo de oro* (Madrid, 2001), pp. 141–2.

[48] Cor van Bree, 'The Development of so-called Town Frisian', in Peter Bakker and Maarten Mous (eds.), *Mixed Languages* (Amsterdam, 1994), pp. 69–82.

Why did some languages decline in this way? There are two rival explanations, one political and the other social: pressure from outside or a change
of mind (what nationalists would call 'treason') from within.

Political explanations stress deliberate acts by governments, which were
as rare before 1789 as they were common after that date. Social explanations,
by contrast, stress the agency of ordinary speakers, who may internalize the
idea that their language is inferior. Especially important is the pressure
of parents on children to learn and use a more prestigious language that
offers more opportunities for social mobility than their own. In sixteenth-
century Wales, some parents began to send their sons to school in England,
to Shrewsbury for instance.[49]

Hence, the children sometimes abandoned their native language altogether, shifting in this period from Welsh and Irish to English, from Breton
and Occitan to French, Catalan to Spanish and so on. More frequently,
though, they practised 'diglossia', using different languages with different
people or in different domains. In early modern Catalonia, for instance, the
elites might use Spanish out of deference to Castilians if they were present,
but Catalan on formal occasions in public, while switching between the
two languages in their family letters.[50]

Within the same group, different languages might be considered appropriate for different purposes. In the sixteenth century, the great Polish poet
Jan Kochanowski once apologized for writing a letter in Polish, while as we
have seen (above, p. 43) cardinal Hosius thought that language inappropriate for writing about theology.[51] Distinctions obviously need to be drawn,
including those between the domains of law and administration, religion,
and literature and learning.

LAW AND ADMINISTRATION

Attempts by governments to impose certain forms of written language
have a long history, especially in the domains of law and administration.
One scholar has spoken of an official 'language policy' in the time of
Charlemagne, since the king tried to impose a reformed version of Latin on
his realm (together with a reformed script, the famous Carolingian minus-
cule), although he also encouraged the use of German for administrative

---

[49] Charles W. J. Withers, *Gaelic in Scotland, 1698–1981: the Geographical History of a Language*
(Edinburgh, 1984), p. 29.
[50] Joan-Lluís Marfany, *La llengua maltractada: El castellà i el català a Catalunya del segle xvi al segle xix*
(Barcelona, 2001), pp. 121, 310, etc.
[51] Backvis, *Quelques remarques*, pp. 6, 8n.

purposes.[52] The phrase 'language policy' has also been used about the actions of the Dutch East India Company, and again about kings Henry IV and Henry V of England, in the course of arguing that their support of English as a chancery language, for instance, at the expense of Latin and French, was a way of gaining legitimacy for their new dynasty.[53]

The problem with the modern phrase 'language policy' is that it implies more than a personal interest by the ruler in linguistic matters, as in Charlemagne's case. It implies planning for change, rather than reacting to problems as they arise. In the case of the Dutch East India Company, its rulings have been described as 'rarely consistent', so that it might be better to speak of 'reactions' rather than of a policy.[54] For this reason it might be wise to avoid the term in the case of Europe before 1789, or at least to emphasize its limitations.[55]

The point is that interest in language on the part of governments was largely confined to two domains. In the first place, it concerned the language of administration, used in departments such as the chancery, an office concerned with the composition, dispatch, receipt and filing of letters. In the fourteenth and fifteenth centuries, there was a shift from Latin to the vernacular in certain chanceries – in the German states, for example, in Milan, and in England in the reign of Henry V, although French was still used in the offices of the Privy Seal and the Signet, so we are told, 'until well into the fifteenth century'.[56]

As for the courts, the royal ordinance of Villers-Cotterêts (1539), replacing Latin by French in this domain, is especially well-known. The ordinance, which refers to *langaige maternel Françoys*, has sometimes been interpreted as 'the first official act of a royal policy of linguistic unification'.[57] However, to see Villers-Cotterêts as a step towards the unification policies of the French Revolution would be a case of the Whig interpretation at its most misleading. According to one famous sixteenth-century lawyer, Pierre

[52] Michael Richter, 'Die Sprachenpolitik Karls des Grossen' (1982: repr. Richter, *Studies in Medieval Language and Culture*, Dublin, 1995), pp. 86–108.
[53] Kees Groeneboer, *Gateway to the West: the Dutch Language in Colonial Indonesia, 1600–1950: a history of language policy* (1993: English translation, Amsterdam, 1998); John H. Fisher, 'A Language Policy for Lancastrian England' (1992: repr. Fisher, *The Emergence of Standard English*, Lexington, KY, 1996, pp. 16–35).
[54] Groeneboer, *Gateway*, p. 59.
[55] Henri Peyre, *La royauté et les langues provinciales* (Paris, 1933), pp. 97, 107, 117, 122, 166, 250.
[56] Maurizio Vitale, *La lingua volgare della cancelleria viscontea-sforzesca nel '400* (Varese-Milan, 1953); Malcolm Richardson, 'Henry V, the English Chancery and Chancery English', *Speculum* 55 (1980), pp. 726–50; on the Privy Seal and the Signet, Helen Suggett, 'The Use of French in England in the Later Middle Ages', *Transactions of the Royal Historical Society* 28 (1946), pp. 61–84, at p. 67.
[57] Danielle Trudeau, 'L'ordonnance de Villers-Cotterêts et la langue française: histoire ou interpretation?' *Bibliothèque d'Humanisme et Renaissance* 45 (1983), pp. 461–72, at p. 461.

Rebuffi, the term 'French' should be interpreted in a wide sense because the ordinance was not intended to exclude other vernaculars from the courts.[58]

The French edict was part of a European trend. In Poland, for instance, the *Sejm* (Diet) ruled in 1539, the year of Villers-Cotterêts, that all laws and edicts should be published in Polish (with a summary in Latin). In 1560, Emmanuel Philibert of Savoy ordered the use of French (*langage vulgaire*) to replace Latin in the courts and the Senate.[59]

In other cases, the exclusion of some 'subordinate' vernaculars from the official domain was less ambiguous than in the case of Villers-Cotterêts. In the Duchy of Burgundy, for instance, French was the dominant language, used at meetings of the Estates and also in the administration. That this dominance was resented became clear on the death of Charles the Bold in 1477, when there was a successful move to make Flemish or Dutch the language of the Estates and also that of the administration in the northern provinces of Holland and Zeeland.[60]

The Act of Union between England and Wales of 1536 required courts to be kept and oaths taken 'in the English tongue', complaining that the Welsh 'have and do daily use a speech nothing like, ne consonant to the natural mother tongue used within this Realm' (in practice, though, Welsh continued to be used in the courts).[61] In similar fashion the 1537 'Act of the English Order, Habit and Language' limited the use of Irish in public. In 1561, the Inquisition made the use of Castilian obligatory in trials in Catalonia.

The trend towards the administrative use of a few vernaculars, whether at the expense of other vernaculars or of Latin, continued after 1600. After the battle of the White Mountain (1620) that led to the suppression of the revolt of Bohemia against the emperor Ferdinand II, Czech was replaced by German in the public sphere. In the Swedish empire in the seventeenth century, the government attempted to restrict the use of Danish and Finnish.[62] In the 1680s, the French state imposed the use of French in the courts and administration of the newly conquered territories of Flanders

---

[58] Peyre, *Royauté*, pp. 58–91; Piero Fiorelli, 'Pour l'interprétation de l'ordonnance de Villers-Cotterêts', *Le français moderne* 18 (1950), pp. 277–88; Pierre Bec, *La langue occitane* (1963: 2nd ed., Paris, 1967).

[59] Geoffrey Symcox, 'The Savoyard State: a Negative Case-Study in the Politics of Linguistic Unification', in Chiappelli, *The Fairest Flower*, pp. 185–91, at pp. 187–8.

[60] Armstrong, 'The Language Question in the Low Countries', pp. 386–409.

[61] Peter R. Roberts, 'The Welsh Language, English Law and Tudor Legislation', *Transactions Cymmrodorion* (1989), pp. 19–75, at p. 27; Jenkins, *Welsh Language*, pp. 69, 153–80.

[62] Peter Skautrup, *Det danske sprogs historie*, vol. II (Copenhagen, 1947); Michael Roberts, *The Swedish Imperial Experience, 1560–1718* (Cambridge, 1979), pp. 109–10; Lars S. Vikør, 'Northern Europe: Languages as Prime Markers of Ethnic and National Identity', in Stephen Barbour and Cathy Carmichael (eds.), *Language and Nationalism in Europe* (Oxford, 2000), pp. 105–29, where it is claimed that the Swedes were 'prohibiting the use of Danish altogether' in Skåne.

and Alsace, and in 1700 in Roussillon (formerly part of Catalonia) as well. In 1696, Polish became the official language in the Lithuanian as well as the Polish part of the Commonwealth. In 1716, Castilian was made obligatory in cases before the Catalan high court, the Audiencia.

LANGUAGE AND POLITICS

If it is anachronistic to speak of conscious 'language policies' at this time, this does not mean that connections between language and politics were lacking. The success of some European vernaculars in this period was as much the consequence of the rise of centralizing states – and the new state churches that emerged from the Reformation – as of the campaigns waged by poets and scholars.

The expansion of the vernaculars into the domain of law and government was not simply a matter of administrative convenience. Once again, community is the clue. This expansion was an act, or succession of acts, of symbolic importance, signalling the rise of new communities or new conceptions of community. We can see this symbolic importance more clearly if we remember that it was only some vernaculars that expanded in this way, and that they did so at the expense of other vernaculars as well as Latin: French at the expense of Occitan, English at the expense of Welsh, Spanish at the expense of Catalan, German at the expense of Czech, Polish at the expense of Ruthenian, Danish at the expense of Norwegian and so on.[63]

The idea that language is the companion of empire became a commonplace in this period, as we have seen (above, p. 20). As the character Eudoxus remarked in the dialogue on Ireland by the poet Edmund Spenser, 'it hath been ever the use of the conqueror to despise the language of the conquered and to force him by all means to learn his'. This assumption is surely the clue to the advice given to Queen Elizabeth in 1582 by Sir John Perrott, President of Munster, to issue orders 'for enlarging the English tongue and extinguishing the Irish'. In 1695, an act went through Parliament 'for rooting out the Irish language' – in other words, what is now known as Scottish Gaelic.[64]

In the case of Spanish, one argument in favour of the public use of Castilian in Catalonia was that it was 'the common idiom of the Spanish

---

[63] On Norwegian, Didrik A. Seip, *Dansk og Norsk i Norge i eldre tider* (Oslo, 1932).
[64] Paul Walsh, 'The Irish Language and the Reformation', *Irish Theological Quarterly* 15 (1920), pp. 239–50, at p. 243; Edmund Spenser, *A View of the Present State of Ireland*, ed. William L. Renwick (Oxford, 1970), p. 67. Cf. Victor Durkacz, *The Decline of the Celtic Languages* (Edinburgh, 1983); Patricia Palmer, *Language and Conquest in Early Modern Ireland* (Cambridge, 2001).

monarchy' (*el idioma común de la Monarquía de España*).[65] Philip II's pro-
hibition of the use of Arabic in Spain (1567) fits in with this idea. However,
the king's main concern was probably with Arabic as the language of Islam,
and his fear was that his Morisco subjects, officially Christian, were really
crypto-Muslims. It is worth noting that in mid-seventeenth-century Spain,
the count-duke of Olivares, despite his commitment to centralization and
his clash with the Catalans, did not concern himself with the language
question.[66]

Again, in 1678, King Karl XI of Sweden ordered Swedish to be used in
Skåne and other southern provinces recently conquered from Denmark.
Teachers were sent to Skåne to teach the children how to speak and write
in the new language. The University of Lund had been founded in 1666
as part of the same campaign to make Skåne more Swedish (for further
details, below, pp. 162ff.).[67]

In France, Louis XIV's minister Jean-Baptiste Colbert recommended the
use of French as a means 'of making the inhabitants of the countries ceded
to the king at the treaty of Westphalia used to our manners and customs'
(*accoustumer les peuples des pays cedés au Roy par le traité de Munster à nos
moeurs et à nos coutumes*).[68] In similar fashion, the secretary of the *intendant*
of Alsace in 1735 declared himself in favour of 'obliging the inhabitants of
this region to speak the language of their sovereign', because they still had
the imperial eagle 'engraved on their hearts'.[69]

In these cases, relatively rare before 1789, we find governments that
are actively concerned with the everyday language of the majority of the
population, a concern that would become much more general in the nineteenth century (below, pp. 163ff.).

THE DOMAIN OF LEARNING

Although it was becoming increasingly common for students to learn modern languages at university, the employment of the vernaculars for teaching
purposes continued to be virtually prohibited, despite protests from a few
academics. In France, scholars of the calibre of Jean Bodin and Louis Le Roy
supported the use of the vernacular in the university, as did Laurentius Fries
and Baltasar Schupp in the German-speaking world. Fries, for instance,

[65] Quoted in García Carcel, *Cataluña*, p. 104.
[66] Alain Milhou, 'Les politiques de la langue à l'époque moderne de l'Europe et l'Amérique', in Marie-
Cécile Bénassy-Berling, Jean-Pierre Clément and Alain Milhou (eds.), *Langues et cultures en Amérique
espagnole coloniale* (Paris, 1993), pp. 15–40, at p. 30.
[67] Vikør, 'Northern Europe'; Skautrup, *Danske sprog*, p. 294.
[68] Quoted in Peyre, *Royauté*, pp. 166–7.   [69] Ibid., pp. 162–3.

suggested that medical books be written in German because that language is 'no less worthy' than Latin, Greek, Italian or Spanish, while Schupp declared that 'it is possible to cure a sick person as well in German as in Greek or Arabic'.[70]

In practice, it was only very slowly that the mother tongues began to infiltrate academic life. It is significant that among the early examples of the shift towards the vernacular we find educational institutions that were not universities. For example, Spanish was the language of a new academy for the discussion of natural philosophy, active in the 1580s. Lectures were given in English at Gresham College London, founded in the 1590s and oriented towards an unusually wide public. The equivalent in Paris of Gresham College was the series of lectures organized by the journalist Théophraste Renaudot between 1633 and 1642. The lectures, which took place on Monday afternoons, discussed a variety of topics, including medicine, agriculture, navigation and politics. The lectures were open to everyone and the use of French was required.[71]

It was in the German-speaking world that the campaign to introduce the vernacular into the universities had most effect. In the early sixteenth century, the physician Paracelsus had insisted on lecturing in German at the University of Basel, but – for this reason among others – his academic career did not last very long. In the late seventeenth century, the polymath Christian Thomasius was allowed to lecture in German at the university of Halle, another new foundation, after causing a scandal by his attempt to do the same in Leipzig (his announcement of a course of lectures in the vernacular in Leipzig in 1687 has been called 'a symbolic gesture reminiscent of Luther's nailing his theses to the door of the church at Wittenberg'). Christian Wolff's creation of a German vocabulary to discuss mathematics and philosophy encouraged the process of vernacularization in the eighteenth century.[72]

In other countries there were similar timid moves towards teaching in the vernacular. In 1588, a lectureship in Tuscan was founded at the University of Siena, and the lecturers presumably gave their lectures in that language. Olof Rudbeck began giving his lectures in Swedish at Uppsala University in

[70] Schiewe, *Macht*, pp. 56–7, 62.
[71] Harald Weinrich, *Wege der Sprachkultur* (Stuttgart, 1985), p. 158; Christopher Hill, *Intellectual Origins of the English Revolution* (Oxford, 1965), pp. 34–5; Howard M. Solomon, *Public Welfare, Science and Propaganda in Seventeenth-Century France* (Princeton, 1972), p. 64.
[72] Richard Hodermann, *Universitätsvorlesungen in deutscher Sprache um die Wende des 17. Jahrhunderts* (Jena, 1891); Irmgard Weithase, *Zur Geschichte der gesprochenen deutschen Sprache*, vol. 1 (Tübingen, 1961), pp. 264–79; Schiewe, *Macht*, pp. 80–7; the comment on Thomasius in Eric A. Blackall, *The Emergence of German as a Literary Language, 1700–75* (Cambridge, 1959), pp. 12–13.

1677. In Paris, an edict of 1680 required lectures on French law to be given in French. At the universities of Pisa and Naples in the seventeenth and eighteenth centuries, a compromise was established, with lectures in Latin followed by explanations in the vernacular outside the lecture-room.[73] In 1734, a chair in Italian eloquence was founded at Turin. In 1765, Antonio Genovesi began to lecture in Italian at the University of Naples, at a time when the Neapolitan elite had chosen to speak as well as write the standard language. In Moscow, Nikolai Popovsky lectured in Russian in the 1750s, while the vernacular became the official language of instruction at the university in 1767.

In the case of learned publications, a gradual decline of Latin is visible, replaced by Italian, French, Spanish, English, and to a lesser extent other languages such as German and Dutch. As was noted in the previous chapter (above, p. 54), there was a steep decline after 1650 in the proportion of Latin books offered for sale in the Frankfurt fairs. Descartes shifted to French for his *Discours de la méthode*, Galileo to Italian for his *Saggiatore* and other works, and Newton to English for his *Optics*, while Robert Boyle, who claimed he had no time to learn languages, always wrote in English.

In the case of natural philosophy, despite the international interest in new discoveries, Latin suffered from two serious disadvantages. It offended the purist because the need to coin new words for new objects and ideas involved departures from the language of Cicero. The use of Latin also excluded many people who were interested in scientific debates, among them a considerable number of artisans. In other words, the new scientific community did not coincide with the latinophone *Respublica Litterarum*.

THE LANGUAGES OF RELIGION

The use of the vernacular in writing and print was also encouraged by the Reformation, and, paradoxically enough, by the Counter-Reformation as well.

The debut in print of some of the smaller European languages owed more to the Reformation than to the Renaissance. For example, the first Estonian book, printed in 1535, was a Lutheran catechism, and so was the first printed book in Romanian (1544), in Lithuanian (1547) and in Slovene (1551). In Romansh too, the first printed book (1557) was a catechism, and in Welsh (1546) it was a prayer-book. The first book printed in Sami, the language of the Lapps, was an ABC published by a Lutheran pastor in Stockholm in 1649.

---

[73] Françoise Waquet, *Parler comme un livre* (Paris, 2003), p. 85.

It is true that only some vernaculars or forms of the vernacular were used in church. Slovak Lutherans, for example, worshipped in Czech, while Occitan-speaking Calvinists worshipped in French and in moments of inspiration their prophets might recite passages from the Bible, more especially from the Psalms, in that language.[74] All the same, their use in the liturgy and in translations of the Bible did much to give certain vernaculars more dignity.

In regions where more than one vernacular was spoken and written, as in Lusatia, the upper classes faced a dilemma. The problem in this Lutheran area was whether to give religious instruction to the peasants in German or in Sorb (a language close to Slovak and Polish). The use of German was supposed to civilize the people, but their difficulty in understanding that language risked the perpetuation of what the clergy called 'superstition' and 'popery'. In the event, German was chosen for Lower Lusatia and Sorb for Upper Lusatia.[75]

In the Catholic world, as we saw in the previous chapter, Latin retained its position as a sacred language. The Council of Trent rejected the use of the vernacular in the liturgy and prohibited further translations of the Bible. All the same, the vernacular might be used for other religious purposes, and it often was. The first printed book in Albanian was a Missal (1555). Vernacular catechisms were printed in large numbers and became a powerful instrument in the service of reformed Catholicism. The catechism of the Italian Jesuit Roberto Bellarmino, for instance, was translated into no fewer than twenty-three European languages between 1600 and 1744.[76]

TRANSLATIONS

The translation of other texts, whether from Latin and Greek into vernacular languages or from one vernacular into another, was a process which accelerated in this period and had important consequences for many languages, as some contemporaries were well aware. The impossibility of finding equivalents for some foreign expressions led to the coining of new words. Hence, the translator Richard Eden observed in 1562 that English was no longer 'indigent' but 'enriched and amplified' by translation.[77]

Translations from one European vernacular into another may be analysed in two ways, according to the text's original language, or according to what

---

[74] Emmanuel Le Roy Ladurie, *Les paysans de Languedoc* (Paris, 1966), p. 621.

[75] Alfred Mietzsche, 'Der Entstehung der obersorbischen Schriftsprache (1668–1728), *Zeitschrift für Slavische Philologie* 28 (1960), pp. 122–48.

[76] Carlos Sommervogel et al., *Bibliothèque de la Compagnie de Jésus* (12 vols., Brussels, 1890–1932), sub voce 'Bellarmine'.

[77] Quoted in Jones, *Triumph*, p. 92.

translators call the 'target language'. The 'balance of trade', as we might call it, between vernaculars is a cultural indicator that deserves more study than it has received so far.[78] Few attempts have been made to compile complete lists of translations from one vernacular into another, so the conclusions that follow are necessarily impressionistic and provisional.[79]

To begin with the 'exports'. In the case of Italy, their high level was only to be expected, especially in the age of the Renaissance, with Ariosto, Boccalini, Guarini, Guicciardini, Machiavelli, Petrarch and Tasso among the authors most frequently translated. Spanish exports were also high in the sixteenth and seventeenth centuries, including works by Cervantes and the devotional writer Luis de Granada, Gracián's conduct books, Guevara's mirror for princes, and the account of China by Gonzalez de Mendoza. The rise of French took place in the seventeenth century and of English in the eighteenth century (with Locke and Richardson among the most popular authors). In other words, the graph of translations from a particular language is a rough indicator of the prestige of that language.

Translations into a particular language, on the other hand, may be read as a sign that that culture was relatively open to foreign ideas. Italian imports were relatively high, especially in the sixteenth century and from Spanish. French imports were also high in the sixteenth century, with 1570–1600 as the peak period for translations from Italian (translations from Spanish peaked a little later).[80] England too had a high level of imports from Italian, Spanish and French (about four hundred and fifty translations from Italian were published between 1550 and 1660).[81]

In the case of Spain, on the other hand, imports seem to have been relatively low, though not as low, in the sixteenth century at least, as traditional stereotypes of the 'closed country' might suggest. As translations into Spanish declined, translations into German began to rise. In East-Central Europe, imports were also low, and they tended to be made from Latin rather than the vernaculars. Erasmus, for instance, was translated into Czech and Polish in the sixteenth century. Latin works by Jean Calvin and the English Puritan William Perkins were translated into Hungarian. Both the *Constancy* and the *Politics* of the humanist Justus Lipsius were translated into Polish and Hungarian.

[78] For the period 1932–77, cf. Daniel Milo, 'La bourse mondiale de la traduction: un baromètre culturel?' *Annales: économies, sociétés, civilisations* 39 (1984), pp. 93–115.
[79] Existing studies include Mary Augusta Scott, *Elizabethan Translations from the Italian* (Boston, 1916); Jean Balsamo, *Répertoire des traductions de l'italien 1570–1600* (Rome, 1992); Frank-Rutger Hausmann, *Bibliographie der deutschen Übersetzungen aus dem italienischen bis 1730* (2 vols., Tübingen, 1992).
[80] Jean Balsamo, 'Traduire de l'italien: ambitions sociales et contraintes éditoriales à la fin du 16e siècle', in Dominique de Courcelles (ed.), *Traduire et adapter à la Renaissance* (Paris, 1998), pp. 89–98.
[81] Scott, *Elizabethan Translations*.

This pattern of linguistic exchange deserves more analysis than it has received so far. Among the factors that need to be taken into account are the attitudes of translators to their own vernacular, whether they considered it appropriate for discussions of philosophy, for instance. Strange as it may now seem, German was a language relatively poor in abstractions in this period, creating an obstacle to certain kinds of translation. Although Leibniz argued that German was an appropriate language for philosophy, it was only in the eighteenth century that his advice began to be taken seriously.

IMPERIALISM

The military metaphor of winners and losers criticized at the beginning of this chapter seems to be inescapable. All the same, we can try to use it without triumphalism, that is, without neglecting the losers and without assuming that the successful languages were intrinsically better.

We might speak of 'linguistic imperialism', both literal and metaphorical. The metaphor of empire appealed to a number of writers in our period, as we have seen (above, p. 20). It is also appropriate to speak of linguistic 'colonization' or 'conquest'. Spanish, Portuguese, Dutch, French and English all found new worlds into which to expand in this period. As a result of conquest and immigration, these languages came to be spoken in Asia, Africa and America. Portuguese, for instance, was spoken in Goa, Ceylon, Macau, Moçambique, Angola and Brazil; Spanish in Mexico, Peru and the Philippines; Dutch in Java, Sumatra, the Cape and New Amsterdam; English in North America and India, and French in Pondichéry and Canada.[82]

The European rulers sometimes tried to impose their languages on the indigenous inhabitants of their empires, at least on the local elites. In 1640, the court or *audiencia* of Guatemala declared that only Indians who could speak Spanish would be allowed to wear cloaks and ride horses. In his commentary on the laws of the Indies, the *Política Indiana* (1648), the Spanish jurist Juan de Solorzano y Pereira explained the thinking behind

---

[82] There is a substantial secondary literature on this theme, including Louis-Jean Calvet, *Linguistique et colonialisme* (Paris, 1974); Angel Rosenblat, *Los conquistadores y su lengua* (Caracas, 1977); José Honorio Rodrigues, 'The Victory of the Portuguese Language in Colonial Brazil', in Alfred Hower and Richard A. Preto-Rodas (eds.), *Empire in Transition* (Gainsville, 1985), pp. 32–64; Victor Kiernan, 'Languages and Conquerors', in Peter Burke and Roy Porter (eds.), *Language, Self and Society* (Cambridge, 1991), pp. 191–210; Walter D. Mignolo, 'On the Colonization of Amerindian Languages and Memories', *Comparative Studies in Society and History* 34 (1992), pp. 301–30; Groeneboer, *Gateway*; Diogo Ramada Curto, 'A língua e o império', in Francisco Bethencourt and Kirti N. Chaudhuri (eds.), *História da expansão portuguesa*, vol. 1 (Lisbon, 1998), pp. 414–33; Palmer, *Language and Conquest*.

this policy, declaring that the conquerors impose their language 'to show in this the justification of their rule and the superiority (*para mostrar en eso el derecho de su dominio y superioridad*).[83]

In similar fashion, the Dutch East India Company, the VOC, tried to impose Dutch in the East Indies. In 1641, an edict of the Governor-General ruled that slaves were only allowed to wear hats or caps if they knew Dutch, the idea being, apparently, to create a linguistic bond between colonizers and colonized. The scheme seems to have failed. Again, in 1659, the Governor of Colombo ordered slaves to learn Dutch.[84] More systematic and probably more effective was the work of missionaries. Many missionaries learned the languages of the regions they had come to convert, but they also taught European languages, the vernaculars as well as Latin.

WINNERS AND LOSERS IN EUROPE

To return to winners and losers in Europe. In 1600, it has been calculated, French was in the lead with about fourteen million speakers, followed by German with ten million, Italian with nine and a half million, Spanish with eight and a half million, English with six million.[85]

A number of smaller languages were in decline in the domain of speech as well as that of writing. For instance, Scottish Gaelic was in retreat as English advanced from the twelfth century. Welsh retreated more slowly, but the gentry began to abandon it in the sixteenth century, just as they abandoned their patronage of the bards. By the eighteenth century, the language was disappearing from some regions, even if, thanks to population growth, the absolute number of Welsh speakers was rising.[86]

On the other side of the Channel, Breton was in retreat as French advanced from the thirteenth century onwards.[87] French was also expanding to the south. Occitan, which had already lost prestige after the defeat of the heretics known as Cathars or Albigensians, was losing ground to French in the fifteenth century, in both the administrative and the literary domains. By the sixteenth and seventeenth centuries, even spoken

---

[83] Amos Megged, *Exporting the Catholic Reformation: Local Religion in Early Colonial Mexico* (Leiden, 1996), p. 65; Lucia Binotti, 'La "lengua compañera del imperio": discursos peninsulares sobre la hispanización de America', in A. Alonso González et al. (eds.), *Actas del III Congreso Internacional de historia de la lengua española* (2 vols., Madrid, 1996), pp. 621–32, at p. 631.

[84] Groeneboer, *Gateway*, pp. 28, 37–8, 51.

[85] Otto Jespersen, *Growth and Structure of the English Language* (1905: revised ed., Leipzig, 1923).

[86] Jenkins, *Welsh Language*, pp. 78–81, 253, 290.

[87] Elmar Ternes, 'The Breton Language', in Donald Macaulay (ed.), *The Celtic Languages* (Cambridge, 1992), pp. 371–452, at pp. 372–5.

Occitan was receding.[88] Basque, almost exclusively a spoken language, was also retreating towards the Pyrenees between 1500 and 1800, although its spread to the Americas via immigration should not be forgotten.[89] Polish advanced eastwards, at least in the domain of writing, after the union of that country with the Grand Duchy of Lithuania in 1569.

It would not always have been easy to predict which languages would expand and which were condemned to contract. This point should become clear from three examples of reversals of fortune, respectively from the Germanic, Slavonic and Romance language groups. In each case, a language that seemed to be on the rise around the year 1500 was overtaken by rivals in the course of the sixteenth and seventeenth centuries.

The first example is that of Dutch. In the later sixteenth century, when the seven provinces of the northern Netherlands became independent, there were signs of a glorious future for the language. Stevin's manifesto in favour of the vernacular was published in 1582, a generation before the praises of English and German by Carew and Opitz. The *Nederduitsche Poëmata* (1616) of Nicholaas Heinsius was an inspiration for the *Teutsche Poëmata* (1624) of Opitz. Dutch purism, in the sense of resistance to words of foreign origin, was a model for German purism (below, p. 151). The rise of the Dutch seaborne empire spread the language to Indonesia, South Africa, North America and for a generation, to the northeast of Brazil as well. All the same, in the course of the seventeenth century Dutch was overtaken by its rivals German and English.

Like Dutch, Czech looked promising in 1500. Legal and administrative documents began to be written in that language in the 1370s. Czech texts on grammar and orthography by Hus and others go back to the early fifteenth century. The first printed book in Czech dates from 1468, fifteen years before Croat and fifty-four years before Polish. The Bible, together with works by Petrarch and Erasmus, was translated into Czech relatively early, before it appeared in other Slavonic languages. The first Czech grammar in print, by Beneš Optát, dates from 1533, thirty-five years before its Polish equivalent, by Peter Statorius. The Kralicy Bible (1579–94) helped to shape the literary language, and some Polish writers, such as Łukasz Górnicki, took Czech as a model. The first Czech dictionary, Beneškovski's *Knižka slov českych*, was published in 1587, seventeen years

---

[88] Auguste Brun, *Recherches historiques sur l'introduction du français dans les provinces du Midi* (Paris, 1923); Brun, *L'introduction de la langue française en Béarn et en Roussillon* (Paris, 1927); Bec, *Langue occitane*; Robert Lafont, *Renaissance du Sud, essai sur la littérature occitane au temps de Henri IV* (Paris, 1970).

[89] Map in Banfi, *Formazione*, p. 486; on the Americas, Milhou, 'politique', pp. 21–2.

before the first English dictionary, Robert Cawdrey's *Table Alphabetical* (1604).

In the later sixteenth century, however, from the time of the poet Kochanowski onwards, Polish was coming to overtake Czech in the domains of literature and print. There was increasing competition between German and Czech. After 1620, when Bohemia was re-incorporated into the Habsburg Empire, German became the language of administration. By the 1740s, the number of books published in Czech had been reduced to 'a mere trickle' to revive only at the end of the century.[90]

The third of these examples of reversal is that of Catalan.[91] In 1500, its future too looked promising. The literary tradition went back to the fourteenth century, assisted by the fact that Catalan was close to Provençal, one of the major literary languages of the Middle Ages. The first printed book in Catalan appeared in 1474, about nine years before the first book in Castilian. The Bible was published in Catalan in 1478, the *Imitation of Christ* in 1491. However, after Ferdinand of Aragon married Isabella of Castille, the court moved to Castille, followed by the Catalan aristocracy. As the language of the court, Castilian acquired overtones of high status. Another reason for the success of Castilian was that after 1492 it became the language of a great empire. Indeed, 'Castilian' was becoming a less and less appropriate name for the language, and from the time of the emperor Charles V onwards, it was increasingly described as 'Spanish'.[92]

Spanish was the language that Joán Boscá, a patrician of Barcelona, used in his famous translation of Castiglione's *Courtier*, thanks to which he became famous as Juan Boscán. It was obviously appropriate for Boscán to translate a book on the perfect courtier into the language of the court. Again, Luis de Milán's dialogue *El Cortesano* (1561), set in Valencia among the ladies and gentlemen of the court of Queen Germana and her husband the duke of Calabria, is written in Spanish except for a few passages representing the speech of people who are not noble. On those occasions the dialogue switches to Catalan, thus communicating a clear social message. The middle class retained Catalan longer, but they too were switching to Castilian in certain domains by the seventeenth century. Although the lawyer Jeroni Pujades wrote the first part of his chronicle in Catalan in 1609, so he explained, 'in order not to be ungrateful to the fatherland and nation by

---

90 Robert Auty, 'Czech', in Alexander M. Schenker and Edward Stankiewicz (eds.), *The Slavic Literary Languages: Formation and Development* (New Haven, 1980), pp. 163–82, at p. 172.

91 García Carcel, *Cataluña*; Marfany, *Lengua*.

92 Amado Alonso, *Castellano, español, idioma nacional: historia spiritual de tres nombres* (Buenos Aires, 1938).

abandoning his own language for another' (*per no ésser ingrat a la Pàtria i nació dexant la pròpia per altra llengua*), he switched to Castilian for the second and third parts of the text.[93]

In the domain of speech, Catalan was not under threat. Indeed, it was claimed in 1621 that outside the main cities of Catalonia, 'Castilian is not well understood by ordinary people' (*no és ben entesa la llengua castellana de la gent comuna*).[94] Hence, some bishops favoured sermons in Catalan, public events that maintained the prestige of the language. All the same, as we have seen, the Inquisition made the use of Castilian obligatory in its trials in 1561, while in 1716 a secret instruction to regional administrators told them to favour Castilian 'in a subtle way'.[95]

Thus, in early modern Catalonia, language became a symbol of class and the ability to speak and write Castilian became necessary to anyone who aspired to rise socially, much like French in Provence or English in Ireland. The gentry followed the model of the aristocracy, distinguishing themselves from commoners by their use of the language of the court.[96] This choice encouraged a sense of community among the Spanish nobility as a whole and at the same time weakened the sense of a Catalan community, increasing the social distance between the nobles and ordinary people.

Among the signs of the international success of certain languages was their study in other countries. Italian was taught in some colleges and universities in the sixteenth century, Spanish in the late sixteenth and early seventeenth centuries, French from the late seventeenth century onwards and English in the eighteenth century. For example, Italian was in use not only at the court of the Italian Catherine de' Medici in France but also at that of Leopold I in late seventeenth-century Vienna. Leopold himself corresponded in that language with Graf Humprecht Jan Černín.[97] Spanish has also been described – with some exaggeration, but not much – as a 'universal language' in the seventeenth century, spoken at the courts of Vienna, France, Brussels and Italy.[98]

FRENCH AS A LINGUA FRANCA

The language whose speakers made the strongest bid for European hegemony was of course French. In the seventeenth and eighteenth centuries, as

---

[93] Quoted in García Carcel, *Cataluña*, p 87; cf. James S. Amelang, *Honoured Citizens of Barcelona* (Princeton 1986), p. 190.

[94] Quoted in García Carcel, *Cataluña*, p. 86.

[95] Josep M. Nadal, 'El català en els segles xvi i xvii', *L'Avenç* 100 (1987), pp. 24–31.

[96] Marfany, *Lengua*, pp. 239, 473.

[97] Leopold I, *Korrespondence*, ed. Zdeněk Kalista (Prague, 1936).   [98] Pastor, *Apologías*, p. xxvii.

we have seen (p. 74), the use of French in the political domain was extended to conquered provinces, where it was not the mother tongue.[99]

Some people had grander ambitions for the language. Cardinal Richelieu, who dominated French politics from 1631 to his death in 1643, was believed to have a plan to make French the language of Europe.[100] There was little that even a statesman like Richelieu could do to turn this ideal into reality, but a trend in this direction among certain groups is visible at about this time.

For example, the regent class of the Dutch Republic often spoke among themselves in French. In German courts, such as Stuttgart in the later seventeenth century, French was spoken, as it was later in Russia under Peter and Catherine the Great.[101] For eighteenth-century Germans with aspirations to status or civilization, French was the language of letter-writing.[102] A funeral oration on Louis XIV noted that 'aujourd'hui dans toutes les cours, on parle la langue de ses sujets'.[103]

The idea that Louis XIV made French the language of diplomacy and international relations is an exaggeration, a 'legend' that makes too much happen too quickly.[104] At the congresses of Westphalia (1647–8) and Nijmegen (1677–8), a good deal of Latin and some Italian and Spanish were spoken.[105] All the same, there was a more gradual trend in this direction. Charpentier quoted a French diplomat at Nijmegen in 1678, the comte d'Avaux, finding that in the houses of all the ambassadors, French was 'used almost as much as their native language' (*presque aussi commune que leur langue naturelle*). In 1682, at Frankfurt, the French diplomats insisted on using French although the imperial envoys expected to hear Latin.[106] In 1714, the treaty of Rastatt was drawn up in French (perhaps because the chief French negotiator did not know Latin), and this precedent was followed in the treaties of Vienna (1735) and Aachen (Aix-la-Chapelle) in 1748.[107]

An important trend was the spread of French books outside France, helped not only by the French contribution to the European Enlightenment but also, ironically enough, by the Huguenot diaspora of the late

---

99 Peyre, *Royauté*; Peter Sahlins, *Boundaries: the Making of France and Spain in the Pyrenees* (Berkeley, 1989), pp. 116–19, 125–7.
100 James Howell, *Ecclesiastical Affairs*, vol. III (London, 1685), pp. 424–47.
101 Tim Blanning, *The Culture of Power and the Power of Culture* (Oxford, 2002), pp. 55–6.
102 Brunot, *Langue française*, vol. V, pp. 360–2.
103 Edme Mongin, *Oraison funèbre de Louis le Grand* (Paris, 1715), p. 14.
104 Brunot, *Langue française*, vol. V, p. 402.
105 Ibid., vol. V, pp. 295, 402–3.   106 Ibid., vol. V, pp. 411–17.
107 Ibid., vol. V, pp. 418–22; cf. André Corvisier, *Arts et sociétés dans l'Europe du 18e siècle* (Paris, 1978), p. 21.

seventeenth century. Both Louis XIV and the Protestants he expelled in 1685 would surely have been surprised to learn about this unintended consequence of the Revocation of the Edict of Nantes. Some German writers published books in French at this time, including Leibniz, Frederick the Great and a number of minor writers of the eighteenth century.[108]

In the earlier seventeenth century, the scholar-magistrate Peiresc's attempt to use French in his correspondence with the imperial librarian in Vienna had met with a rebuff.[109] By 1685, on the other hand, the refugee scholar Pierre Bayle's claim that French was a 'langue . . . transcendantelle', the language of communication between 'tous les peuples de l'Europe' was becoming a reality, assisted by the publication – outside France – of newspapers in French, such as the *Gazette de Leyde*, which lasted from 1677 to 1811.[110]

Learned periodicals in French, whether produced in France or the Dutch Republic, were being read all over Europe, the *Nouvelles de la République des Lettres*, for instance, the *Bibliothèque Universelle et Historique* (1686–93), and its successors the *Bibliothèque Choisie* (1703–13), the *Bibliothèque Ancienne et Moderne* (1714–27) and so on, published in Amsterdam, and the *Nouveau Journal des Savants* (1696), published in Berlin.[111] When Frederick the Great ordered that the language of the Berlin Academy of Sciences be changed from Latin to French in 1744, he was recognizing a trend rather than imposing his personal preference.

There was, inevitably, resistance to the rise of French. In his Wiles Lectures, delivered over twenty years ago, Michael Roberts told the story of Johan III of Sweden, 'who once rebuked the impertinence of a king who wrote to him in French by answering him in Finnish'.[112] Johan's Francophobe successors ranged from the Viennese librarian mentioned above to the imperial envoys at Frankfurt and to Dr Samuel Johnson, who insisted on speaking Latin to his French visitors. Treaties in Latin continued to be drawn up in the eighteenth century.[113]

All the same, by the eighteenth century the French could reasonably think of their language as potentially universal, the successor of Latin, as

[108] Brunot, *Langue française*, vol. v, pp. 381–5.
[109] Peter Miller, *Peiresc's Europe* (New Haven, 2000), p. 163.
[110] Quoted in Paul Hazard, *The European Mind, 1680–1715* (1935: English translation, London, 1953), p. 61.
[111] Jean Sgard (ed.), *Dictionnaire des journaux, 1600–1789* (2 vols., Paris, 1976).
[112] Roberts, *Imperial Experience*, p. 21. Cf. Nils Ahnlund, *Svenskt och Nordiskt* (Stockholm, 1943), p. 114, where Johan responds to a letter from Philip II in Spanish. A similar story is told about Roberts himself during his time in Belfast, receiving a letter in Gaelic from Dublin and replying in Swedish.
[113] Ahnlund, *Svenskt*, pp. 114–22.

Anglophones think of their language – or languages – today. In 1782, the Berlin Academy could propose as the subject for a prize essay, 'Qu'est-ce qui a fait la langue française la langue universelle de l'Europe?' The prize was shared between two candidates, Johann-Christoph Schwab, who wrote his essay in German, and Antoine Rivarol, whose *Universalité de la langue française* contained the famous phrase, 'ce qui n'est pas clair n'est pas français'.[114]

The simultaneous expansion of a number of European vernaculars into an increasing number of linguistic domains led to more contacts between them. The contacts led in turn to mixing. Linguistic encounters and mixtures are the subject of the following chapter.

---

[114] Antoine Rivarol, *De l'universalité de la langue française* (1784: ed. T. Suran, Paris, 1930), p. 255.

CHAPTER 4

Standardizing languages

The more the domain of the vernaculars, at least some vernaculars, expanded, the more necessary it was for those vernaculars to be standardized. 'Standardization' is an ambiguous term that refers not only to the process of becoming more uniform (*uniformidad*, Nebrija called it) but also to following rules. The purpose of standardization in this period was also double. It was partly pragmatic, to facilitate communication between regions, and partly honorific, to give Italian, or Spanish, or German, or English some of the prestige or dignity associated with Latin. When Du Bellay, for example, wrote about the *illustration* of the French language, he was discussing how to make it illustrious, on the model of the *volgare illustre* recommended by Dante. His wish was to elevate French (*élever nostre vulgaire*) to the level of more famous languages. The Spanish humanist Cristóbal de Villalón explained that he wrote his grammar to make his nation great (*engrandecer las cosas de mi nación*).

A language without a standard was regarded as 'in a manner barbarous', as the poet John Dryden remarked in 1660. Civilization implied following a code of behaviour, including linguistic behaviour. The sociologist Norbert Elias's idea of a 'civilizing process' in early modern Europe might therefore be extended to include attempts to reform language.[1] Using the approved or standard variety of language was, for many speakers at least, a form of self-control, since what came 'naturally' (or at least habitually) to them was another variety, such as dialect.

Another purpose of standardization, besides uniformity across space, was fixity over time. For a language to gain the kind of prestige accorded to Latin, it had to be stable. For this reason, Dryden found it embarrassing that while 'from the time of Boccaccio and of Petrarch, the Italian has varied

---

[1] Norbert Elias, *The Civilizing Process* (1939: English translation, 2 vols., Oxford, 1981–2). There are some perceptive remarks on language in vol. 1, pp. 11, 108–13, but no explicit link is made between language and the civilizing process itself.

very little', in the English case, on the other hand, Chaucer 'is not to be understood without the help of an old dictionary'. Jonathan Swift disliked what he called 'the perpetual variations of our speech' and hoped 'to fix it for ever'.[2] We might call this reaction 'the anxiety of instability'. On the other side of the Atlantic, Hugh Jones, a professor at William and Mary College, expressed the wish in 1721 'that a public standard were fix'd'. As the journalist Antoine de Rivarol wrote at the end of our period, 'fixity is necessary' (*il faut de la fixité*).[3]

The desire for fixity was one important reason for the foundation of academies in Florence (the Crusca, 1582), Paris (1635), Madrid (1713), Copenhagen (1742), Lisbon (1779), Moscow (1783) and Stockholm (1786), all of them responsible for dictionaries (although the Portuguese did not get beyond the letter A). The motto of the Spanish academy was (and is) 'it purifies, it fixes and it gives splendour' (*limpia, fija y da esplendor*).

Many grammars of European vernaculars were published in this period, often written in Latin to facilitate their use by foreigners learning the language, but also intended to propose rules to native speakers. By 1550 there were printed grammars of Italian, Spanish, French, Portuguese, German and Czech. Between 1550 and 1599, additions to the list included Dutch, English, Polish, Welsh, Slovene and Church Slavonic. Between 1600 and 1649, Basque, Croat, Danish, modern Greek (called 'popular' Greek), and Latvian. Between 1650 and 1699, Breton, Estonian, Frisian, Lithuanian, Russian, Sorb and Swedish. Between 1700 and 1749, Albanian, Romansh and Sami. In 1757, Romanian.

The publication of a grammar of a given vernacular does not of course mean that even a minority of the speakers of that vernacular were actually following the rules. All the same, the spread of the grammars is impressive and, in the case of a few vernaculars, the rules appear to have been taken seriously by elites.

It might be said that certain vernaculars won the battle with Latin by ceasing to be vernaculars, by creating a sort of 'authorized version' of language that was distant from colloquial speech. The question, which variety of vernacular ought to be authorized, whether for writing, or for conversation among cultivated people, was much debated in early modern Europe.

---

[2] Hermann M. Flasdieck, *Der Gedanke einer englischen Sprachakademie* (Jena, 1928), pp. 39, 71.

[3] Villalón quoted in Amado Alonso, *Castellano, español, idioma nacional: historia spiritual de tres nombres* (Buenos Aires, 1938), p. 34; Jones quoted in Allen W. Read, 'American Projects for an Academy to Regulate Speech', *Publications of the Modern Language Association* 51 (1936), pp. 1141–79, at p. 1141; Rivarol quoted in Alexis François, *La grammaire du purisme et l'Académie Française au 18e siècle* (Paris, 1905), p. 14.

The competition discussed in the previous chapter recurs here at another level.

In the course of the Renaissance, the humanists, following their usual procedures of imitation and emulation, mainly of Latin and sometimes of Greek, attempted to reform a number of vernaculars (including Italian, Spanish, French, Portuguese and English) in order to make them more suitable for literary use. The movement of reform spread still more widely in the seventeenth and eighteenth centuries. Writers in one country were often inspired to emulate what was going on elsewhere. For example, Du Bellay borrowed from the dialogue on the vernacular by Speroni, the supporters of the literary use of Welsh were aware of Italian and French precedents, while the Spanish Academy and the Russian reformer Vasily Trediakovsky were both inspired by the French critic Vaugelas.[4]

The trend to 'grammatization', as it is sometimes called, looks – at least at first sight – like a remarkable example of the power of scholars and intellectuals, but it might be more realistic to offer a social explanation for their success. Standard forms of vernacular were expressions of the values of new communities – or communities of increasing importance – the national communities of lay elites who were distancing themselves not only from learned or Latin culture but from popular, regional or dialect culture as well.

In any case, there was in this period a collective, co-operative European enterprise aimed at raising the status of the vernaculars, codifying them, enriching them and so turning them into languages appropriate for literature. This enterprise was greatly assisted by a new medium of communication, print.

THE ROLE OF PRINT

Some historians of printing regard the fixity or standardization of language as a virtually automatic outcome of the mass production of identical texts from Johann Gutenberg onwards. As Lucien Febvre and Henri-Jean Martin put it in their classic study of the rise of the book, printing 'played an essential role in the formation and fixing of languages'. Sigfrid Steinberg agreed: 'Having fortified the "language walls" between one nation and another', he wrote, 'the printers proceeded to break down the minor differences of speech . . . within any given language group'.[5]

---

[4] R. Brinley Jones, *The Old British Tongue: the Vernacular in Wales, 1540–1640* (Cardiff, 1970), pp. 12–13.
[5] Lucien Febvre and Henri-Jean Martin, *The Coming of the Book* (1958: English translation, London, 1976), pp. 319–32, at p. 319; Sigfrid H. Steinberg, *Five Hundred Years of Printing* (1955: revised ed., Harmondsworth, 1961), p. 88; cf. Michael Giesecke, *Der Buchdruck in der frühen Neuzeit* (Frankfurt, 1991), pp. 489–97.

There is a good deal to be said in favour of this view. It is clear that a standard language suited the economic logic of the printing industry, the need to sell identical texts to the maximum number of readers. The shift from the variety of spellings of the same word in the late Middle Ages, for instance, to the uniform standards of the nineteenth and twentieth centuries is a dramatic one. Similar points can be made about regional variations in vocabulary. The idea that the spread of printed books influenced writing habits – and, later, speaking habits – seems an inherently plausible one.

One of the most convincing examples comes from outside Europe. It is the role of missionaries, especially Jesuits, in fixing indigenous languages such as Nahuatl in Mexico, Quechua and Aymara in Peru, Tupí in Brazil, Tagalog in the Philippines and so on, by writing these languages down for the first time as well as compiling dictionaries and writing grammars such as Alonso de Molina's Nahuatl-Spanish vocabulary (1555), Diego González Holguín's dictionary of Quechua (1586), José de Anchieta's grammar of Tupí (1595), or Ludovico Bertonio's dictionary of Aymara (1612). In these regions there was a shift from orality to print without passing through an age of manuscript.

All the same, we cannot assume that the press was the only actor in this drama. Four general observations should serve to make the story more complicated.

1. The first point is a conceptual one. The concept of 'standardization' is less simple than it looks, and it is necessary to distinguish official varieties of language from those with most prestige and those most widely understood.[6] The formal codification of a language is not the same thing as the rise to dominance of a particular dialect or sociolect. Standardization of practice, whether in writing or speech, is a matter of degree and to this day German, for instance, is less standardized than English or French.

2. The second point is a chronological one. The process of standardization is older than the printing-press. In the case of some European vernaculars, it began long before 1450. In England, for example, West Saxon was widespread in the eleventh century as a literary language. Scholars debate the question whether this 'Standard Old English' was the work of King Alfred or the bishop of Winchester, Aethelwold.[7] In Spain, the process

[6] John E. Joseph, *Eloquence and Power: the Rise of Language Standards and Standard Languages* (Oxford, 1987), p. vii.

[7] Helmut Gneuss, 'The Origin of Standard Old English', *Anglo-Saxon England* 1 (1972), pp. 63–83; John H. Fisher, *The Emergence of Standard English* (Lexington, 1996), p. 75. My thanks to Simon Keynes for drawing my attention to this debate.

becomes visible in the thirteenth century.[8] In Bohemia, Jan Hus reformed Czech orthography in the early fifteenth century. More generally, as Febvre and Martin were well aware, the chanceries of Europe played an important part in the history of the vernaculars from the fourteenth century onwards. In the German-speaking world, written norms were influenced by the practice of the chanceries of Prague, Vienna, and later Meissen in Saxony. In England, a chancery standard began to spread from the year 1417 onwards.[9]

3. In the third place, print was a two-edged weapon that could be used to promote rival standards. In the case of Britain, it is relatively easy to forget this point, since for much of this period presses were virtually confined to London. The result of this quasi-monopoly was to spread the hegemony of south-eastern English not only to the north and west of England, but to the Lowlands of Scotland as well, leading to what has been called 'the sudden and total eclipse of Scots as a literary language' around the year 1500.[10] In France too, despite the importance of Lyons during the Renaissance, a high proportion of books came to be published in Paris.

However, the story is very different in the German-, Spanish- or Italian-speaking worlds, where printing was polycentric. In Spain, the arrival of the press in Valencia, Seville, Salamanca, Barcelona and elsewhere led, so we are told, as much to 'chaos' as to 'general uniformity'.[11] In Germany, the period before 1550 has been described as one of competing 'printer's languages' (*Druckersprachen*) in Augsburg, Frankfurt, Leipzig, Basel, Wittenberg and elsewhere.[12] Books printed in sixteenth-century Venice, Milan, Florence, Rome and other cities also promoted different varieties of language. It was only in the early seventeenth century that Tuscan forms became the typographical standard.[13] In the German- and

---

[8] Roger Wright, 'Linguistic Standardization in the Middle Ages in the Iberian Peninsula: Advantages and Disadvantages', in Stewart Gregory and David A. Trotter (eds.), *De mot en mot* (Cardiff, 1997), pp. 261–75.

[9] Malcolm Richardson, 'Henry V, the English Chancery and Chancery English', *Speculum* 55 (1980), pp. 726–50; John H. Fisher, 'European Chanceries and the Rise of Standard Languages' (1986: repr. in *Emergence*), pp. 65–83.

[10] J. Derrick McClure, 'English in Scotland', *Cambridge History of the English Language* vol. v (Cambridge, 1994), pp. 23–93, at p. 36.

[11] Wright, 'Standardization', p. 272.

[12] John Waterman, *A History of the German Language with Special Reference to the Cultural and Social Forces that Shaped the Standard Literary Language* (Seattle, 1966), p. 128.

[13] Pietro Trifone, 'La lingua e la stampa nel '500', *Storia della Lingua Italiana*, vol. i (Turin, 1993), pp. 425–46, at p. 441; Paolo Trovato, *Con ogni diligenza corretto: la stampa e le revisioni editoriali dei testi letterari italiani, 1470–1570* (Bologna, 1991); Brian Richardson, *Print Culture in Renaissance Italy: the Editor and the Vernacular Text, 1470–1600* (Cambridge, 1994).

Italian-speaking worlds in particular, the sense of regional community remained strong, and encouraged an attachment to dialect that extended to the upper classes.

France may have lacked such regional variations but it was not exempt from deviations from the standard. Even the famous *Dictionary* of the *Académie Française* (1694), which was supposed to set orthographic standards, spelled the same words differently on different pages according to the compositor employed.[14]

4. In the fourth place, there is the problem of agency. The defenders of the thesis of a 'print revolution' have stressed the medium of communication at the expense of the messages of those writers, printers and readers who used the new technology for their own purposes.[15] On the other hand, the critics of the 'revolution' thesis view print as a technology that may be employed by different individuals or groups for different purposes in different locales.

The determinism implicit in the 'revolutionary' position and the voluntarism of some critics are equally one-sided. It is surely more illuminating to speak, like the Canadian media theorist Harold Innis, of a built-in 'bias' to be found in each medium of communication.[16] In other words, print may be viewed as a catalyst, assisting changes rather than initiating them, and requiring certain cultural or social preconditions in order to succeed. Although print has its economic logic, derived from the need to sell a uniform product in as large a market as possible, it is always possible for printers and their patrons to defy that logic, until funds run out.

Returning to the first of these four problems, the conceptual one, the following pages will distinguish codification and unification, discussing the two trends in order.

CODIFICATION

There were many codifiers or would-be codifiers active in this period, although they often disagreed about the standard to be adopted. Here, as elsewhere in this study, it may be useful to adopt a comparative approach. The 'language question', *la questione della lingua* as Italian scholars call it, was a European debate, not just an Italian one, although it was more

---

[14] Nina Catach, *Histoire de l'orthographie française* (Paris, 2001), p. 175.
[15] Elizabeth Eisenstein, *The Printing Press as an Agent of Change*, 2 vols. (Cambridge, 1979).
[16] Harold Innis, *The Bias of Communications* (Toronto, 1951).

intense in some places than others. It was, for instance, relatively muted in Spain.[17]

In the course of the Renaissance a number of humanists and other writers, caught between their admiration of Latin and their ambitions for their own vernacular, dreamed of making the later more dignified by discovering or inventing its rules. They began to publish grammars of the vernacular modelled on the rules for Latin and Greek.

The first of these was the *Gramática castellana* written by Antonio Nebrija and published in 1492, the first printed grammar in a vernacular language (a grammar of Italian had been written in the 1430s by the humanist Leonbattista Alberti, but it was not published until 1495). Alberti's *Regole della lingua fiorentina* was followed by the *Regole grammaticali della volgar lingua* (1516), by Gianfrancesco Fortunio, and by the book destined to have the greatest success, the *Prose della volgar lingua* (1525) by Pietro Bembo.

Grammars of other languages soon followed. The importance of the 1530s, a decade before the rise of treatises in praise of the vernacular (above, p. 65) is worth noting. Publications included a French grammar by the physician Jacques Dubois (1531), a Czech grammar by Beneš Optát and his collaborators (1533), a German grammar by the Protestant pastor Valentin Ickelsamer (1534), a grammar of Portuguese by the Dominican friar Fernão de Oliveira (1536) and a Hungarian grammar by János Sylvester (1539).

Thirty-five grammars of French had appeared in print by the year 1600, while grammars of ninety-eight languages, European and extra-European, had been published by 1782.[18]

ORTHOGRAPHY AND PUNCTUATION

It was especially of the written language that many rule-givers were thinking. One of their principal concerns was to codify spelling and punctuation.

Treatises on Czech and Polish orthography go back to the early fifteenth century. In the case of Italian, French, Spanish and English, on

---

[17] Luciana Stegagno Picchio, 'La questione della lingua in Portogallo', in João Barros, *Diálogo* (1540: new ed., Modena, 1959), pp. 5–54; Riccardo Picchio (ed.), *Studi sulla questione della lingua presso gli slavi* (Rome, 1972); Picchio, 'Guidelines for a Comparative Study of the Language Question among the Slavs', in Picchio and Goldblatt, *Aspects*, vol. 1, pp. 1–42.

[18] John H. Rowe, 'Sixteenth- and Seventeenth-Century Grammars', in Dell Hymes (ed.), *Studies in the History of Linguistics* (Bloomington, 1974), pp. 361–79, at p. 361.

the other hand, the standard was debated most vigorously in the sixteenth century.[19]

In Italy, for instance, the debate began in the 1520s, launched by the humanist Gian Giorgio Trissino, who had strong ideas about the reform of spelling. In Spain, the controversy was spread out over a longer period. Nebrija's rules of orthography were published in 1517, while Gonzalo Correas, a professor of Greek at the University of Salamanca, proposed reforms rather like Trissino's in his *Ortografía kastellana* (1630). In France, the great debate took place around 1550, the year in which Jacques Peletier published a dialogue on orthography and Louis Meigret his *Tretté de la grammaire françoeze* (the spelling of the title gives some sense of the reforms he proposed). In England, John Hart's *Orthographie* was published in 1569 and William Bullokar's *Amendment of Orthography* in 1580. Among the would-be reformers of English spelling in the sixteenth and seventeenth centuries were the writers Gabriel Harvey, James Howell and John Evelyn.[20]

The Germans, the Dutch and the Portuguese also debated these questions in the sixteenth and seventeenth centuries. A treatise on Danish spelling was published in 1678, while Peter the Great personally reformed Russian orthography at the beginning of the eighteenth century (the tsar's corrections of a draft scheme have survived).

The principal aim of the reformers was uniformity. They tried to ensure that every sound was rendered in writing in just one way. With the model of ancient Greek in mind, they suggested the introduction of new letters (*omega* into Italian, *kappa* into Spanish, *theta* into English and so on), the abolition of traditional letters (removing *q* or *y* from English, for instance), the suppression of silent letters (such as the final *g* in 'ung' in French), and the adoption of accents (such as the grave, acute and circumflex). The French borrowed the cedilla from Spanish at this time.[21]

Many of the reforms were unsuccessful. Spaniards, for instance, do not call their language 'Kastellano', as Correa wished. On the other hand, the acute, grave and circumflex accents did become part of everyday writing practice in a number of languages. At much the same time, signs for punctuation were introduced into Italian, thus simplifying the task of reading

[19] Ferdinand Brunot, *Langue française*, vol. II, pp. 93–123; Richard F. Jones, *The Triumph of the English Language* (Stanford, 1953), pp. 142–67; Nina Catach, *L'orthographie française à l'époque de la Renaissance* (Geneva, 1968); Brian Richardson, 'La riforma ortografica dal 1501 al 1533', in Mirko Tavoni (ed.), *Italia e Europa* (Ferrara, 1996), pp. 257–66; Vivian Salmon, 'Orthography and Punctuation', in Lass, *History of the English Language*, vol. III, pp. 13–55.

[20] Flasdieck, *Gedanke*, pp. 9, 23, 31.

[21] Malcolm B. Parkes, *Pause and Effect: an Introduction to the History of Punctuation in the West* (Aldershot, 1992).

aloud. The printer Aldo Manuzio introduced the apostrophe, borrowing it from ancient Greece, while his son Paolo Manuzio introduced the semi-colon. These signs soon spread to French and other languages. Spelling became more uniform – though not completely so – in one language after another, with Spanish and Italian in the lead and the sixteenth century as the crucial period.[22]

A second debate concerned linguistic unification and the comparative merits of different varieties of the vernacular. This debate had two main outcomes. On one side, we see the victory of one dialect over its rivals, as in the cases of Spain, Italy, France and England, and on the other the triumph of a mixed variety or *koine*.

THE VICTORY OF A DIALECT

In Spain, the spread of a standard form of Castilian was linked to the Reconquest. The variety spoken in Burgos became the standard, accepted in Toledo when that old capital was retaken from the Muslims or 'Moors' and then spreading southwards. In 1235, King Alfonso X, 'the Wise', declared Toledo to be 'the measure of the Spanish language' (*metro de la lengua castellana*).[23] A further stage in standardization was reached around 1500, in the age of the joint monarchs Ferdinand and Isabella and also of the humanist Antonio Nebrija, although Nebrija's grammar was criticized by a fellow-humanist, Juan de Valdés, for its Andalusianisms.[24] As a result, early modern Castille was unusually homogeneous from the linguistic point of view. There were no dialects.[25]

In the Italian case, many voices were heard in this debate, including that of Machiavelli, while the solutions proposed ranged from a mixed or common language associated with the court (*lingua commune, lingua cortigiana*) to the spoken language of Florence or Tuscany. In the victory of the Tuscan norm, it appears to have been the literary achievement of Dante, Petrarch and Boccaccio, without parallel in other regions of Italy, which weighed most heavily in the balance, thanks in particular to the efforts of Pietro Bembo.

---

[22] Attilio Bartoli Langeli, *La scrittura dell'italiano* (Bologna, 2000), pp. 8, 77–104.

[23] Wright, 'Standardization'. Cf. Hans-Josef Niederehe, *Die Sprachauffassung Alfons des Weisen* (Tübingen, 1975), pp. 98–100.

[24] Ramón Menéndez Pidal, 'La lengua en tiempo de los Reyes Católicos', *Cuadernos Hispanoamericanos* 13 (1950), pp. 9–24; Juan de Valdés, *Diálogo de la lengua* (written c. 1536: ed. Juan M. Lope Blanch, Madrid, 1969), p. 46.

[25] Alain Milhou, 'politiques', in *Langues et cultures*, pp. 15–40, at p. 18.

Bembo was a Venetian patrician, a humanist and finally a cardinal. He was still better known as a literary pope or arbiter of good style in both Latin and Italian. In Latin, he was a Ciceronian. In the case of Italian, it was Bembo who canonized Petrarch and Boccaccio, presenting them as models for anyone who wished to write and speak with elegance and purity (below, p. 145), thus ending what he called the 'Babel' of competing varieties of vernacular.[26] From the regional point of view, Bembo was something of an oddity. A Venetian living in Rome, the variety of language that he promoted was Tuscan. This looks like one of many cases of an outsider's over-identification with a norm, although it should be noted that the Tuscan standard advocated by Bembo was that of the fourteenth century.[27]

The literary achievement of Dante, Petrarch and Boccaccio might be exploited for political reasons, and was so exploited by Cosimo de'Medici, Grand Duke of Tuscany, who used this 'cultural capital' to legitimate his regime, sending an ambassador to the Council of Trent to prevent the banning of Boccaccio's *Decameron* as well as founding an academy in Florence concerned with questions of language.[28] All the same, the appeal of Tuscan was cultural rather than political or religious in origin.[29] The religious route to standardization was closed in the middle of the sixteenth century, when vernacular Bibles were banned.

The price of the cultural route to the standard, lacking the support of either the state or the Church, was that it was only taken by a tiny minority of the population, living mainly in Tuscany and in Rome – although the upper classes elsewhere might employ the Tuscan standard to mark special occasions, and the eighteenth-century Neapolitan elite used it more generally. Hence, the eighteenth-century Lombard writer Carlo Gozzi called Italian a 'dead language', like Latin. It has been calculated that when Italy became a single nation in 1860, only 2.5 per cent of the population knew and used the standard language.[30]

In France and England, on the other hand, the victory of the dialects of the Ile de France and the Home Counties seems to have been the result of a mixture of urbanization and political centralization.

---

[26] Robert A. Hall, Jr, *The Italian questione della lingua* (Chapel Hill, 1942); Maurizio Vitale, *La questione della lingua* (1960: revised ed. Palermo, 1984); Brian Richardson, 'Gli italiani e il toscano parlato nel '500', *Lingua Nostra* 48 (1987), pp. 97–107.

[27] Carlo Dionisotti, *Gli umanisti e il volgare fra quattro- e cinquecento* (Florence, 1968).

[28] Sergio Bertelli, 'Egemonia linguistica come egemonia culturale', *Bibliothèque d'Humanisme et Renaissance* 38 (1976), pp. 249–81.

[29] It has been argued that Tuscan won thanks to Florentine banks: Fisher, 'Chanceries', p. 80.

[30] Tullio De Mauro, *Storia linguistica dell'Italia unita* (1963: revised ed., Rome, 1991), pp. 14, 43, 78.

Already in the sixteenth century the humanist Benedetto Varchi, like Bembo an authority on language, recognized that 'the language of Paris' (*la lingua parigina*) could not be described as barbarous. The seventeenth-century poet François de Malherbe might be described as a new Bembo. Like Bembo, he was an outsider, who came not from Paris but from the South. Malherbe wanted, as he put it, to 'degasconize' French, to lay down rules for language, as well as for poetry. As in the case of Bembo, his ideals were institutionalized. Bembo's work was carried on by the Accademia della Crusca, and Malherbe's by the Académie Française, founded by Cardinal Richelieu on the Florentine model. Some of the early members of the Académie were followers of Malherbe, and one of the tasks of the institution was to reform the language, excluding from polite usage not only regionalisms but also foreign words and the technical terms used by artisans.[31]

The successful varieties of French were those of *la cour et la ville*, as people said in the seventeenth century, the court and the capital, or as Claude de Vaugelas, another member of the Académie Française, put it, 'the sound-est part of the court' (*la plus saine partie de la cour*), including women and those townspeople who were in contact with the court and so 'partic-ipate in its culture' (*participent à sa politesse*). The 'remarks' of Vaugelas, as he called them, proved controversial, and the years around the middle of the seventeenth century were the height of the French *questione della lingua*, but the standard he proposed was effectively adopted.[32]

As a model speech community, the term 'court' should be understood in a wide sense, including not only the noblemen and women surrounding the king but the clerks in the chancery as well. Chancery language was not infrequently taken as a model for writing by private individuals. In the case of German, for instance, the imperial chanceries at Prague and Vienna and the Saxon chancery at Meissen had most prestige (below, p. 101). In England, 'chancery English' was spreading in the mid-fifteenth century. A hundred years later, the printer Robert Estienne claimed in his grammar – written and published in Geneva in 1557 – that the chancery was one of the places where the best French could be heard. As late as 1599 a book was published called *Le tresor du stile de la Chancellerie*, suggesting that the style of the royal officials remained a model for good writing.

---

[31] Brunot, *Langue française*, vol. III (1909), pp. 3–9.
[32] Claude de Vaugelas, *Remarques sur la langue française* (Paris, 1647), preface: Erich Auerbach, 'La cour et la ville' (1951: English translation in his *Scenes from the Drama of European Literature*, New York, 1959, pp. 133–79); Wendy Ayres-Bennett, *Vaugelas and the Development of the French Language* (London, 1987).

By the seventeenth century, on the other hand, the key locales were the royal court and the *salons* of some noble ladies in Paris, notably that of Madame de Rambouillet, frequented by both Malherbe and Vaugelas. It is tempting to conclude that despite their bad press (above, p. 35) the *précieuses* may well have had the last word. Although they wrote little and published even less on the subject, the role of aristocratic women in the purification of language should not be underestimated. As sociolinguists have often pointed out, women in many societies are more polite than men, as well as displaying a tendency to hypercorrectness.[33]

England had no Bembo and no academy, although Daniel Defoe, among others, called for one 'to polish and refine the English tongue'. The Royal Society set up a committee 'for improving the English language' in the later seventeenth century and the Society's first historian, Thomas Sprat, also supported an English language academy on the model of the Académie Française.[34] In the eighteenth century, Dr Johnson's *Dictionary* was not only a work of reference but also a deliberate attempt 'to refine our language'.

All the same, social change probably had more effect on the language than the efforts of any individual. The growth of London and the fact that the court was located nearby encouraged the adoption of the south-eastern dialect as the standard, first in the chancery and then more generally. The Elizabethan writer George Puttenham advised poets to follow 'the usual speech of the court and that of 'London and the shires lying about London within 60 miles'. It has been calculated that between 1650 and 1750 one adult in six had experience of London life. Migration to the capital is likely to have been of great assistance to the process of linguistic unification.[35]

In other countries too, a standard was advocated based on the speech of the court or the capital. The Polish writer Jan Seklucjan supported what he called 'courtly language' (*dworski mowy*). Henrik Gerner wrote in favour of a standard Danish based on the usage of Copenhagen. Mikhaylo Lomonosov suggested that the dialect of Moscow be taken as the Russian standard, not only as the language of the court but also 'on account of the importance of the capital'.[36] Turning to practice, Rome, the headquarters of the Catholic Church, acted as a kind of capital for early modern Italy, and helped to spread the Tuscan standard.

---

[33] Janet Holmes, *Women, Men and Politeness* (London, 1995).   [34] Flasdieck, *Gedanke*, pp. 30–7.

[35] George Puttenham, *The Arte of English Poesie* (1588: ed. Gladys D. Willcock and Alice Walker, Cambridge, 1936), p. 145; E. Anthony Wrigley, 'A Simple Model of London's Importance, 1650–1750', *Past and Present* 37 (1967), pp. 44–70.

[36] Antoine Martel, *Michel Lomonosov et la langue littéraire russe* (Paris, 1933), pp. 36–7.

THE RISE OF THE KOINE

In Italy, which lacked a capital in this period, the phrase 'courtly language' (*lingua cortigiana*) referred to a *koine* or common language (otherwise known as a *lingua commune*) that combined elements from different dialects. This solution to the language problem was proposed by various participants in the debate, but proved unable to compete with the Tuscan standard.

On the other hand, in German, and also in Swedish, Dutch and Finnish, we see the victory of the mixed solution. In the Dutch case, this mixture may have been the result of urbanization, especially the rapid growth of Amsterdam in the seventeenth century, due in part to immigration from Antwerp. Irritating to traditional Amsterdammers at the time, as Bredero's satire suggests (above, p. 39) in the long run the language of the immigrants made an important contribution to standard Dutch.

The most famous and best-studied case of the creation of an early modern *koine* is that of German.[37] The difference between the dialects of North and South (Hamburg and Munich, for instance), or East and West (Leipzig and Cologne, say) was so great as to present formidable obstacles to interregional communication, written as well as spoken. When the imperial chancery and those of some leading princes adopted the vernacular in the fourteenth century, they had to decide what form of vernacular to choose. After the chancery of the emperor, based first in Prague and later in Vienna, that of the elector of Saxony at Meissen had most prestige. Eastern Germany was relatively unified linguistically because it had been colonized relatively recently, in the twelfth and thirteenth centuries.

All the same, the language of the Saxon chancery incorporated elements from other forms of German in order to be more widely intelligible – after all, the purpose of a chancery was to send letters to other places.[38] We might refer to this process of incorporation as 'pragmatic standardization'. It led to the creation of what was known at the time as a 'common language' (*lingua communis*).

[37] John Waterman, *German Language*, pp. 128–35; Erwin Arndt and Gisela Brandt, *Luther und die deutsche Sprache* (1983: second ed., Leipzig, 1987); Max L. Baeumer, 'Luther and the Rise of the German Literary Language: a Critical Reassessment', in Scaglione (ed.), *Emergence*, pp. 95–117; G. Arthur Padley, 'Germany: Luther and the Dialects', in his *Grammatical Theory in Western Europe 1500–1700*, vol. II (Cambridge, 1988), pp. 244–318.
[38] William F. Twaddell, 'Standard German', *Anthropological Linguistics* I, no. 3 (1959), pp. 1–7, at p. 2; Gerhard Kettmann, *Die kursächsische Kanzleisprache zwischen 1486 und 1546* (Berlin, 1967); cf. Fisher, *Emergence*.

In his attempt to reach ordinary people with his message, Martin Luther decided to write in the vernacular (though he also wrote in Latin for fellow-scholars). He was a Saxon but he did not want to limit his audience to Saxony. He could not write in German, for a standard German did not exist at this time. As he once remarked, 'Germany has so many dialects that people living only thirty miles apart do not understand one another' (*Germania tot habet dialectos, ut in triginta miliaribus homines se mutuo non intelligant*).[39]

Luther's solution to this problem was to follow the model of his local chancery. 'I speak in the style of the Saxon chancery', he once declared (*Ich red nach der sechsischen cantzeley*).[40] The emphasis on speaking rather than writing is worth noting. Luther believed that people do not learn languages from books as well as 'orally, at home, in the marketplace and from preaching' (*aus der mundlichen rede, im Hause, auff dem marckt und in der predigt*). In practice, Luther used expressions from his own dialect in writing as well as in speech, but he gradually followed the chancery model more closely. To speak more exactly, he followed different chancery models, imperial as well as Saxon.[41]

It was once again for pragmatic reasons that the Diet of Upper Lusatia set up a committee in 1691 to ensure that a standard language was employed in Protestant texts written in Sorbian. For similar reasons to the Protestants, in their attempt to reach as many people as possible with their religious message, the Jesuits in Bohemia adopted a kind of *koine*, midway between Czech and Slovak. Associated with the Jesuit University of Trnava between 1635 and 1777, this language became known as 'Jesuit Slovak' (*jezúitska slovencina*). It was the equivalent of the so-called 'general languages' (*línguas gerais, lenguas generales*) based on Tupí, Quechua and other Indian languages that the Jesuit missionaries used in Brazil and Peru.

In the struggle for the souls of ordinary people, the Protestants had a major advantage over the Jesuits and other Catholic missionaries: the vernacular Bible.

THE LANGUAGE OF THE BIBLE

The Danish scholar Peter Skautrup has spoken of 'the Reformation of language' (*Sprogets reformation*).[42] The Reformation was associated at one level with centrifugal forces, with what might be called the breakup of the

---

[39] Martin Luther, *Tisch-Reden*, 5 vols. (Weimar, 1912), no. 6146.
[40] Luther, *Tisch-Reden*, no. 1040.   [41] Baeumer, 'Luther', pp. 100–3.
[42] Skautrup, *Danske sprog*, vol. II, pp. 175–203.

Roman ecclesiastical empire, but at another level it was associated with centripetal forces, with the creation of national vernaculars as opposed to regional dialects.

The logic of missions was like the logic of print. To reach as many people as possible, it was necessary to speak and write in a language that the maximum number of listeners or readers could understand. Hence, Luther had recourse to the *koine* of the Saxon chancery not only in his sermons but also in the translation of the Bible that he published between 1522 and 1534.

It should be emphasized that this *koine* was only a regional standard, current in central and eastern Germany. Luther's Bible was not intelligible all over the German-speaking world, as the printer Georg Erlinger of Bamberg, among others, realized. Erlinger added a glossary to his edition of the Luther version of the Epistles and Gospels 'because I have observed that not everyone can understand some words' (*weil ich gemerckt hab daz not yederman verston mag etliche wörter*).[43] In the north they understood still less, so Luther's translation had to be retranslated into Low German.

Despite these problems, the Luther Bible became a linguistic model. A German grammar, published in Latin by Johannes Clavius in 1578, declared on the title-page that its examples would be taken 'from the Luther Bibles' (*ex bibliis Lutheri*). Conversely, the Catholic Church's opposition to the translation of the Bible was a major obstacle to the success of a rival solution supported by Luther's opponent Johann Eck, a standard based on Swabian.[44]

Elsewhere in Europe, translations of the Bible, often made by committees of scholars, also played a crucial part in the creation of a *koine*. Take Scandinavia, for instance.[45] In Sweden, King Gustav Vasa's Bible (1541) followed the Luther model and used a language that could be understood all over Sweden, although a majority on the committee of translators came from Uppsala or Stockholm. In Denmark, the committee was asked by the king to follow the example of Luther, and so Christiern III's Bible (1550), as it was called, provided a written norm for Danish that later became a spoken norm.[46]

[43] Karl Schottenloher, *Die Buchdruckertätigkeit Georg Erlingers in Bamberg* (Leipzig, 1907).

[44] Werner Besch et al. (eds.), *Sprachgeschichte: Ein Handbuch zur Geschichte der deutschen Sprache und ihre Erforschung* (Berlin, 1984).

[45] Lillemor Santesson, 'Ecclesiastical History III: Luther's Reformation', in Oskar Bandle (ed.), *The Nordic Languages*, vol. 1 (Berlin, 2002), pp. 412–24.

[46] Elias Wessén, 'Studier over språket i Gustav Vasas Bibel', *Nysvenska studier* 7 (1927), pp. 251–63; Skautrup, *Danske sprog*, pp. 210–6.

In Finland, the story is a little more complicated. Mikael Agricola, the Lutheran bishop of Turku, who had studied in Wittenberg, translated the New Testament (1548) and part of the Old, basing himself on the dialect of the Turku area and also introducing new words into Finnish. His text has been described as 'a sort of pot-pourri of dialects'. However, in 1642, the Bible was re-translated by a committee headed by Eskil Petraeus that aimed at writing in a language that could be understood all over the country.[47]

Turning to Dutch or Flemish, we find a similar situation. Jan Utenhove's New Testament aimed, we are told, at 'a Dutch text that would be comprehensible to readers from all parts of the Netherlands'.[48] It was not successful, so the work was done again in the Calvinist 'States' Bible' (*Statenbijbel*) of 1637, commissioned by the States-General. This translation was, like the English Authorized Version, the work of a committee, but a committee in which different regions and their dialects were represented.[49]

The influence of the scriptures on the standardization of vernacular writing and even speech is also perceptible in Czech, Danish, English, Hungarian and other languages. The story does not begin with the Reformation. John Wyclif's earlier contribution to the development of English, like that of Jan Hus to Czech, was an important one. A Catalan Bible was printed as early as 1478 and a Czech Bible in 1488. However, the Bible played a more important part in the history of the European vernaculars after 1520.

The English part of this story is well-known, from the New Testament of William Tindale (1525–6) to the Authorized Version (1611). Tindale, for instance, enriched the language with words such as 'Passover' and 'scapegoat', and phrases such as 'broken-hearted', 'peace-maker' and 'stumbling-block'.[50] The Authorized Version contributed 'clear as crystal', 'fat of the land', 'root of all evil', 'still small voice' and proverbs such as 'the wages of sin is death' and 'sufficient to the day is the evil thereof'.

However, translations of the Bible were also important in the history of many other vernaculars, including Icelandic, in which the New Testament appeared in 1540, Romansh, in which it came out in 1560, and Basque, in

47 Haugen, *Scandinavian Languages*; Aurélien Sauvageot, *L'élaboration de la langue finnoise* (Paris, 1973); Sauvageot, 'Le finnois de Finlande', in István Fodor and Claude Hagège (eds.), *Language Reform*, vol. III (Hamburg, 1984), pp. 173–90, at p. 179.
48 Andrew Pettegree, *Emden and the Dutch Revolt* (Oxford, 1992), p. 90.
49 Cornelis G. N. de Vooys, *Geschiedenis van de Nederlandse taal* (1931: fifth ed., Antwerp and Groningen, 1952), pp. 108–10. Robert B. Howell, 'The Low Countries', in Stephen Barbour and Cathy Carmichael (eds), *Language and Nationalism in Europe* (Oxford, 2000), pp. 130–50, at p. 143, doubts the influence of this Bible on the language.
50 Gavin D. Bone, 'Tindale and the English Language', in Stanley L. Greenslade, *The Work of William Tindale* (London, 1938), pp. 50–68.

which it was published in 1571 (the work of a French Calvinist missionary). It was in the context of translations of the Bible that a controversy broke out in Poland in the 1540s about the best model for the literary language, whether it should come closer to Czech or remain pure Polish.

The influence of the Geneva Bible of 1588 on the spoken French of Protestants at least is suggested by the seventeenth-century phrase describing their speech as 'the *patois* of Canaan' (a variant of the biblical phrase *lingua Canaan*, Isaiah 19.18). In Bohemia, literary Czech was shaped by the Kralicy Bible (1579–93), leading to the development of what was known in the eighteenth century as 'Bible language' (*biblictina*). In Wales, Morgan's Bible (1588) has been described as the basis of modern literary Welsh. The Hungarian Protestant Bible of 1590 was important for the development of literary Hungarian.

Bible translations were one of the principal means by which printers aided the process of linguistic standardization, to which some of them were committed. For example, the printer Gáspár Heltai contributed to the standardization of Hungarian orthography by the books he produced in the later sixteenth century. As in the cases of Bembo, Malherbe and Vaugelas, we see the importance of the outsider, since Caspar Helth, as he was originally known, was a German who only learned Hungarian at the age of twenty.

The story of the Bible in Illyria, the lands of the South Slavs, is an unusually complex one. In the mid-sixteenth century Primoz Trubar, a Protestant exile in Germany, worked on a Bible translation into Slovene while his assistants worked on Croat. The Italian Protestant humanist Pier Paolo Vergerio suggested translating the Bible into a language that could be understood by all South Slavs, but Trubar considered this task to be impossible. By 1561, however, Trubar was concerned to publish books which Croats, Dalmatians, Serbs, Bosnians and even Bulgarians could all understand, a popular and Protestant version of Church Slavonic. The New Testament translated by Antun Dalmatin and Stjepan Konzul (printed 1562–3), drew on Croatian, Istrian and Dalmatian dialects.[51]

In the case of Sorb, or, as it was known at the time, 'Wend', we find a political assembly intervening in the language question, in a manner reminiscent of nineteenth-century Norway. The Estates of Lusatia was concerned with the variety of translations of religious literature from German and so

---

[51] Martin Dimnik, 'Gutenberg, Humanism, the Reformation and the Emergence of the Slovene Literary Language 1550–1584', *Canadian Slavonic Papers* 26 (1984), pp. 141–59, at p. 154; Dimnik, 'Primoz Trubar and the Mission to the South Slavs (1555–64)', *Slavonic and East European Review* 66 (1988), pp. 380–99, at pp. 389, 392.

supported what they called 'the new Sorbian style' (*dem neuen wendischen Stylo*).[52] In the case of Romanian, the metropolitan of Transylvania, Simeon Stefan, argued in 1648 (in the preface to a translation of the New Testament) in favour of a common literary form of the language. However, it would take centuries for such a form to be established. Similarly, in the case of Czech, Slovak, Slovene, Serbian, Croat, Bulgarian and Greek, the age of linguistic standardization was the late eighteenth and early nineteenth centuries, the age of Josef Dobrovský, Ľudovít Štúr, Jernej Kopitar, Vuk Stefanović Karadžić, Ljudevit Gaj and Adamantios Korais.

THE ROLE OF THE PRINTERS

In some discussions of the importance of print, the printers themselves are almost invisible, 'unsung heroes', squeezed out between the famous writers on one side and impersonal forces on the other.[53] However, in many parts of Europe we find individual printers playing leading roles in the standardization of the vernacular.

In late fifteenth-century England, for instance, William Caxton decided to print in chancery English and so encouraged its wider use, although he was not consistent in the spellings he favoured.[54] In the German-speaking world, Sebastian Franck was a printer who was personally involved in the language question, like his colleagues Hieronymus Wietor and Jan Malecki in Poland. In Paris and Geneva, Geoffroy Tory, Etienne Dolet and Robert and Henri Estienne were all at work as reformers of language as well as printers.[55] In the Slav world, the Ruthenian Pamva Berynda was at once a monk, a printer and the compiler of a dictionary. In sixteenth-century Hungary, a key role was played by Gáspár Heltai, as we have seen. Since only a few Hungarian presses were in operation, the efforts of an individual like Heltai could have a disproportionate effect.

The success of Tuscan was also aided by print – once the printers were persuaded to adopt Tuscan norms – while certain printers, notably Aldo Manuzio, Bembo's printer, and his son Paolo Manuzio, were involved in the movement of codification. The edition of Dante published by Aldo in 1501 illustrates the process. The spelling of the manuscript Aldo used and

[52] Alfred Mietzschke, 'Der Entstehung der obersorbischen Schriftsprache (1668–1728)', *Zeitschrift für Slavische Philologie* 28 (1960), pp. 122–48, at p. 135.
[53] Richard Cole, 'Reformation Printers: Unsung Heroes', *Sixteenth-Century Journal* 15 (1984), pp. 327–39.
[54] John H. Fisher, 'Caxton and Chancery English' (1984: repr. Fisher, *Emergence*), pp. 121–44; Thomas Cable, 'The Rise of Written Standard English', in Scaglione, *Emergence*, pp. 75–94, at pp. 81–3.
[55] Catach, *Orthographie*, pp. 31–50, 51–70, 245–59.

the published version of Dante differ in a systematic way, showing that Aldo wanted to make Italian look more like Latin. Hence *anno,* 'they have', became *hanno, giusticia* became *giustitia, silencio* became *silentio,* and *scuola* became *schola* (in all but the last case, modern Italian follows Aldo).[56]

In three further cases, one of them Spanish, one German and one English, the happy survival of a manuscript, along with the text printed from it, allows us to enter the printer's workshop and observe the decisions taken there. The *Gran Conquista de Ultramar,* a thirteenth-century Spanish translation of a twelfth-century Latin chronicle, was published in 1503. A comparison with the manuscript has shown that variations in orthography and syntax have been eliminated, and also that the choices adopted have often survived into the Spanish of today: *calle* rather than *call, dignidad* rather than *dignitat, imperio* rather than *emperio,* etc.[57]

In the German-speaking world, the different 'printer's languages' of the early sixteenth century yielded to the norms of Wittenberg and Frankfurt after 1550.[58] The survival of a manuscript printed by Sigmund Feyerabend of Frankfurt allows a comparison of the same kind as the *Gran Conquista.* Ulrich Schmidl's account of his adventures in the New World was written in Bavarian dialect, and it was also highly inconsistent in spelling and grammar. The version published in 1567 not only modified the Bavarianisms but also made the verbal forms more consistent, and again, on occasions, closer to the modern German: from *warden* to *warten,* for instance, *pleibt* to *bleiben, friedt* to *Fried.*[59] Feyerabend also printed Luther's translation of the Bible, but in his editions the language was modified to make it less Saxon.[60]

An English example of the same process is that of John Harington's translation of Ariosto, published in 1591. Yet again the changes made the printed version closer to modern English, changing *bee* to *be,* for instance, *greef* to *grief, noorse* to *nurse* and *swoord* to *sword.*[61]

As Ferdinand Brunot once argued, the printers had more influence on the way that French was written than Malherbe or Vaugelas.[62] In the case of England and France, the organization of printing, itself a reflection of the

[56] Ambroise Firmin-Didot, *Alde Manuce et l'Hellénisme à Venise* (Paris, 1875), p. 195.
[57] Ray Harris-Northall, 'Printed Books and Linguistic Standardization in Spain', *Romance Philology* 50 (1996), pp. 123–46.
[58] Waterman, *German Language,* p. 128.
[59] Marion L. Huffines, 'Sixteenth-Century Printers and the Standardization of New High German', *Journal of English and Germanic Philology* 73 (1974), pp. 60–72.
[60] Baeumer, 'Luther', p. 115.
[61] Fernand Mossé, *Esquisse d'une histoire de la langue anglaise* (Lyon, 1947), p. 140.
[62] Brunot, *Langue française,* vol. IV, p. 119; Henri-Jean Martin, *Print, Power and People in Seventeenth-Century France* (1969: English translation, Metuchen, NJ, and London, 1993).

centralization of government, assisted the process of linguistic unification. In England, printing was centralized – indeed, it was virtually confined to London, Oxford and Cambridge until the eighteenth century. In France, as in England, the capital city dominated the printing industry, and the supremacy of Paris was strengthened by government intervention in the age of Louis XIV.

THE SPOKEN LANGUAGE

A second wave of standardization affected the spoken language. Its chronology is more difficult to establish, but it seems that the common practice of reading aloud contributed in the long term to bringing the spoken language closer to the written.

In sixteenth-century Italy and seventeenth-century France, in particular, language debates were concerned with the speech of educated people as well as with the written language. Indeed, Malherbe and Vaugelas were more concerned with speech than with writing. The debates extended to pronunciation as well as vocabulary. Renaissance writers on pronunciation were mainly concerned with Latin and Greek, but Jacques Peletier and Theodore Beza discussed French, John Rhys Italian, and Juan López de Velasco Spanish.

In England, where accent was already a social shibboleth, as we have seen (above, p. 41), Robert Robinson's *The Art of Pronunciation* (1617) was an early contribution to the debate, but the mid-eighteenth century was probably the turning-point, as the success of the works on correct speech by Thomas Sheridan bear witness. William Johnston's *Pronouncing and Spelling Dictionary* (1764) offers further evidence of the increasing concern with speaking correctly. So does John Walker's *Critical Pronouncing Dictionary* (1791), which made the famous claim that London pronunciation was 'the best' because it was 'more generally received' than its rivals.

In some parts of Europe, from the Dutch Republic through the German states to Russia, the use of French by the upper classes probably delayed the rise of a standardized vernacular, since it was less necessary for distinguishing between people of high and low status. In Denmark, German performed a similar function. All the same, a concern for the spoken vernacular was developing, and a Danish grammarian wrote in 1679 that 'our corrupt speech should adapt itself to our cultivated writing in order that we may also get a cultivated speech'.[63]

[63] Henrich Gerner, quoted in Haugen, *Scandinavian Languages*, p. 418.

CENTRIPETAL VERSUS CENTRIFUGAL

The power of centrifugal forces must not be underestimated. Mikhail Bakhtin has written eloquently about the long history of competition between standard or official languages and their unofficial alternatives, such as dialects and jargons, part of the rivalry or indeed the conflict between official culture and popular culture.[64] Such conflict is endemic, and it would doubtless be a disaster for both varieties of language if it did come to an end.

Two hundred years after Luther, in the middle of the eighteenth century, Frederick the Great, writing in French, could still dismiss German as an unrefined language, 'semi-barbaric and divided into as many dialects as Germany has provinces'. In the eighteenth century, the language debate was still raging among German men of letters. Johann Christoph Adelung, for instance, supported a south Saxon standard, some Bavarians proposed their own dialect, Joachim Campe favoured a *koine*, while Johann Christoph Gottsched advocated a written standard based on the usage of Meissen in Saxony.[65] To this day, German is a less unified language than, say, English or French.

In short, the story of standardization was subject to considerable variation in different parts of Europe. In Italy and Germany, in particular, there was resistance, the centrifugal tendencies being as strong as or stronger than the centripetal ones.[66] In Eastern Europe, the great age of standardization was the nineteenth century (below, p. 168). Where standardization was successful in the early modern period, it took different routes. In the case of France, scholars have spoken of 'linguistic absolutism', noting the involvement of the state with the official arbiter of language, the Académie Française (imitated in Spain, Russia and Sweden). In England, on the other hand, we see the rise of a standard by informal means.

Returning to the question raised at the beginning of the chapter, we may now say that standardization owed something to conscious planning but that the unification of national languages owed more to forces outside human control, including the medium of print and the rise of certain courts and cities. The rise of a codified language, praised at the time as refined,

---

[64] Mikhail Bakhtin, 'From the Prehistory of Novelistic Discourse' (1975: English translation, *The Dialogic Imagination*, Austin, 1981), pp. 41–83.

[65] Eric A. Blackall, *The Emergence of German as a Literary Language, 1700–75* (Cambridge, 1959).

[66] W. Theodor Elwert, *Studi di letteratura veneziana* (Venice-Rome, 1958); Luca Serianni, 'La lingua del Seicento: espansione del modello unitario, resistenze ed esperimenti centrifughi', in Enrico Malato (ed.), *Storia della letteratura italiana*, vol. v (Rome, 1997), pp. 561–96.

urbane or 'polite', should surely be viewed as part of the 'civilizing process' which Norbert Elias described and linked to state-building in France and elsewhere. The warrior nobility were gradually tamed and turned into courtiers. They lost their local accent and their local loyalties at about the same time.

As in the case of table manners, to which Elias devoted particular attention, the glamour of the court and its influence on provincial elites encouraged the adoption of the new form of language, which became a sign that its users were distinct from and superior to ordinary people. The reform of speech was part of a wider change, the withdrawal from participation in many forms of popular culture on the part of European elites. Culture was becoming more important as a status symbol at a time when older social hierarchies were breaking down, especially in large cities such as London or Paris. In the anonymity of such cities, status was coming to depend less on birth and more on the 'culture of politeness', which included speaking the right variety of language as well as wearing the right clothes.[67] As Vaugelas remarked in the preface to his *Remarques*, one wrong word was sufficient for someone to lose face in good company (*pour faire mespriser une personne dans une compagnie*).

As the supporters of different vernaculars liked to point out, their languages deserved praise because they were rich, abundant or copious. More exactly, they were becoming richer by borrowing words, whether from Latin or from other vernaculars. The languages of Europe were becoming more mixed. The process of mixing is the subject of the following chapter.

---

[67] Elias, *Civilizing Process*; Peter Burke, *Popular Culture in Early Modern Europe* (1978: second ed., Aldershot, 1994), pp. 270–80; Lawrence E. Klein, *Shaftesbury and the Culture of Politeness* (Cambridge, 1994).

CHAPTER 5

Mixing languages

Chapter 3 referred to 'winners' and 'losers' in the competition. However, in the history of language, as in the case of history in general, this contrast should not be made too sharp. The losers sometimes influence the winners to some extent, producing some kind of mixture, whether this is conscious or unconscious, pragmatic (as in the case of a *lingua franca*) or playful, as in the case of macaronic literature.

This process of linguistic exchange, as well as expressing the increasing cultural unification of Europe, contributed to its 'Europeanization', or at least offered some compensation for the gradual decline of communication in Latin. The participation of the elites of different European countries in a common culture that extended from music to warfare was marked by the creation of what the nineteenth-century Italian poet Giacomo Leopardi called 'europeisms' (*europeismi*).[1] All the same, historians of Europe have so far had little to say about this aspect of cultural encounters, preferring to leave this topic to their colleagues the linguists. Inspired by some recent work on 'language encounters' in North America in particular, I have tried in what follows to extend the approach to Europe.[2]

When there are contacts between speech communities, the influences flow in both directions and the result is cultural 'hybridization' or 'trans-culturation'.[3] In the case of language, the process of hybridization produces pidgins, creoles and other mixed languages. Pidgins may be described as languages without native speakers, languages that have been simplified, pruned to the minimum in order to allow people from different speech communities to understand one another. Creoles are pidgins that have grown back, in other words acquired native speakers and become complex again. Some linguists also refer to 'mixed languages', which combine

[1] Tullio De Mauro, *Storia linguistica dell' Italia unita* (1963: new ed., Rome-Bari, 1991), pp. 9, 283.
[2] Edward G. Gray and Norman Fiering (eds.), *The Language Encounter in the Americas, 1492–1800* (New York, 2000).
[3] Fernando Ortiz, *Cuban Counterpoint* (1940: English translation, New York, 1947).

the vocabulary of one language with the syntax of another, like the *media lengua* of Ecuador, which is Spanish in lexicon but follows Quechua rules of syntax.[4]

The process of globalization is contributing to language mixing today, most visibly – or audibly – in the invasion of so many languages, from Portuguese to Japanese, by English or Anglo-American words and phrases. However, the mixing of languages at global level began centuries ago. In early modern times it was a consequence of the invasion of the rest of the world by Europeans, otherwise known as 'discovery' or 'empire-building'. Portuguese was the first to expand its domain, followed by Spanish, French, Dutch and English.[5]

Similar processes of hybridization had been taking place within Europe for a long time. In medieval England, for example, English, French and Latin were in constant interaction, and the borrowing of Scandinavian words was so important that some linguists speak of 'pidginization' and 'creolization' in Middle English. However, this chapter will argue that borrowing and mixing increased in the early modern period. A language spoken by relatively few people, Maltese for example, reveals the mixing process more clearly than a language spoken by millions. In the later fifteenth century, Maltese was essentially a dialect of Arabic. By the late eighteenth century, on the other hand, it bore many traces of Sicilian, Catalan, French and north Italian.[6]

There were at least two main reasons for an increase in language mixing at this period. In the first place, mixing was encouraged by migration, including the three great diasporas of the period. The Greeks left the Byzantine Empire for Italy around 1453, the Ladino-speaking Jews left Spain for Italy and the Netherlands around 1492, and the French Protestants left France for London, Amsterdam or Berlin around 1685. Migration was also a response to the religious wars of the period 1568–1648. The religious refugees who fled to Poland in the sixteenth century and brought their languages with them included speakers of Italian, French, Flemish and Hungarian. Thanks to the immigration in the later sixteenth century of Protestants fleeing persecution, 'Norwich was a trilingual city for perhaps as much as two hundred

[4] Alexandru Rosetti, 'Langue mixte et mélange de langues', *Acta linguistica* 5 (1945), pp. 73–9, distinguishing 'langue mixte' from 'langue mélangée'; cf. Antonio Quilis, 'Le sort de l'espagnol au Philippines: un problème de langues en contact', *Revue Linguistique Romane* 44 (1980), pp. 82–107; Bakker and Mous, *Mixed Languages.*
[5] Richard W. Bailey, *Images of English: a Cultural History of the Language* (Ann Arbor, 1991), p. 60.
[6] Geoffrey Hull, 'Maltese, from Arabic Dialect to European Language', in Fodor and Hagège, *Language Reform*, vol. VI, pp. 331–46.

years', in which nearly 40 per cent of the inhabitants spoke French or Flemish as their first language.[7]

In the second place, the gradual decline of Latin was making it necessary for more Europeans to study one another's vernaculars than before. There was also a rise of translations from one vernacular into another from the sixteenth century onwards. An unintended consequence of the processes of learning and translation was mixing. Linguists have pointed out that whenever a person regularly speaks or writes two languages, some kind of 'interference' is virtually bound to occur.[8]

Two figures, one fictional and one real, preside over this chapter. The fictional character is Salvatore, a character in Umberto Eco's *The Name of the Rose*, who is described by a colleague as 'the monk who looks like an animal and speaks the language of Babel', which turns out to be a mix of Latin, French, Italian, Provençal and Spanish. The real person is the Russian Mikhail Bakhtin, who was fascinated by what he variously called – in Russian, of course – 'polyglossia', 'polyphony' or 'heteroglossia', the dialogue between different languages or varieties of language, including what he called their 'interanimation', the idea being that mixing encourages language consciousness and so linguistic and literary creativity.[9]

LANGUAGE LEARNING

A number of early modern rulers, ministers and diplomats are known to have spoken several European languages. William the Silent, for instance, who governed the Netherlands during the struggle for independence from Spain, knew French, Dutch, German and Spanish. The emperor Leopold knew Latin, Italian and Spanish as well as his native German. Erik XIV of Sweden is said to have known five foreign languages – German, Italian, Spanish, French and Finnish.[10]

Like their masters, ambassadors knew languages better than most. John Hackett, Henry VIII's ambassador in the Low Countries, is said to have spoken six languages, English, Latin, French, Spanish, Flemish and Italian).[11] In the reign of Louis XIV, when French was becoming the common language

[7] Peter Trudgill, 'Third-Person Singular Zero' (1997: repr. Jacek Fisiak and Peter Trudgill (eds.), *East Anglian English* (Cambridge, 2001), pp. 179–86, at p. 183.

[8] Max Weinreich, *History of the Yiddish Language* (1973: English translation, Chicago, 1980).

[9] Mikhail Bakhtin, *Rabelais and his World* (1965: English translation, Cambridge, MA, 1968), pp. 81–2; Bakhtin, 'From the Prehistory of Novelistic Discourse' (1975: English translation, *The Dialogic Imagination*, Austin, 1981), pp. 41–83, p. 81.

[10] Michael Roberts, *The Early Vasas: a History of Sweden, 1523–1611* (Cambridge, 1968), p. 199.

[11] Joycelyne G. Russell, *Diplomats at Work* (Stroud, 1992), p. 125.

of diplomacy, François de Callières recommended entrants to this profession to learn Italian, Spanish and German – though not English – as well as Latin.[12] In Denmark, the three Ulfeldt brothers, leading members of the political elite, were said by a French visitor to have spoken six or seven languages and to have understood still more.[13]

Some scholars and men of letters also achieved a respectable score. The botanist Charles de l'Écluse (Clusius) knew Dutch, German, Italian, Spanish and French. The Hungarian poet Bálint Balassa was said to have known as many as nine languages, including Turkish and three languages from the Slavonic family.

It has been argued that an interest in learning modern foreign languages was on the increase in a number of European countries in this period, for example in France and Spain (despite the local traditions of xenophobia) between 1650 and 1700.[14] It was certainly becoming easier to study these languages, thanks to the rise of a number of institutions.

One key institution, in the broad sense of that term, was the Grand Tour, on the course of which many young aristocrats learned Italian and French. The Tour has been studied most carefully in the case of England, although French, Dutch, German, Polish and Scandinavian aristocrats followed similar routes in the seventeenth and eighteenth centuries. It was generally, though not always, a case of the northern Europeans exploring the south. The Tour made the knowledge of foreign languages necessary and at the same time offered a convenient means of learning them.

Foreign languages were also taught in some European schools, colleges and universities. In towns in the Netherlands, for instance, both boys and girls were not infrequently taught French.[15] Spanish was often taught in France in the seventeenth century, and Dutch sometimes, at the Collège de Guyenne, for instance, perhaps on the principle that it is necessary to understand one's enemies. German was also taught in France at this time.[16] In London, the way to learn foreign languages was to go to a private tutor, like the French-speaking Protestant refugees established near St Paul's

[12] François de Callières, *De la manière de négocier avec les souverains* (Paris, 1716).

[13] Peter Skautrup, *Danske sprog*, vol. II, p. 305.

[14] Henri-Jean Martin, *Print, Power and People in 17th-Century France* (1969: English translation, Metichen, NJ, and London 1993), p. 544; Asensio Gutierrez, *La France et les français dans la littérature espagnole: un aspect de la xénophobie en Espagne 1598–1665* (St-Etienne, 1977), pp. 129–45.

[15] Kornelis J. Riemens, *Esquisse historique de l'enseignement du français en Hollande du 16e au 19e siècle* (Leiden, 1919).

[16] Sabina Collet Sedola, 'L'étude de l'espagnol en France à l'époque d'Anne d'Autriche', in Charles Mazouet (ed.), *L'âge d'or de l'influence espagnole: la France et l'Espagne à l'époque d'Anne d'Autriche* (Mont-de-Marsan, 1991); Paul Lévy, *La langue allemande en France*, vol. I, *Des origines à 1830* (Lyon, 1950); on Dutch, see pp. 93–5, 126–31.

Churchyard.[17] In similar fashion in Danzig (now Gdańsk), French schools were opened by French refugees in the seventeenth century.

In Oxford and Cambridge, language teaching, mainly of Italian, Spanish and French, was informal, with private tutors operating outside the university system.[18] In some continental colleges for nobles, on the other hand, modern languages were part of the curriculum. This was the case at the Collegium Illustre at Tübingen in the late sixteenth century, for instance, and at the Danish noble academy at Sorø in the early seventeenth century.[19] Gradually the teaching of modern languages infiltrated the universities. Italian was taught at the University of Halle in the seventeenth century, and the romance languages at Ingolstadt and Leipzig. French was taught at the University of Uppsala from 1637, and at the University of Lund from 1669.[20]

Hundreds of grammars and dictionaries were produced in this period to allow speakers of one language to learn another. A few of them were multilingual, notably 'Calepino', a dictionary first published in 1502, regularly reprinted until late in the eighteenth century, and gradually enlarged so that it finally included eleven languages.

THE CASE OF ENGLISH

Readers, especially anglophone readers, may have been surprised by the lack of reference to English in the preceding section. The point is that learning English was not a high priority for continental Europeans at this time, at least not until the eighteenth century. An Italian treatise on diplomacy, Ottaviano Maggi's *De legato* (1596), declared that an ambassador should know seven languages – Latin, Greek, Italian, French, Spanish, German and Turkish – but not English. As a distinguished historian of the Renaissance has commented, 'Nobody in the sixteenth century except an Englishman was expected to speak English, not even the perfect ambassador'. The main exception was that of the Netherlanders, north and south, who learned English for commercial reasons.[21]

---

[17] Kathleen Lambley, *The Teaching and Cultivation of the French Language in England during Tudor and Stuart Times* (Manchester and London, 1920).
[18] Mark H. Curtis, *Oxford and Cambridge in Transition, 1558–1642* (Oxford, 1959), pp. 137–41.
[19] Hans Helmut Christmann, 'Italienische Sprache in Deutschland', in Konrad Schröder (ed.), *Fremdsprachenunterricht 1500–1800* (Wiesbaden, 1992), pp. 43–56.
[20] Elisabet Hammar, *L'enseignement du français en Suède jusqu'en 1807* (Stockholm, 1980).
[21] Garrett Mattingly, *Renaissance Diplomacy* (London, 1955), p. 217; Petrus L. M. Loonen, *For to Learne to Buye and Sell: Learning English in the Low Dutch Area between 1500 and 1800* (Amsterdam-Maarssen, 1991).

The regret expressed by the French scholar Nicolas Fabri de Peiresc in a letter of 1628, that the accounts of travel edited by Samuel Purchas were unintelligible to him, expressed a common situation among continental scholars. Even in the early eighteenth century, when *The Spectator* was being read almost all over Europe, we find the German-Swiss writer Johann Bodmer and his friends studying the periodical in French translation.[22]

One reason that relatively few books were translated from English into other European languages before the middle of the seventeenth century was the lack of people with sufficient knowledge of the language. The few translators often had special reasons for acquiring English. The French noblewoman Geneviève Chappelain, for example, the translator of Philip Sidney's *Arcadia*, spent time at the English court in the suite of the Countess of Salisbury. Pierre de Mareuil, a Jesuit who translated Milton, had an unusual and unwelcome opportunity to learn English – in captivity.

Other examples of foreigners who mastered English before the year 1700 include the Swedish Princess Cecilia and the Transylvanian noble-man Miklós Bethlen, who records in his autobiography the fact that he studied English in the Netherlands for five to six weeks in preparation for a visit to England in 1663.[23] All the same, the continental men of letters who could read English were so rare, at least before 1700 or so, that they can virtually be listed in a paragraph.

Italians included the historian Giovanni Francesco Biondi, who lived in London and wrote on the Wars of the Roses, and the natural philosopher Lorenzo Magalotti, who visited England and made, but did not publish, a translation of the poems of Edmund Waller. The Dutch scholar Constantijn Huygens studied English on a visit to England in 1618 in the suite of an embassy, and learned it well enough to translate nineteen poems by John Donne.[24] In the case of Germany, the poet Georg Weckherlin knew English even before settling in that country in 1619, while the polymath Gottfried Wilhelm Leibniz, to judge from the books he ordered, had at least a reading knowledge of the language.

The situation began to change from the late seventeenth century onwards. References to the teaching of English now multiply, from the academy for diplomats founded in Paris in 1712, through the German

[22] Eric A. Blackall, *The Emergence of German as a Literary Language, 1700–75* (Cambridge, 1959), p. 69.

[23] István G. Tóth, *Literacy and Written Culture in Early Modern Europe* (1996: English translation, Budapest, 2000), p. 136.

[24] Rosalie L. Colie, *Some Thankfulness to Constantine: a Study of English Influence upon the Early Works of Constantijn Huygens* (The Hague, 1956), pp. 52–71.

colleges for noblemen to the University of Göttingen, which appointed a certain John Tompson professor of English in 1732.[25] Among the eighteenth-century German writers who knew English were Johann Georg Hamann, Johann Gottfried Herder and Johann Wolfgang von Goethe. In the case of Sweden, it has been suggested that 'Among the eighteenth-century travellers to England, the ability to make their way with at least broken English was general'.[26] Translations of English books into French, German (often via French) and into other languages also multiplied from this time onwards.[27]

LOCALES OF ENCOUNTER

Like other cultural encounters, linguistic contacts are more intense in some places than others, notably frontier zones and large polyglot cities. At worst, the inhabitants of frontier zones spoke no language well. More exactly, they were sometimes perceived as speaking no language well, as in the case of eighteenth-century Wales, where the borderers were described as 'a sort of Mongrels that cannot speak Welsh or English correctly'.[28] As for Ireland, the inhabitants of Wexford in the age of Elizabeth were described by the Englishman Richard Stanyhurst as speaking neither good English nor good Irish, but instead as making 'a mingle mangle or gallamaufrey of both the languages and have in such a medley or checkerwyse . . . crabbedly jumbled them together'.[29]

At best, though, the people who lived on frontiers dominated two or more languages. In sixteenth-century Switzerland, for instance, one finds members of the Salis family writing letters in Latin, Italian, German, Romansh and French.[30] The story of Cardinal Granvelle, who came from another border area, Besançon in Franche-Comté, dictating to six secretaries in as

[25] Wilhelm Aehle, *Die Anfänge des Unterrichts in der englischen Sprache, besonders auf den Ritter-akademien* (Hamburg, 1938); Thomas Finkenstaedt, 'John Tompson', in Schröder, *Fremdsprache-nunterricht*, pp. 57–74.
[26] Sven Rydberg, *Svenska Studieresor till England under Frihetstiden* (Uppsala, 1951), p. 421.
[27] Mary B. Price and Lawrence M. Price, *The Publication of English Literature in Germany in the Eighteenth Century* (Berkeley, 1934); Bernhard Fabian, 'Englisch als neue Fremdsprache des 18. Jahrhunderts', in Dieter Kimpel (ed.), *Mehrsprachigkeit in der deutschen Aufklärung* (Hamburg, 1985), pp. 178–96.
[28] Quoted in Geraint H. Jenkins (ed.), *The Welsh Language before the Industrial Revolution* (Cardiff, 1997), p. 105.
[29] Quoted in Patricia Palmer, *Language and Conquest in Early Modern Ireland* (Cambridge, 2001), p. 42.
[30] Randolph C. Head, 'A Plurilingual Family in the Sixteenth Century', *Sixteenth-Century Journal* 26 (1995), pp. 577–93.

many languages at the same time may be apocryphal, but it is at least plausibly located, since Granvelle's correspondence offers supporting evidence for his command of French, Spanish and Italian.[31]

As for the Netherlands, the English traveller Fynes Moryson – himself no mean performer in this respect, speaking Italian, Spanish, French and German – commented on 'the Flemings general skill in strange languages'.[32] It is not difficult to cite instances of this skill. The ambassador Ogier Ghiselin de Busbecq spoke six modern languages – Dutch, German, Italian, Spanish, French and Croat – besides writing a famous account of the Ottoman Empire in Latin. The painter Rubens corresponded in four languages, Italian, French, Spanish and Flemish.

Extreme examples of this fluency include the Antwerp patrician Jan van der Noot and the Ghent patrician Karel Utenhove. Noot published his *Verscheyden Poetische Werken/Divers Oeuvres Poetiques* in 1580, including poems in French and Dutch and commentaries in Italian and Spanish, while Utenhove published a book of poems in twelve languages. These men were unusual even in their own culture, but they were, predictably, Flemings rather than Frenchmen, Spaniards, Englishmen or Italians.[33]

Then there were polyglot cities, generally ports, such as Venice with its Greek, Jewish and Slavonic quarters, Antwerp with its Italians, French, Spaniards and Englishmen, or Amsterdam with its Germans, Scandinavians, Jews, Huguenots and others. Thanks to their immigrants, these three cities became centres of publishing in a number of languages. Sixteenth-century Antwerp printers produced books in French, German, Spanish and English as well as Latin and Flemish. The printers of Venice had a still wider range that included Greek (demotic as well as ancient), Hebrew, Spanish, Church Slavonic and Croat. However, even the Venetians were surpassed by the printers of seventeenth-century Amsterdam, with a linguistic repertoire that included French, English, Spanish, German, Yiddish, Russian, Hungarian and Georgian. The rise of large cities – that is, cities with one hundred thousand people or more, which was large by the standards of the time – was a major social change in the early modern period, and its linguistic consequences have still to be worked out.

The linguistic map of East-Central Europe was particularly fragmented, contrasting with Western Europe on one side and Russia on the other. As one Central European scholar puts it, the most variegated map of languages

[31] Théodore Juste, *La Révolution des Pays-Bas sous Philippe II* (Paris, 1860–3), p. 230; Edmond Poullet (ed.), *Correspondance du cardinal de Granvelle* (Brussels, 1877).

[32] Fynes Moryson, *Shakespeare's Europe* (London, 1903), p. 378.

[33] Leonard W. Forster, *The Poet's Tongues: Multilingualism in Literature* (Cambridge, 1970), pp. 30–5.

was to be found in 'the lands between the Elbe and Dob, from the Baltic to the Aegean'. In moving from one village to its neighbour in Hungary or Transylvania, for example, it might be necessary to switch between German, Hungarian, Slovak, Slovene or Romanian.[34]

Again, the Czech-speaking scholar Jan Komenský, better known internationally as Comenius, described the Hungarian town of Sárospatak in the middle of the seventeenth century as one in which at least five languages were spoken, so that unless Latin is used, 'one person understands another no more than in the Tower of Babel'.[35] From the point of view of the study of community, it would have been good to know whether the five languages were spoken by five groups of people or in five kinds of situation. In any case, it is no wonder that Comenius, who spent much of his life moving between speech communities in the Netherlands, England, Poland and elsewhere, was much concerned with the best way to teach language, or that he was obsessed with the need to see beneath the veil of language and to study things rather than words.

Other polyglot areas could be found in early modern Europe. In the north of Italy, there were places where French or German or a South Slav language could be heard, and in the south there were villages where the inhabitants spoke Greek or Albanian. In Sardinia in 1561, a Spanish Jesuit noted 'the diversity of languages', with Sardinian competing with Italian, Spanish and – in the cities of Alghero and Cagliari – Catalan.[36] In eighteenth-century Finland, four languages coexisted, with each of the three 'foreign' languages (Swedish, Latin and German) performing a different function.[37]

In the British Isles, besides English and five Celtic languages (Irish, Welsh, Scottish Gaelic, Cornish and Manx, still the language of most people on the island until the beginning of the eighteenth century), there was also a pocket of Flemish, thanks to immigration in the twelfth century. When the painter Lucas de Heere visited Pembrokeshire in the 1570s, he spoke to some people 'who still spoke Flemish well, as they have learned it from their parents and from father to son' (*die noch gued vlaemsch spraken tzelfde aen haer ouders ende als van vader tot kinde gheleert hebbende*).[38]

[34] János Bak, 'Linguistic Pluralism in Medieval Hungary', in *The Culture of Christendom*, ed. Marc A. Meyer (London, 1993), pp. 269–79, at p. 270; Tóth, *Literacy*, pp. 54, 138.

[35] Quoted in Jean Béranger, 'Latin et langues vernaculaires dans la Hongrie du 17e siècle', *Revue Historique* 242 (1969), pp. 5–28, at p. 5.

[36] Raimondo Turtas, 'La questione linguistica nella Sardegna del '500', *Quaderni sardi di storia* 2 (1981), pp. 55–86, at pp. 60–1.

[37] Aurélien Sauvageot, *Elaboration de la langue finnoise* (Paris, 1973).

[38] Lucas de Heere, *Beschrijving der Britsche Eilanden* (Antwerp, 1937), p. 48. Cf. Lauran Toorians, 'Wizo Flandrensis and the Flemish Settlement in Pembrokeshire', *Cambridge Medieval Celtic Studies* 20 (1990), pp. 99–118, at p. 115, a reference I owe to my Emmanuel colleague Liesbeth Van Houts.

PERCEPTIONS OF MIXTURE

These coexisting languages naturally influenced or 'interfered' with one another. As Martin Luther once remarked in the course of his 'table talk', anticipating the modern linguists quoted earlier, 'All languages are mixed up' (*Omnes linguae inter se permixtae sunt*: no. 2758). The idea seems to have been something of a commonplace, for the Alsatian humanist Beatus Rhenanus made the same point in a somewhat more qualified way (*puto linguas omnes nonnihil esse mixtas, et puram nullam*).[39] In the eighteenth century, the Italian writer Melchiorre Cesarotti concurred, writing in his essay on Italian that 'no language is pure' (*Niuna lingua è pura*).[40] A good many contemporaries were aware of the mixing process, which they described in metaphors that were always vivid and often pejorative.

The French scholar-printer Henri Estienne, for instance, spoke of 'incompetent householders' (*mauvais ménagers*), who borrow from their neighbours what they already have at home. References to borrowing, 'robbing' and to 'pilfered' words' were legion at this time.[41] Others spoke of aping, *la singerie*.[42] Yet others used the metaphor of 'patching', like those who compared English to 'a beggars patched cloak'.[43] Or they used the image of 'broken' language, like the German humanist Aventinus, who rejected a German with 'broken Latin words' (*zerbrochen lateinischen Worten*).[44] Or they spoke in English of 'mingle-mangle', in German of *Mischmasche*.[45] Or they spoke of 'bastard' words, like the Dutch humanist Hendrik Spieghel.

Culinary metaphors were particularly common.[46] Corrupt Latin was known as 'kitchen Latin'. Luther, for example, spoke of the *küchenlatein* of the papal letters, while Italian humanists had already referred to *culinarius Latinus* or to *coquinaria latinitas*.[47] Another common term was 'macaronic'

---

[39] Quoted in Monika Rössing-Hager, 'Küchenlatein und Sprachpurismus im frühen 16. Jahrhundert', in Nikolaus Henkel and Nigel F. Palmer (eds.), *Latein und Volksprache im deutschen Mittelalter, 1100–1500* (Tübingen, 1992), pp. 360–86, at p. 364.

[40] Melchiorre Cesarotti, *Saggio sopra la lingua italiana* (1785: repr. in Emilio Bigi (ed.), *Dal Muratori al Cesarotti*, Milan and Naples, 1960), pp. 304–468, at p. 308.

[41] Quoted in Blank, *Broken English*, pp. 33, 45, 177.

[42] Quoted in Brunot, *Langue française*, vol. ii, p. 201.

[43] Moryson, *Europe*, p. 437; cf. Carew, quoted in Blank, *Broken English*, p. 33.

[44] Quoted in Rössing-Hager, *Küchenlatein*, p. 361.

[45] Quoted in Jürgen Schiewe, *Die Macht der Sprache: Eine Geschichte der Sprachlichkeit von der Antike bis zur Gegenwart* (Munich, 1998), p. 77.

[46] Michel Jeanneret, *A Feast of Words: Banquets and Table Talk in the Renaissance* (1987: English translation, Cambridge, 1991), pp. 199–227.

[47] Paul Lehmann, 'Mittelalter und Küchenlatein' (1928: repr. in *Erforschung des Mittelalters*, 5 vols., Leipzig, 1941), vol. i, pp. 46–62, at p. 57; Rudolf Pfeiffer, 'Küchenlatein' (1931: repr. *Ausgewählte Schriften*, Munich, 1960), pp. 183–7.

Latin, referring not to what we know as macaroni but to *gnocchi*, which were considered to be coarse and rustic food.[48] The inventive translator Johann Fischart rendered this term as *Nudelverse*.[49] A sixteenth-century Frenchman complained that French was becoming 'une fricassée des mots de divers pays'.[50] An English term was 'hotch-potch' (a fifteenth-century word for a pudding). An anonymous German pamphlet the *Sprachverderber* ('Corrupter of Language', 1643), criticized the Frenchified German as 'half-baked' (*Halbgebachenen Teutscher Frantzös*). Today, Javanese describe the mix of Indonesian and Javanese that is sometimes spoken as a 'language salad'.[51]

Some languages were more mixed than others, or at least perceived as such. Italian was described by Pierfrancesco Giambullari as 'a combination of different languages' (*un componimento di varie lingue*), including Etruscan, Greek, Latin, German and French.[52] Spanish was both praised and blamed for its borrowings from Latin, Arabic, Hebrew and the language of the Visigoths, who invaded the peninsula when the Roman Empire declined. Juan de Valdés called it a 'mixed language' (*lengua mezclada*), while Martin Viziana described it as 'a mixture of many languages' (*mezcla de muchos lenguas*).[53] Portuguese too was known to have borrowed many Arabic words, some of which were listed in the history of the language by Nunes de Leão.[54]

Yiddish is another obvious case of mixture, and its speakers were denounced in 1699 because 'they have mutilated, minced, distorted [*gestümmelt, geradbrecht, verkehret*] the good German words . . . and mixed into German countless Hebrew words and phrases'.[55] German itself was perceived in the seventeenth century as a mixture that included words from Latin, French, Spanish and Italian.[56]

English offers another frequently-cited example of mixing. According to the Swiss humanist Conrad Gesner, 'Today, the English language is of all the

---

[48] Ugo E. Paoli, *Il latino maccheronico* (Florence, 1959); Lucia Lazzerini, 'Per latinos grossos: studio sui sermoni mescidati', *Studi di Filologia Italiana* 29 (1971), pp. 219–339; Lazzerini, 'Aux origines du macaronique', *Revue des langues romanes* 86 (1982), pp. 11–33; Ivano Paccagnella, 'Mescidanza e macaronismo', *Giornale Storico della Letteratura Italiana* 150 (1973), pp. 363–81.

[49] Quoted in Jeanneret, *Feast*, p. 213.   [50] Quoted in Brunot, *Langue française*, p. 166n.

[51] J. Joseph Errington, *Language Shift* (Cambridge, 1998), p. 98.

[52] Giambullari quoted in Marie-Lucie Demonet, *Les voix du signe. Nature et origine du langage à la Renaissance (1480–1580)* (Paris, 1992), p. 375.

[53] Juan de Valdés, *Diálogo de la lengua* (written c. 1540: ed. Juan M. Lope Blanch, Madrid, 1969), p. 53; Martin Viziana, *Libro de alabanças de las lenguas castellana y valenciana* (Valencia, 1574), sig. A5, verso.

[54] Nunes de Leão, *Origem*, pp. 243–5.

[55] Quoted in English in Weinreich, *Yiddish Language*, p. 103, and in German in Solomon A. Birnbaum, *Yiddish* (Toronto, 1979), p. 45.

[56] Strassner, *Sprachkultur*, p. 66.

most mixed and corrupt' (*Anglica omnium maxime mixta hodie corruptaque videtur*).[57] As we have seen, some foreigners described it as the scum that emerged when other languages were mixed in a pot (above, p. 68). It was 'a language confused, bepieced with other tongues' as the Anglo-Italian translator John Florio famously complained, 'so that if every language had his own words again, there would but few remain for Englishmen'.[58] It is indeed fortunate for us all that loanwords do not have to be repaid.

Even some natives agreed with this description of English. It was 'part Dutch, part Irish, Saxon, Scotch, Welsh and indeed a gallimaufry of many', according to Thomas Heywood. Fynes Moryson linked borrowing to wealth or copiousness and asserted that 'The English language . . . being mixed is therefore more and not less to be esteemed'.[59]

ENCOUNTERS AND EXCHANGES

A study of linguistic hybridity in Europe cannot afford to neglect the encounters between Europeans and the inhabitants of other continents, the global level of what Pierre Bourdieu called the 'economy of linguistic exchanges'.[60] The importance of certain kinds of individual in these exchanges should be noted, especially translators and interpreters or more generally people in motion, individually or in diasporas – merchants, pilgrims, soldiers and refugees.

The importance of linguistic imports to Europe from Asia, Africa and the Americas is well-known, especially the local terms for fauna, flora and foods. 'Chocolate', 'avocado' and 'tomato' and similar words in Spanish, Portuguese, French and other European languages all derived from Nahuatl. 'Jaguar', 'cashew' and 'manioc' came from Tupí. 'Condor', 'puma' and 'quinine' came from Quechua. New words to describe tropical weather ranged from the 'hurricane' to the 'typhoon' or the 'monsoon'.

It should be noted that the European languages in which African and American terms are first attested are usually the languages of imperial powers – Spanish, Portuguese, Dutch, English and French. In German or the Scandinavian or the Slav languages, these words generally appear later. The story is rather different in the case of another imperial power, the Ottoman Empire. Turkish borrowed extensively from other languages in the early modern period, but mainly from Arabic and Persian, while

[57] Conrad Gesner, *Mithridates* (Zurich, 1555), p. 3.
[58] Heywood quoted Blank, *Broken English*, p. 31; John Florio, *First Fruits* (London, 1578), chapter 27.
[59] Moryson, *Europe*, p. 479.
[60] Pierre Bourdieu, *Language and Symbolic Power* (1982: English translation, Cambridge, 1991).

Hungarian, Greek, Serbian, Bulgarian and other languages spoken by sub-ject peoples within the Ottoman Empire borrowed from Turkish.[61]

Words referring to items of material culture that were new in Europe include: 'pagoda', an Indian term that was taken up first by the Portuguese and then in French, Italian and English; 'palanquin', a word from Malay or Javanese that made its way through Portuguese into English, Italian, French and Spanish; 'kris', a Malay term for a special kind of curved sword that entered Portuguese and then Italian in the sixteenth century; 'veranda', an Indian word adopted first by the Portuguese and then, in the eighteenth century, by the English and the French; 'caftan', from Turkish, first used in English to describe Russian costume, and 'assagai', the Arabic name for a spear used in Africa, already recorded in English by 1625.

From the New World came such terms as 'canoe', originally a Taíno word from Hispaniola that passed into Spanish, English and French, and 'wampum' and 'wigwam', which entered English from the language of the Amerindian neighbours of the settlers in Massachusetts.

Of special interest to social historians are terms that refer to local customs and social roles and so testify to an increasing European knowledge of non-European societies. For example, a cluster of terms from the Muslim world entered a number of European languages in the sixteenth century. They include: *cadi*, the Arabic word for a Muslim judge; *sheikh*, recorded in Italian and in English; *aga*, a Turkish word for 'lord', found in French and in Italian; *sultan*, a Turkish word that entered Italian and English; *pasha*, a Turkish word found in Italian, English (in the form 'bashaw') and French; *dervish*, a Persian term found in French; *imam*, an Arabic word for a religious leader that is recorded in French in 1559 and in English in 1613, and *muezzin*, the Arabic or Turkish word for the man who calls the faithful to prayer, which entered both French and English.

Neologisms from other regions describing social roles were less com-mon, a fact that may well be significant. They included: *bonze*, a Japanese term that entered Portuguese and then Italian before spreading to other languages, such as English; *mandarin* (used in English in 1589, borrowed from the Portuguese), and *cacique*, a term for a 'big man' that originated in Santo Domingo and was adopted into Spanish and later into English.

Turning to the language of institutions, we find the same preponderance of words from the world of Islam, including: *caravanserai*, a Persian term that passed into Italian, French and English; *bazaar*, taken into Italian

[61] Kemal H. Karpat, 'A Language in Search of a Nation: Turkish in the Nation-State', in Scaglione (ed.), *Emergence*, pp.175–208, at pp. 188–92.

and then into English, and *harem*, current in English by 1634. *Casta* was the word the Portuguese adopted to describe the Indian social system, later borrowed by the Italians, the French and the English. From North America came *powwow*, taken into English by 1642.

The idea of the 'Columbian exchange' in ecology might be extended to the case of language.[62] The fortunes in the New World of Spanish and English have been studied in particular detail.[63] The studies concentrate on the words that the Europeans took from Indian languages, but they include movement in the other direction, from Spanish into Nahuatl, for instance. By the late sixteenth century, we learn, Spanish loanwords 'were asserting their presence strongly in Nahuatl': *alcalde*, for example ('mayor'), *anima* ('soul'), *caballo* ('horse'), *compadre* ('godfather'), *dios* ('god'), *firma* ('signature'), *misa* ('Mass'), *queso* ('cheese') and *virrey* ('viceroy'). The number of words borrowed from the religious and political domains is worth noting.[64] At much the same time, in the world of trade, some Basque words were becoming current in the Gulf of St Lawrence. They included *anaia*, 'brother', and the phrase *Nola zaude?*, 'how are you?'[65]

European intervention also disturbed what might be called the 'ecological balance' between local languages in the New World. The missionaries, especially the Jesuits, employed and encouraged the use of a *koine*, the so-called *língua geral* in Brazil, based on Tupí, and the *lenguas generales* in Mexico, based on Nahuatl, and in Peru, based on Quechua and Aymara. It is true that Quechua had been used in this way by the Incas before the Spaniards arrived, but the Jesuits employed it more extensively.[66] The point was – as in the Europe of the Reformation and Counter-Reformation – to reach as many people as possible with the least effort.

---

[62] Alfred W. Crosby, *The Columbian Exchange: Biological and Cultural Consequences of 1492* (Newport, CT, 1972).

[63] On Spanish, Rufino J. Cuervo, 'El Castellano en América', *Bulletin Hispanique* 3 (1901), pp. 35–62; Angel Rosenblat, 'La hispanización de América. El castellano y las lenguas indígenas desde 1492', in *Los conquistadores y su lengua* (Caracas, 1977), pp. 91–136; Emma Martinell Gifre, *Aspectos lingüísticos del descubrimiento y del conquista* (Madrid, 1988); Maria Beatriz Fontanella de Weinberg, 'La lengua española in América durante el periódo colonial', in Ana Pizarro (ed.), *América Latina: Palavra, Literatura, Cultura* (São Paulo, 1993), pp. 493–500; Juan Antonio Fraso Gracia, *Historia del español de América* (Madrid, 1999). On English, Joey L. Dillard, *Toward a Social History of American English* (Berlin, 1985); Gray and Fiering, *Language Encounter*.

[64] James Lockhart, *The Nahua after the Conquest* (Stanford, 1992), pp. 100, 291.

[65] James Axtell, 'Babel of Tongues: Communicating with the Indians in Eastern North America', in Gray and Fiering, *Language Encounter*, pp. 15–60, at pp. 30–2.

[66] Pedro de Ribera y Chaves wrote in 1586 of 'the Quechua *lengua general*': quoted in Bruce Mannheim, *The Language of the Inka since the European Invasion* (Austin, 1991), p. 45. On *lenguas generales* before the Spanish arrived, Yakov Malkiel, 'A Linguist's View of the Standardization of a Dialect', in Scaglione, *Emergence*, pp. 51–73, at p. 61.

THE CASE OF PORTUGUESE ABROAD

Since the fortunes of English and Spanish in the New World have been studied quite intensely, it may be more useful to concentrate attention on Portuguese. In his praises of his vernacular, published in 1540, João de Barros drew attention to borrowings from Asian languages in particular, referring to these appropriations as examples of Portuguese 'conquest'. Among his examples were *lascarim*, a soldier, and *sumbaya*, derived from a Malay word that means to bow with one's arms crossed.[67] In what follows, however, the emphasis will fall on the triangular relations of Portuguese with the Amerindian languages of Brazil and the African languages spoken by the slaves who were brought to the New World from about 1600 onwards to work on the sugar plantations.[68]

The Jesuit José de Anchieta, who wrote hymns in Tupí, introduced into the language words for concepts that the Indians apparently lacked, such as 'grace' (*graça*), 'virgin' (*virgem*) and 'sin' (*pecado*).[69] Conversely, some Tupí words entered Portuguese and later, other European languages: words for animals, such as the jaguar (*iagûara*) or the anteater (*tamanduá*), birds, such as the *tucan*, fish, such as the *piranha*, fruit, such as the *maracujá*, plants, such as *mandioca*, and vegetation, such as the *caatinga*, the prickly bushes of the desert or backlands. Even now, many Brazilians speak Tupí every day without realizing that they are doing so, since the names of many places are Tupí names. The famous falls of Iguaçu, for instance, include the term *açu*, meaning 'large'; the state of Pará derives its name from the Tupí word for 'sea', while the state of Paraíba takes the final part of its name, *iba*, from the word for 'tree'.

Brazilian Portuguese also borrowed about three hundred words from the different Central or West African languages spoken by the slaves – words for food, such as palm oil (*azeite de dendê*), or for housing (*mucambo*, 'shanty', or *senzala*, 'slave quarters', or *quilombo*, a village founded by slaves who had fled from the plantations). Words for music and dance often came from Africa, including *samba* and *afoxê*, 'rattle'. So did words for religious practices, such as *candomblé*, or for holy people, such as *orixá*,

---

[67] João de Barros, *Diálogo* (1540: ed. Luciana Stegnano Picchio, Modena, 1959), pp. 81, 103.

[68] João H. Rodrigues, 'The Victory of the Portuguese Language in Colonial Brazil', in Alfred Hower and Richard A. Preto-Rodas (eds.), *Empire in Transition* (Gainsville, 1985), pp. 32–64; Edith Pimentel Pinto, 'O português no Brasil: época colonial', in Pizarro, *América Latina*, pp. 515–26; Diogo Ramada Curto, 'A língua e o império', in Francisco Bethencourt and Kirti Chaudhuri (eds.), *História da expansão portuguesa*, vol. I (Lisbon, 1998), pp. 414–33.

[69] José de Anchieta, *Lírica portuguesa e Tupí*, ed. Armando Cardoso (São Paulo, 1984), pp. 157, 171, 178.

'god' or 'saint', and *babalorixá*, literally 'father of the saint', a person who is regularly possessed by an African divinity.

As a result of colonisation and the slave trade, a number of creoles developed in the early modern period, based on French (in Haiti, Louisiana etc.), on Dutch (in the Virgin Islands and perhaps in South Africa), on English (the Krio of the Guinea Coast and the Patwa of Jamaica), and especially on Portuguese, in Malacca, Macau, Goa, São Tomé and other places.[70] For example, a French visitor to Senegal in the late seventeenth century remarked that the inhabitants of that country spoke not only their own language but also 'a certain jargon that has only very little resemblance to Portuguese and is known as creole' (*un certain jargon qui n'a que très peu de resemblance à la langue portugaise et qu'on nomme langue créole*), comparing it to the *lingua franca* of the Mediterranean.[71]

The next stage was the development of what has been called 'plantation creole', and finally that of distinctive dialects of Portuguese, English or French, which still retain traces of their origins. For instance, the use in African American English of the phrase 'too much' for 'very much' is a borrowing from the Portuguese *demais*, which has both meanings, while the syntax as well as the vocabulary of some Black Englishes is marked by Africanisms, derived from West African languages, such as Yoruba.[72] Some sixteenth-century Portuguese plays, like the *Auto das regateiras*, by António Ribeiro Chiado, reproduced Black Portuguese, the so-called 'língua de preto'. For example, the sentence 'I have not finished dressing', *Eu não acabei de me vestir*, turned into *A mi não cabá besí*, simplifying the grammar, dropping parts of words and pronouncing the v as a b. In other plays blacks are represented as using a simplified form of Portuguese in which verbs are reduced to infinitives and the question, *Como chamar terra vosso?'* ('how call your country?') receives the answer, *Terra meu nunca saber* ('my country never know').[73]

MIXING IN EUROPE

European languages also displayed a tendency to mix. As we have seen (above, p. 97), the rise of some standard written vernaculars was often the

---

[70] John A. Holm, *Pidgins and Creoles*, 2 vols. (Cambridge, 1988), vol. II.

[71] Quoted in Robert Chaudenson, *Les créoles français* (Paris, 1979), p. 9.

[72] Gilberto Freyre, *The Masters and the Slaves* (1933: English translation, New York, 1946); Melville J. Herskovits and Frances S. Herskovits, *Suriname Folklore* (New York, 1936), pp. 117–35; Joey L. Dillard, *Black English: its History and Use in the United States* (New York, 1972); Dillard, *American English*, pp. 108–27.

[73] António Ribeiro Chiado, *Auto das regateiras*, ed. Giulia Lanciani (Rome, 1970), p. 61; Anthony J. Naro, 'A Study on the Origins of Pidginisation', *Language* 54 (1978), pp. 314–47; cf. Curto, 'A língua e o império'.

result of the mixing of dialects. Again, in Europe, as in other continents, the existence of several pidgins or trade languages can be documented from the early modern period. The original *lingua franca*, a mix of Venetian, Portuguese and Arabic that was known in the Mediterranean world in the Middle Ages, was even more important in the so- called 'age of piracy', between 1600 and 1830.[74]

Again, around the year 1500, Low German was widely used as a commercial language in northern Europe, in the area where the German-dominated Hanseatic League operated. It was used so frequently in Scandinavia that it produced 'interference', dissolving some of the case endings in Danish and Swedish. In Denmark, High German was employed in the early modern period in a number of domains, such as the court and the army as well as commerce, and mixtures of Danish and German were not uncommon.[75] In Eastern Europe too, at least in cities, German could often be heard, because a substantial proportion of the urban population was German in origin.

These well-known examples do not exhaust the repertoire. During the Renaissance, Italian might be used as a *lingua franca* among scholars and artists, as French would be used later. For example, the French scholar Nicholas-Claude Fabri de Peiresc and the Flemish painter Peter Paul Rubens wrote to one another in Italian in the 1620s, and Peiresc used the same language to write to the imperial librarian of Vienna after the librarian had explained that he lacked expertise in French.[76] It is unlikely that many people spoke the Basque-Icelandic pidgin documented from the seventeenth century, but it was important for sailors, fishermen and whalers.[77]

With travel and translation and the rise of language learning came what might be called the 'invasion' of some languages by others in certain domains such as commerce or the arts. Italy was especially important in both domains. In the case of commerce, one thinks of the term *banco* (originally 'bench', where the money-changers sat) and the related terms *banchiere* and *bancarotto*, adopted into English ('bank', 'banker',

---

[74] Keith Whinnom, 'Lingua Franca: Historical Problems', in Albert Valdman (ed.), *Pidgin and Creole Linguistics* (Bloomington, 1977), pp. 295–310; Manlio Cortelazzo, 'Lingua franca', in Hans Georg Beck, Manoussos Manoussacas and Agostino Pertusi (eds.), *Venezia centro di mediazione tra Oriente e Occidente* (Florence, 1977), pp. 523–35; Guido Cifoletti, *La lingua franca mediterranea* (Padua, 1989), p. 23.

[75] Olav Brattegard, *Die mittelniederdeutsche Geschäftsprache des hansischen Kaufmanns zu Bergen* (Bergen, 1945); Willy Sanders, *Sachsensprache, Hansesprache, Plattdeutsch: Sprachgeschichtliche Grundzüge des Niederdeutschen* (Göttingen, 1982); Vibeke Winge, *Dänische Deutsche – deutsche Dänen. Geschichte der deutschen Sprache in Dänemark 1300–1800* (Heidelberg, 1992), pp. 130–46; Jahr, *Language Change*, pp. 127–8.

[76] Nicholas-Claude Fabri de Peiresc, *Lettres*, ed. Philippe Tamizey de Larroque, 7 vols. (Paris, 1888–98); Peter N. Miller, *Peiresc's Europe* (New Haven, 2000), p. 163.

[77] Peter Bakker, 'A Basque Nautical Pidgin', *Journal of Pidgin and Creole* 2 (1987), pp. 1–30.

'bankrupt'), French, German, Spanish, and so on. Again, *cassa*, 'chest' and *cassiere*, the person looking after the chest, came to mean 'cash' and 'cashier'. *Bilancia*, 'balance', in its financial sense, was also a term that was widely adopted.

In architecture, technical terms such as *arcada, architrava, balcone, casamatta, colonna, cornice, cupola, facciata, pedimento, piazza, pilastro, portico* and *villa* entered a number of European languages at the Renaissance. In music, the invasion came later, mainly in the eighteenth century, and included *allegro, andante, cantata, concerto, opera, oratorio, pianoforte, solo, sonata* and *soprano*.[78]

Conquest too played its part within Europe, as in the case of the Spanish terms which entered Italian in Lombardy, in the south, and also in Genoa, for example the word *menino*, 'boy' (in the sense of 'page'), a reminder of the influence of early modern courts on linguistic practices. Around two hundred Spanish and Portuguese words are known to have established themselves in Italian in the course of the sixteenth century.[79] When the island of Gotland was incorporated into the Swedish Empire, its inhabitants, like those of Skåne (below, p. 162) were expected to make the transition from Danish to Swedish. Letters written by Gotlanders in the seventeenth century show that the way from one language to the other was via a mixture of the two.[80]

Not only words but whole phrases were transplanted from one language to another. In England, what was known from Milton's time onwards as 'law French' was a kind of mixed language, French in structure but increasingly English in vocabulary (to say nothing of pronunciation). The sub-titles of two famous legal works of the fifteenth and sixteenth centuries are perhaps sufficient to reveal the flavour of the language: Thomas Littleton's *Tenures: ouesque certain cases addes per auters de puisne temps*, and Edmund Plowden's *Commentaries: ou reports de divers cases esteant matters en ley*.

Again, phrases from foreign languages, notably Latin, Italian and French, were in regular use as symbols of prestige or cosmopolitanism. In the seventeenth and eighteenth centuries, Germans who belonged to the upper classes or wished to be taken to be upper-class might introduce into

[78] Marjatta Wis, *Ricerche sopra gli italianismi nella lingua tedesca* (Helsinki, 1955), pp. 75–87; Gianfranco Folena, 'L'italiano come lingua per musica', in *L'italiano in Europa: esperienze linguistiche del Settecento* (Turin, 1983), pp. 228–9, 262–4.

[79] Gian Luigi Beccaria, *Spagnolo e spagnoli in Italia* (Milan, 1968); Mari D'Agostino, *La Piazza e l'altare: momenti della politica linguistica della chiesa siciliana* (Palermo, 1988), p. 806.

[80] Jens Lerbom, *Mellan två riken: Integration, Politisk kultur och förnationella identiteter på Gotland 1500–1700* (Lund, 2003), pp. 128–32. My thanks to Hanne Sanders for drawing my attention to this book and sending me a copy.

everyday conversation French phrases such as *épée à la main* or *mon treschere ami*.[81]

For a case-study of this kind of invasion, it may be interesting to look not at the domain of the arts, which has been studied so often, but that of warfare. The military speech community deserves to be taken seriously, since the armies of the period were polyglot, extremely mobile and also increasing rapidly in size in the course of the period. Unlike the social history of armies, which flourishes, military language seems to be relatively neglected by historians of early modern Europe and even by linguists.[82]

The first point to make here is that armies were often international organizations. The Spanish army in the Netherlands, for example, included Englishmen, Irish, Germans and Italians. Its language was probably transmitted along the 'military corridors' of the Army of Flanders, including the famous 'Spanish Road' from Milan to Brussels.[83] At a time when soldiers were billeted on civilians rather than confined to barracks, military terms could spread relatively rapidly through the civilian world: official terms, such as the names of ranks, from corporal to Field Marshal; technical terms for weapons, such as arquebus or bayonet, and unofficial, perhaps slang terms, like 'forage', 'plunder', or 'deserter'.

The Thirty Years' War in particular, in which not only German states but also France, Spain, the Dutch Republic, Denmark and Sweden took part, encouraged the rise of an international military language that was current from Portugal to Poland or even beyond, although at the frontiers of the Ottoman Empire it yielded to a rival military language of Arabic-Turkish origin. The Western variety of military language was composed in the main of romance words, though disentangling the Italian, French and Spanish elements is not always easy.

In this domain, the French, for instance, seem to have contributed a number of terms for military hardware, including *arquebus, artillerie, bayonette, cartouche* and *pique*, as well as words for vanguard and rearguard (*avant-garde, arrière-garde*). The share of the Italians included *bastione,*

---

[81] William J. Jones, *A Lexicon of French Borrowings in the German Vocabulary 1575–1648* (Berlin, 1976); Richard J. Brunt, *The Influence of the French Language on the German Vocabulary, 1649–1735* (Berlin, 1983).

[82] For exceptions, see William A. Coates, 'The German Pidgin-Italian of the Sixteenth-Century *Lanzichenecchi*', *Papers from the Fourth Annual Kansas Linguistics Conference* (1969), pp. 66–74; Robert A. Verdonk, *La lengua española en Flandes en el siglo XVII* (Madrid, 1980).

[83] Geoffrey Parker, *The Spanish Road* (Cambridge, 1972), esp. pp. 50–105.

battaglione, infanteria, moschetto (musket), *scaramuccia* (skirmish), *sentinello* and *squadrone*. For their part, the Spaniards contributed *alférez* (ensign), *amotinarse* (to mutiny), *bandolero, casco* (casque), *guerrilla, merodear* ('maraud'), *morrión* ('morion', a kind of helmet) and *tercio* (a body of troops) together with a number of terms recognizable by their distinctive ending in – ada, such as *armada, camarada, emboscada* ('ambuscade'), *escalada, parada* and *retirada* ('retreat').

Well over a hundred military terms came into German from romance languages, mainly French, between 1575 and 1648.[84] A number of these were transmitted to Scandinavia and Eastern Europe via military treatises such as Wilhelm Dilich's *Kriegsbuch* (1607) or Johann Wallhausen's *Kriegskunst* (1615). It is likely that the Swedish *infanteri*, for instance, the Danish *pik*, the Hungarian *dragonyer*, the Polish *kasarnia* (*Kasern*, 'barracks') and the Russian *mushket* were transmitted in this way.

It was also from German or Dutch (directly or via Polish or Ruthenian), that a number of naval, administrative and technical terms entered Russian from the middle of the seventeenth century onwards. The new naval vocabulary was mainly Dutch, including *matroos* (sailor), *mast, stuurboord* and *zeil* (sail), while the English contributed 'brig'. The vocabulary of ranks and institutions was mainly German, including *admiral, advokat, akademiya, baron, dekret, president* and *senator*. Borrowing went so far that even Peter the Great, who generally approved of learning from the West, once complained about a Russian diplomat who used 'very many Polish and other foreign words and terms'. The process continued after Peter's time, although borrowing from French overtook borrowing from German around the middle of the eighteenth century.[85]

This process of borrowing and mixing may be shown in action with the help of a case-study within this case-study, the letters of General Albrecht von Wallenstein during the Thirty Years' War. Wallenstein's letters are peppered with Italian, Spanish or French words, such as *abociren* (from *s'aboucher*, 'to enter into discussion'), *ambasciada, armada, campagnia, capo, cavaliero, commando*, and so on. Sometimes the general uses whole phrases, such as *per inganiarme meglio* (hispanizing the Italian *ingannare*), but mixed phrases are more common, such as *meine disegni, ein posto, solchen travaglio, dem basta, kein tregua* or *Guberno-sachen*.[86]

---

[84] I counted 124 such terms (omitting rare uses) in Jones, *Lexicon*.

[85] Vinogradov, *Russian Literary Language*, pp. 33, 36; Gerta Hüttl-Worth, *Foreign Words in Russian: A Historical Sketch, 1550–1800* (Berkeley, 1963), esp. pp. 9–11.

[86] 'the better to deceive me'; 'my plans'; 'a post'; 'such labour'; 'the sufficient'; 'no truce'; 'matters of state': Albrecht von *Wallenstein, Briefe*, ed. Ferdinand Tadra (Vienna, 1879), *passim*.

PRAGMATIC MIXING

Wallenstein also made use of Latin phrases in his letters, as was common in his day, especially though not exclusively among German speakers from Luther to Leibniz. In similar fashion, in parts of Europe where Latin was not in use, Ruthenia for instance, clerks sometimes produced documents in a mixture of Church Slavonic with the local vernaculars.[87]

Luther, for instance, in his table talk, asserting that war simply takes away what God gives, such as religion, political order, marriage, wealth, dignity, studies and so on, says *Bellum nimbt simpliciter als hin weg, was Got geben kan, religionem, politiam, coniugium, opes, dignitatem, studia, etc* (no. 282). Attempts have been made to work out the – presumably unconscious – rules which Luther followed in his rapid switches between languages, using German, for instance, to speak of more personal matters, Latin for public issues and also for abstractions such as *accidentia, allegoria, causa, consequentia* and so on.[88] As for Leibniz, he took a considerable interest in the German language, and argued on occasion (as Schupp had done earlier, p. 76 above) that it was an appropriate language for philosophy. All the same, he went on using Latin and French, in order to reach a wider audience and also, in all probability, so as to avoid neologisms.[89]

As Lucien Febvre pointed out long ago in the case of French, words such as 'absolute' and 'relative', 'abstract' and 'concrete' were lacking in most vernaculars in the sixteenth century and the deficiency was supplied from Latin.[90] There was a similar problem in German. Today we are accustomed to think of German as the language of abstractions *par excellence*, at least in Europe. The concepts which are central to this book, notably 'speech community' (*Sprachgemeinschaft*), 'language culture' (*Sprachkultur*), or 'language consciousness' (*Sprachbewusstsein*), often originated in German. It is something of a shock to discover how poor in abstractions the German language was until the eighteenth century, the age of the philosophers Christian Wolff and Immanuel Kant. Latin filled a serious gap.

In Wallenstein's case, which was not untypical, abstract ideas were expressed with Latin nouns such as *praeparatoria* and set Latin phrases

---

[87] Antoine Martel, *La langue polonaise dans les pays ruthènes, Ukraine et Russie Blanche, 1569–1667* (Lille, 1938), p. 147.

[88] Birgit Stolt, *Die Sprachmischung in Luthers Tischreden* (Stockholm, 1964), especially the list of Latin nouns, pp. 59–73; Els Oksaar, 'Social Networks, Communicative Acts and the Multilingual Individual', in Jahr, *Language Change*, pp. 3–19, at p. 14.

[89] Yvon Belaval, 'Leibniz et la langue allemande' (1947: repr. *Etudes Leibniziennes*, Paris, 1976), pp. 25–36.

[90] Lucien Febvre, *The Problem of Unbelief in the Sixteenth Century: the Religion of Rabelais* (1942: English translation, Cambridge, MA, 1982), p. 385.

such as *pro forma* or *in summa*. Documents of the period were often written in a similar mixture of Latin and the vernacular. That military and
civilian officials often spoke in this way too is suggested by the minutes
of meetings of the imperial privy council, like the meeting in which one
of Wallenstein's colleagues switched from German to Latin in the course of
arguing that 'as regards how many troops to put in the field the conference
of war should decide, because they are experts in military affairs' (*So viell die
Anzahl des Kriegsvolcks anlangt, gehöre ad militarem conferentiam, ad quam
belli periti*).[91]

German was not the only language into which people mixed Latin in this
way. The Swedish chancellor Axel Oxenstierna regularly used Latin phrases
in addressing the Council of State (*Riksråd*) about the war in Germany,
referring to the *principalis scopus* of the war, *arma spiritualia, status publicus*
and so on.[92] This was not a parade of learning. Like German, Swedish still
lacked these useful abstractions.[93]

A similar point may be made about Polish and Hungarian in the seventeenth century. For example, the journal kept by the Polish gentleman Jan
Chryzostom Pasek is full of Latin words and phrases, *per nexum sanguinis*
('through a blood relationship'), for instance, *omnibus modis* ('in all ways'),
sub praetextu ('under the pretext'), *verba pro verbis* ('word for word') and so
on.[94] No wonder that satirists such as Krzysztof Opaliński mocked Poles
who spoke 'macaronically' (*macaronice*). The autobiography of the Hungarian aristocrat Miklós Bethlen, a generation later than Pasek's, employs
Latin phrases on almost every page: *ab anno* ('from the year'), *ex dictamine
conscientiae* ('following the dictates of conscience'), or *experientia teste* ('as
experience testifies').[95]

Latin phrases could also be heard in the debates in the English House
of Commons. A speech delivered by Sir Edwin Sandys on 8 March 1621
included the words and phrases *iniuria* ('injury'); *crimen lesae Maiestatis*
('the crime of lese-majesty'); *nihil utile quod inhonestum* ('nothing that is
dishonourable is useful'; *meum et tuum* ('mine and thine'); *coram domino
rege* ('in the presence of the king'). However, these phrases are less frequent
than in the continental texts quoted above. They tend to be either phrases
from Roman law or quotations from classical authors.[96]

[91] Albrecht von Wallenstein, *Briefe*, ed. Hermann Hallwich (Vienna, 1912), pp. 126–7.
[92] Michael Roberts, *Gustavus Adolphus*, vol. II, *1626–32* (London, 1958), p. 419. Further examples in
N. A. Kullberg (ed.), *Svenska Riksrådets Protokoll* (Stockholm, 1878) and Stolt, *Sprachmischung*,
pp. 263–5.
[93] On Danish, Skautrup, *Danske sprog*, pp. 301–2.   [94] Jan Pasek, *Pamiętnik* (Cracow, 1929).
[95] Miklós Bethlen, *Önéletírása*, 2 vols. (Budapest, 1955).
[96] Wallace Notestein (ed.), *Commons Debates 1621*, vol. 2 (New Haven 1935), pp. 191–5.

Conversely, university lectures, which were supposed to be delivered in Latin, might include phrases in a vernacular, so that an English student who attended Guy Patin's lectures on medicine in Paris in 1664, recorded that 'I was much disappointed in my expectation of understanding all he said by reason he used the French tongue so much'. Sermons too might be mixed, as they often were in the later Middle Ages in England, France, Italy and elsewhere: based on Latin but with frequent expressions in the vernacular.[97]

Mixing could be found in print as well as in speech and writing. Indeed, in some books the use of Latin phrases in a vernacular text was emphasized by printing them in Roman type where the rest of the text was in black letter.

Still more common was the practice of taking Latin words and naturalizing them into the vernacular, making it richer and more dignified at the same time. Many words in the languages of Western Europe which have Latin roots were coined in the sixteenth and seventeenth centuries, though we tend to notice only the coinages that have not survived, like 'idoneus' (suitable), as in the Scottish phrase 'apt and idoneus for the ministry'. In the case of Russian, on the other hand, the vernacular was enriched and elevated by borrowings from Church Slavonic. Indeed, the German scholar Heinrich Ludolf claimed that Russians used slavonicisms in speaking as a way of showing off.[98] In these cases we should speak not so much of pragmatic mixing as of borrowed majesty.

PLAYFUL MIXING: THE RISE OF MACARONICS

A knowledge of this everyday mixing of Latin with the vernacular makes it easier to see the point of the more elaborate and playful mixing in literature which might be called 'macaronics' on the analogy of 'ebonics'.

It may be useful to distinguish two senses of the term 'macaronic'. In the broad sense, it refers to any kind of code switching or code mixing in a literary work. This was a not uncommon medieval practice, especially in poetry. In the more precise sense of the term, though, 'macaronic' Latin, with its partly vernacular vocabulary combined with Latin syntax, was an invention of the fifteenth century. It seems to have developed out of student slang at the University of Padua. A famous example is that of the mock-epics of the poet Teofilo Folengo in early sixteenth-century Italy, but other

[97] Edward Browne, *Journal* (London, 1923), p. 3; Lazzerini, 'Sermoni'; Siegfried Wenzel, *Macaronic sermons: bilingualism and preaching in late Medieval England* (Ann Arbor, 1994).
[98] Vladimir V. Vinogradov, *The History of the Russian Literary Language from the Seventeenth Century to the Nineteenth* (1949: condensed adaptation, Madison, 1969), p. 4.

examples of macaronic Latin are not hard to find, in Germany, for instance, in Spain (where practitioners of the genre included the humanist Juan de Vergara), and in Scotland, where Ben Jonson's friend John Drummond of Hawthornden wrote a mock-heroic poem about the conflict between two feudal ladies, in which he used hybrid phrases such as *crossare fenestras* for 'go past the windows'.[99]

Macaronic verses were particularly common in France. The lawyer Jean Germain wrote a poem mocking Charles V's invasion of Provence, a poem which he described as being in *mesclatas linguas*, a phrase neatly exemplifying the phenomenon to which it refers. It contains lines such as *"drinc drinc" clamant omnes tunc lansaquaneti* (the German mercenaries or *Lanzknechten*).[100] Another lawyer, Jean Richard of Dijon, described the French religious wars in a poem which refers to *Suyssos, Lansqnettos . . . cum vestris picquis tremulis* ('wavering pikes') and *pistoliferos Reistros* (pistol-bearing cavalry, the notorious German *Reiter*).[101]

A slightly macaronic prose was deployed for satirical purposes in the famous *Epistolae Obscurorum Virorum* or 'Letters of Obscure Men', written by humanists in Germany in the 1520s to ridicule the culture or lack of culture of their conservative opponents in the universities.[102] Later in the century, the Calvinist humanist Theodore Beza would use the same technique in his satire on the Church of Rome, the *Passavant*. Texts such as these well illustrate the interanimation of three languages or varieties, classical Latin, medieval Latin and the vernacular.[103]

In similar fashion, the mixing of different vernaculars, whether languages or dialects, was deployed for comic effect by writers and especially by playwrights.

Panurge, for example, when he first meets Pantagruel in chapter nine of Rabelais's romance, speaks to him in two invented languages and ten real ones, German, Italian, English, Basque, Dutch, Spanish, Danish, Hebrew, Greek and Latin. Rabelais was extremely interested in language and in the linguistic debates of his day, as various chapters of *Gargantua* and *Pantagruel* show quite clearly.[104]

In France in the fifteenth century, the farce *Maître Pierre Pathelin* had already employed the mixture of languages as a comic device. Pathelin

[99] Antonio Torres-Alcalà, *Verbigratia: los escritores macarronicos de España* (Madrid, 1984), pp. 77, 90; John Drummond, *Polemo-Middinia inter Vitaruam et Bebernam* (c. 1645), quoted in Robert H. MacDonald (ed.), *William Drummond: Poems and Prose* (Edinburgh, 1976), pp. 196–7.

[100] Jean Germain, 'Historia bravissima Caroli Quinti' (1537: in Fausta Garavini and Lucia Lazzerini (eds.), *Macaronee provenzali*, Milan-Naples, 1984), pp. 251–78, at p. 267.

[101] Octave Delepierre, *Macaronéana*, vol. II (London, 1862–3), pp. 109–11.

[102] Bakhtin, *Rabelais*, pp. 81–2.   [103] Bakhtin, 'Prehistory', p. 81.

[104] Claude-Gilbert Dubois, *Mythe et langage au 16e siècle* (Bordeaux, 1970); Demonet, *Voix*, pp. 178–9.

buys some cloth and does not pay for it. When the draper visits Pathelin to demand his money, the rogue pretends not to understand him and speaks in Limousin, Picard, Flemish, Norman, Breton and Latin in order to create confusion. Rabelais was inspired by this scene and acknowledges his fifteenth-century predecessor by slipping in a reference to *langaige patelinois*. *Pathelin* did not stand alone in late medieval French drama in its use of different languages for comic effect. The anonymous *Valet qui vole son maître* includes passages in Picard and Lombard. In what has been called the Occitan Renaissance of the later sixteenth century, plays were composed in a mixture of French and Provençal. In some of these plays, the negative characters speak French while the positive ones speak *patois*.[105]

In Venice, the playwright Andrea Calmo reproduced the carnival of dialects to be heard on the streets of the city.[106] Thus in Calmo's *Spagnolas* (c. 1549), we hear a peasant speaking his local dialect, a German coal-heaver, a schoolmaster from Ragusa (Dubrovnik), a soldier speaking Bergamask with occasional Spanish words and another soldier, from Albania, speaking a mixture of Venetian and a little Greek (described by another comic writer of the time as 'this Greek-Italian language of ours', *chesta nostra lingua gresesca talianao*). If we include the urban Venetian of the other characters, that makes six speech varieties altogether. In another text one of Calmo's characters speaks what is called 'turco', in other words Venetian with a Turkish accent and the odd Turkish word.[107]

The *commedia dell'arte*, which has been described as a comedy of dialects, carried on this tradition, with Pantalone speaking Venetian, Dottore Bolognese, Capitano Neapolitan and so on. Another Venetian, Carlo Goldoni, revived this tradition in the eighteenth century, with plays such as *I Rusteghi* and *Sior Todero* in Venetian and *Le Baruffe Chiozziote* in the dialect of Chioggia, a small town a few miles from Venice.[108] In Spain, polyglot comedies were written by Juan de Timoneda and by Lope de Vega, who wrote bilingual scenes in Spanish and macaronic Latin, Italian, French and Flemish, as well as introducing phrases in Arabic, Turkish, German, Catalan and Basque.[109] The Portuguese playwright Gil Vicente wrote his plays in Spanish as well as in his native language, and introduced characters speaking French and Italian.[110]

[105] Halina Lewicka, 'Le mélange des langues dans l'ancien théâtre du Midi de la France', *Mélanges Jean Boutière*, 2 vols. (Liège, 1971), vol. 1, pp. 347–59.
[106] Ivano Paccagnella, *Il fasto delle lingue: plurilinguismo letterario nel '500* (Rome, 1984).
[107] Giorgio Padoan, *La commedia rinascimentale veneta* (Vicenza, 1982), pp. 154–83, at pp. 158–9, 165.
[108] Bakhtin, 'Prehistory', p. 82; Folena, 'L'italiano', pp. 364–6.
[109] Elvezio Canonico-de Rochemonteix, *El poliglotismo en el teatro de Lope de Vega* (Kassel, 1991).
[110] Paul Teyssier, *La langue de Gil Vicente* (Paris, 1959), pp. 230–54.

In Denmark, sixteenth-century comedies such as *Kort Vending* (1570) by Hans Christensen Sten, included soldiers speaking Low German mixed with some High German and Danish.[111] An opera for the king's birthday in 1699 included Cupid singing in Italian, Diana in French, Mars in High German, Mercury in Low German, and Neptune in Danish.[112] In Russia, the multilingual comedy arrived in the mid-eighteenth century. Denis Ivanovich Fonvizin's *The Brigadier* (1766) represents an official, the Councillor, who speaks a mix of chancery Russian and Church Slavonic, while the Brigadier's son, the fop Ivanushka, laces his Russian with French phrases such as *je vous prie* or *vous avez raison*, enabling Fonvizin to satirize Westernization while himself borrowing from the West (he was inspired by the Italian *commedia dell'arte*).[113]

Rome was of course a major centre of linguistic encounters which left their mark on literature. The polyglossia of the city was exploited to particularly good effect in the *Tinelaria*, a play by the émigré Spaniard Bartolomé de Torres Naharro, performed before pope Leo X, published in 1517 and set in the servant's hall (*tinello*). Six main languages, all romance, are spoken on stage. The chef is a Frenchman, 'Metreianes' (*Maître Jean*), and his staff consists of an Italian, a Portuguese, a Valencian, a Basque (who speaks Castilian), and a German (who speaks Latin). Since the characters sometimes try to speak one another's languages in broken fashion, the result is not difficult to imagine. 'No meat for me, by God', in the mouth of the German, becomes *Nite carne yo, bi Got*.[114] Incidentally, the play offers good evidence of the capacity of the audience to understand varieties of romance language as if they were so many dialects of Latin. They would have had no problem making sense of Salvatore.

A similar point might be made about the readers of or listeners to the sonnets of the period that were written in two or three romance languages (like some medieval poems). On the marriage of the Duke of Savoy with a Spanish *infanta*, Lope de Vega, for instance, produced a sonnet in Latin, Spanish and Italian.

> Sit, o sante Himenee, haec dies clara
> Eas bellas Ninphas, en alegre coro
> Ornen le tempie con ghirlande di oro
> Al dulce esposo y a su esposa cara.[115]

[111] Winge, *Dänische Deutsche*, pp. 125–6, 222–3.   [112] Skautrup, *Danske sprog*, p. 305.
[113] Denis I. Fonvizin, *Dramatic Works* (Bern, 1974), pp. 49–86.
[114] Bartolomé de Torres Naharro, *Obra Completa* (Madrid, 1994), pp. 337–410.
[115] Otto Jörder, *Die Forme des Sonetts bei Lope de Vega* (Halle, 1936), pp. 239–67.

In similar fashion, the southern French poet Du Bartas welcomed Catherine de'Medici to Nérac with a dialogue between three nymphs, one of whom spoke Latin, another French and a third Gascon.[116]

Private letters may be located on the frontier of literature and everyday life. Some people wrote letters in foreign languages but switched to their native tongue from time to time, perhaps because they could not easily find the phrase they wanted. The emperor Leopold I, for instance, used Italian to write to Graf Humprecht Jan Černín, but from time to time slipped into German. For instance, when Leopold wanted to say 'I expect him to return here within a few days and will tell him what I think', he wrote *l'attendo qui fra pochi giorno di ritorno und will ihm die meinung sagen.*[117]

The letters of two polyglot composers offer particularly fine examples of code-switching and code-mixing, thanks perhaps to the well-tuned ears of the writers. The letters of Mozart, written in a mix of Italian, French, Latin and different dialects of German, have been described as a sort of 'linguistic concerto', a marvellous example of 'linguistic polyphony'.[118]

An even more remarkable example of language mixing, two hundred years before Mozart, comes from the letters of the musician Roland de Lassus, otherwise known as Orlando di Lasso. Lasso was a francophone from Mons, who had lived in Italy before entering the service of Wilhelm Duke of Bavaria. He wrote French *chansons*, Italian madrigals, German *Lieder* and Latin hymns with apparently equal ease. He was on intimate though deferential terms with his young patron (the duke was in his twenties at the time), playing the role of a court fool (*poltrone* is his own term).

Forty-eight letters from Lasso to the duke survive from the period 1572–9, written in a wonderful mix of languages, mainly French, Latin (liturgical in flavour), Italian (with traces of Venetian) and German, spiced with puns, deliberate mistakes and a few words of Spanish. They represent a form of clowning, an extension into the domain of the private letter of the polyglot comedy, the *commedia dell'arte* with which Lasso was associated at the court. Like a sophisticated Salvatore, Lasso mixes languages within sentences and occasionally within a single word, as in the case of a term of his invention, *trégrandissamente.*

Here is a passage describing Lasso's return to Munich, dog-tired (*lasso*), but finding his family in good health and joining with him in kissing his master's hands. 'Cum adiutorium altissimi, siamo arrivati a Monaco pero tanto lassi e strachi quanto mi sia mai ritrovato in diebus vite mee . . . ma

---

[116] Philippe Gardy, *La leçon de Nérac* (Bordeaux, 1999).
[117] Leopold I, *Korrespondence*, ed. Zdeněk Kalista (Prague, 1936), p. 96.
[118] Folena, 'L'italiano', p. 434.

femme, mon petit guillaume, se portent Zimlich wol got sei lob, et tres humblement baisons tous la main de votre Excellence'.[119]

LINGUISTIC EXCHANGES

A remarkable collective achievement of this period was the increase in European knowledge of non-European languages revealed by the many grammars and dictionaries published in the period.[120] This was also a time of increasing linguistic contacts within Europe, revealed by similar sources. However, in the case of the languages of Europe, the increased concern to teach modern languages should probably be viewed not as a simple result of increasing interest in the neighbours but rather as an attempt to find a substitute for Latin as its use declined.

Within Europe, the vernaculars were enriched by borrowing from one another as well as from Latin. The Italians, for instance, borrowed 661 words from French between 1650 and 1715, in the domains of clothes, furniture, politics and diplomacy in particular. They also borrowed heavily from Spanish at this time.[121] For their part, the French borrowed over seventeen hundred words from other vernaculars between 1400 and 1800, with the trend reaching its peak in the sixteenth century (595 loanwords). Loans diminished only slightly in the seventeenth century (549 words).[122] The new French expressions were taken above all from Italian (688 words), 462 of them in the sixteenth and 203 in the seventeenth century.[123] There were 242 words taken from Spanish, especially in the seventeenth century (116), many of them refer to the fauna, flora and customs of the Americas.[124] There were 221 words taken from English, especially in the eighteenth century. As one scholar has noted, this amount of borrowing 'does not quite match up to accepted notions about seventeenth-century French linguistic nationalism'.[125]

English has been studied in particular detail from this point of view. The sixteenth century marked an important phase in the construction of

[119] Orlando di Lasso, *Briefe*, ed. Horst Leuchtmann (Wiesbaden, 1977), no. 16.
[120] W. Keith Percival, 'La connaissance des langues du monde', in Sylvain Auroux (ed.), *Histoire des idées linguistiques*, 2 vols. (Liège, 1989–92), vol. II, pp. 226–38.
[121] Thomas E. Hope, *Lexical Borrowing in the Romance Languages*, 2 vols. (Oxford, 1971), p. 346; Beccaria; *Spagnolo*; Andrea Dardi, *Dalla provincia all'Europa: l'influsso del francese sull'italiano tra il 1650 e il 1715* (Florence, 1992), pp. 39–46, 51.
[122] Brunot, *Langue française*; Pierre Guiraud, *Les mots étrangers* (Paris, 1965), p. 6.
[123] Bartina H. Wind, *Les mots italiens introduits en français au 16e siècle* (Deventer, 1926), corrected by Hope, *Borrowing*.
[124] Hope, *Borrowing*, p. 322n.   [125] Hope, *Borrowing*, p. 323.

a cosmopolitan vocabulary.[126] The 'amazing hospitality' of early modern
English to foreign words has often been noted.[127] A study of a 2 per cent
sample of the *Oxford English Dictionary* shows nearly two thousand new
words coming into use between 1500 and 1700. About four hundred of
these were derived from Latin, but 120 came from French, 16 from Italian
and 16 from Spanish.[128]

If we describe English as 'hospitable' to foreign words, it is difficult to
say what adjective should be used about German. The Germans borrowed
about nine hundred Italian words between 1350 and 1600, more than half
of these in the sixteenth century and especially in the domains of commerce
and seafaring.[129] However, this total is far surpassed by the more than two
thousand French words that Germans adopted in just over a hundred and
fifty years, or to be more precise between 1575 and 1735.[130]

The chronology of the borrowing process brings us back to the ideas of
Mikhail Bakhtin, mentioned earlier in this chapter. Bakhtin argued that
it was in the sixteenth century that 'this inter-animation of languages . . .
reached its highest point'. In the course of the interaction between Latin
and the vernacular, in particular, 'each became more aware of itself, of
its potentialities and limitations'.[131] Bakhtin does not say what happened
after 1600, but he seems to have believed that heteroglossia declined in
the seventeenth and eighteenth centuries, to revive in the age of the classic
European novel.

The great value of this idea of inter-animation is that it links lexical
borrowing and macaronic literature to the praises of particular vernaculars
(above, p. 65) and even, perhaps, to the codification of language on the
model of Latin and Italian, although this codification discouraged further
borrowing and mixing. As for the chronology, the suggestion that the sixteenth century was the high point of inter-animation is supported by many
examples already quoted in this chapter, from macaronic Latin and Italian
dialect comedy to Rabelais and his translator Fischart, not forgetting the
letters of Lassus, which Bakhtin would surely have enjoyed had he known
about them.

[126] Richard Wermser, *Statistische Studien zur Entwicklung des englischen Wortschatzes* (Bern, 1976), pp. 59–61.
[127] Robert W. Burchfield, *The English Language* (Oxford, 1985), p. 25.
[128] Charles L. Barber, *Early Modern English* (Cambridge, 1976), pp. 166–95; on French, Brunot, *Langue française*, pp. 208–14, 232–6.
[129] Wis, *Italianismi*.
[130] Calculated from the dictionaries in Jones, *Lexicon*, and Brunt, *Influence*, totalling over 2,500 but with a considerable overlap between the two studies.
[131] Bakhtin, *Rabelais*, pp. 81–2; cf. Gary S. Morson and Caryl Emerson, *Mikhail Bakhtin: Creation of a Prosaics* (Stanford, 1990), pp. 139–45.

However, the process of inter-animation did not come to an end in 1600. When multilingual plays ceased to be popular, in the early seventeenth century, they were succeeded by comedies displaying the varieties of speaking associated with different social groups, as in the case of Molière or his equivalents in eighteenth-century Venice and Scandinavia, Carlo Goldoni and Ludvig Holberg (above, pp. 39, 135).

In some languages, as we have seen, lexical borrowing was at its height in the seventeenth and eighteenth centuries. Indeed, another Russian scholar, Vladimir Vinogradov, referred to what he called the 'crisis' of Russian in the seventeenth century, a crisis that was due to the 'collision' between the Slavonic and Western European languages. What is the difference between 'interanimation' and 'collision'? Why did seventeenth-century Russia not produce a Rabelais? Bakhtin's theory raises at least as many questions as it solves.

The English virtuoso John Evelyn approved of many of the words that were entering English in his day from Italian or French. Giving the old metaphor of words as immigrants a new twist, he suggested that his compatriots 'make as many of these do homage as are like to prove good citizens'.[132] However, Evelyn's open attitude was not shared by everyone. Indeed, the seventeenth century was the time that European movements for linguistic purification really gathered force. These centripetal movements, a reaction against the centrifugal tendencies we have been discussing, are the topic of the following chapter.

---

[132] Quoted in Manfred Görlach, *Introduction to Early Modern English* (1978: English translation, Cambridge, 1991), p. 256.

CHAPTER 6

Purifying languages

One reason for believing that the mixing of languages was increasing in the early modern period comes from the vehemence of the reaction against such mixing. Scholarly discussions of the movements for linguistic purity of the nineteenth and twentieth centuries are relatively common. Some of these movements were nationalist, like the Greek and the German crusades against foreign words (below, p. 169). Others were essentially literary, efforts by poets such as Stéphane Mallarmé 'to purify the dialect of the tribe' as he put it (*donner un sens plus pur au mots de la tribu*). Mallarmé dreamed of an ideal world described in an ideal language.[1]

Although they have attracted much less scholarly attention, movements of linguistic purification in early modern Europe were neither uncommon nor unimportant. They were the negative side of the standardization and codification of language described in chapter 4. Attempts to make the vernaculars more uniform and more dignified entailed rejecting many words and certain forms of syntax and pronunciation.

At least three different kinds of purity were advocated. Language had to be morally pure, as opposed to 'talking dirty': the *Dictionary* of the French Academy excluded what the preface called 'swearwords or those which offend modesty' (*termes d'emportement ou qui blessent la pudeur*). Language also had to be socially pure, in other words to follow the usage of the upper classes. For this reason the Academy's dictionary normally excluded the technical terms used by craftsmen, sending readers in search of explanations of these terms to a special dictionary compiled by Thomas Corneille. Finally, language had to be what might be described today as 'ethnically' pure, employing native expressions in the place of foreign ones. It is this third form of purity that will be the main focus of attention in the following pages.

---

[1] On linguistic purism in general, see Björn Jernudd and Michael Shapiro (eds.), *The Politics of Language Purism* (Berlin, 1989); George Thomas, *Linguistic Purism* (London, 1991).

CAMPAIGNS FOR PURITY

Before focusing on language, it may be illuminating to take a broader view and discuss contemporary conceptions of purity and campaigns for purification in a more general way. A concern with purity is to be found in many domains in early modern Europe – one is tempted to say, everywhere except in the literal sense of hygiene. When plague struck Cambridge in the early seventeenth century, the Master of Emmanuel, Lawrence Chaderton, declared that 'it is not the clean keeping and sweeping of our houses and streets that can drive away this fearful messenger of God's wrath, but the purging and sweeping of our consciences'.[2]

Baths were rare in early modern Europe, and they were becoming rarer as the public bath-houses of the later Middle Ages were closed down as morally dangerous. The luxurious bathrooms in the Vatican decorated by Raphael went out of use during the Counter-Reformation. Philip II of Spain forbade his subjects to take regular baths, which he interpreted as a symbol of Muslim sympathies (he may well have been correct in his interpretation). The Dutch stood out from the rest of Europe by their concern for clean streets and houses, noted with surprise by one foreign visitor after another.[3] No wonder then that India seemed a strange place to European visitors, who commented on the frequency of baths there.

The principal domain in which a concern with purity was visible in this period was that of religion. Erasmus wrote a treatise on the purity of the Church, *De puritate ecclesiae*. Luther spoke and wrote about the 'pure gospel'. The Dutch Anabaptist Menno Simons dreamed of a pure community 'without spot or stain'.[4] Calvinist iconoclasm was justified in France by the desire 'to see the Christian religion in its original purity and whiteness' (*de voir la religion chrétienne en sa pureté et blancheur première*).[5]

On the other side, Catholics viewed heresy as a kind of poison or disease. A good deal of the violence of the religious wars of the sixteenth century in France and elsewhere was justified, if not motivated, by the need to purify society from this infection.[6] Officially, heretics were burned, in other words

---

[2] On hygiene in this period, Georges Vigarello, *Concepts of Cleanliness* (1985: English translation, Cambridge, 1988).

[3] Simon Schama, *The Embarrassment of Riches* (London, 1987).

[4] Quoted in Guido Marnef, *Antwerp in the Age of Reformation: Underground Protestantism in a Commercial Metropolis 1550–77* (Baltimore, 1996), p. 73.

[5] Jean-Loys Micqueau (1564), quoted in Olivier Christin, *Une révolution symbolique* (Paris, 1991), p. 64. Cf. Solange Deyon and Alain Lottin, *Les casseurs de l'été 1566* (Paris, 1981), pp. 147–64.

[6] Janine Estèbe, *Tocsin pour un massacre* (Paris, 1968); Natalie Z. Davis, 'The Rites of Violence', (1971: repr. in her *Society and Culture in Early Modern France*, Stanford, 1975, pp. 152–88); Denis Crouzet, *Les guerriers de Dieu*, 2 vols. (Paris, 1990).

purified by fire. Unofficially, they were often drowned, or purified by water. Witches, who were sometimes viewed as a kind of heretic, were also killed in both these ways.

The ideal of a pure society may also be illustrated by a variety of secular examples. In Spain, the concern with 'purity of blood' (*limpieza de sangre*) was becoming more acute in the sixteenth and seventeenth centuries.[7] In this case pure blood was 'old Christian' blood, uncontaminated by that of Jews or Muslims. Another common idea in this period was that noble blood was more pure than that of commoners.[8]

When plague struck a region, as it so often did in early modern Europe, the attempts to purify the city or village concerned – including disinfection with sulphur and perfumes, burning clothes and the contents of houses, washing and quarantine (in other words, the segregation of the unclean) – were as much symbolic acts as examples of hygiene. The example of the Italian city of Pistoia in 1630 makes this symbolic element particularly clear. To fight the plague, the municipal government decreed the expulsion of foreigners, mountebanks and Jews.[9]

At a more everyday level, the preoccupation with purity may be illustrated by the idea of the so-called 'infamous occupations', described as 'dirty' and generally located on the periphery of cities. In the case of dyers, for instance, this regulation appears to be utilitarian, but in the case of executioners, it was surely symbolic.[10] In Bologna, a law of 1564 which mentioned both cleaning streets and driving away vagabonds implies, so it was recently suggested, 'a revealing association between physical dirt and social dirt'.[11]

In the political sphere too there was a concern with purity, as a further three examples may suggest. After the revolt of the fisherman Masaniello against the Spanish regime in Naples in 1647–8, exorcism was considered to be necessary in order to purify the city from the taint of rebellion.[12] In England at much the same time, Colonel Pride carried out his 'purge' of the House of Commons, perhaps the first of many political purges.[13] During the French Revolution, the expulsion of twenty-two Girondins

---

[7] Albert A. Sicroff, *Les controverses des statuts de 'pureté de sang' en Espagne aux 16e et 17e siècles* (Paris, 1960).

[8] André Devyver, *Le sang épuré* (Brussels, 1973); Arlette Jouanna, *L'idée de race en France, 1498–1614* (Paris, 1976).

[9] Carlo Cipolla, *Fighting the Plague in Seventeenth-Century Italy* (Madison, 1981), p. 53. Cf. Colin Jones, 'Plague and its Metaphors in Early Modern France', *Representations* 53 (1996), pp. 97–127.

[10] Werner Danckert, *Unehrlich Leute* (Munich, 1963); Anton Blok, 'Infamous Occupations' (1981: English translation in *Honour and Violence*, Cambridge, 2001), pp. 44–68.

[11] Ercole Sori, *La città e i rifiuti* (Bologna, 2001), pp. 164–5.

[12] Peter Burke, 'The Virgin of the Carmine and the Revolt of Masaniello' (1983: repr. in *Historical Anthropology of Early Modern Europe*, Cambridge, 1987), pp. 191–206, at p. 206.

[13] David Underdown, *Pride's Purge: Politics in the Puritan Revolution* (Oxford, 1971).

from the Convention on 15 April 1793 was followed by the declaration that 'the majority of the convention is pure'.

PURIFYING LATIN

It is time to move from the language of purity to the purity of language. The humanists of the Renaissance were extremely interested in the purity of the ancient languages, especially Hebrew, Greek and Latin. Hebrew was described by Conrad Gesner as the only pure language. The decline of pure or 'Attic' Greek into impure, 'Asiatic' or Hellenistic Greek as a result of contact with other languages was studied by some humanists, notably Claude de Saumaise (above, p. 20).[14]

It was Latin that was most often discussed from this point of view. Ancient Romans such as Cicero had already defended what they called a pure, plain or clear form of the language against more elaborate and obscure varieties. Cicero had compared Latin to those women who are most beautiful when unadorned. Quintilian, a leading writer on oratory, had objected to the invasion of Latin by Greek and Carthaginian words.[15] Following these models, a number of Renaissance humanists defended the purity of classical Latin against threats which Cicero and Quintilian could scarcely have imagined.

The humanist historians of Latin, discussed earlier in this book (above, p. 20) both described and lamented the loss of purity in Latin, dating this loss as early as the first century AD, noting the rise of provincial barbarisms and other offences against what one seventeenth-century scholar called *mundities sermonis* – because he had doubts about the purity of the term *puritas* itself.[16]

If first-century Latin could be described as barbarous, it is easy to imagine how Italian humanists reacted to medieval Latin, which they rejected as smelling of the kitchen (above, p. 120), and as impure. Leonardo Bruni, for instance, declared that the purity of Latin should be preserved and not defiled by Greek or barbarous diction.[17] Pietro Corsi wrote about 'polluted' Latin (*inquinata Latinitas*). The case for and against purism was neatly summed up in an early dialogue by Claudio Tolomei, in which the lawyer Giasone del Maino defended the use of technical terms while the humanist poet Poliziano attacked them.[18] Pietro Bembo claimed in 1525 that Latin

[14] Simon Swain, *Hellenism and Empire: Language, Classicism and Power in the Greek World, AD 50–250* (Oxford, 1996), pp. 1–64.

[15] Quintilian, *De Oratore* (Cambridge, MA, 2001), book 1, chapter 5, section 55.

[16] Gerard Jan Voss, *De vitiis sermonis* (Amsterdam, 1645).

[17] Leonardo Bruni, *Epistolae*, ed. Lorenzo Mehus (Florence, 1741), book 10, no. 24.

[18] Claudio Tolomei, *De corruptis verbis* (Siena, c. 1516).

had recovered its splendour because it had been 'purified from the rust of the unlearned centuries' (*purgata dalla rugine degl'indotti secoli*).[19] Tolomei, less optimistic, declared in 1555 that modern Latin still had to regain 'the brightness, the purity . . . of the language of the Romans' (*il candore, la purità . . . de la romana lingua*).[20]

Outside Italy these arguments were repeated. The German Johann Reuchlin spoke of 'the purity of the language' (*puritas linguae*). The Portuguese Arias Barbosa wrote of 'the brightness [or whiteness] of the Roman language' (*Romanae linguae candor*). The Englishman John Colet, the founder of St Paul's school, required the choice of a headmaster who was learned in 'the good and clean Latin literature'.[21] In this case it is not clear whether Colet was thinking of moral purity, excluding Plautus, say, or Catullus from the curriculum, or of purity of language, excluding medieval authors.

For some of these humanists, notably Bembo, writing pure Latin meant more than abandoning medieval conventions and trying to emulate the manner of the Romans of the late Republic. It meant writing in the style of one individual, Cicero. The humanists Christophe de Longueil and Etienne Dolet offer extreme and explicit examples of this tendency – Longueil was said to refuse to use any Latin word that could not be proved to have been used by Cicero – but in a milder form the tendency was widespread among the humanists of the sixteenth century.

Turning to the vernacular, it may be useful to distinguish two forms of purism. The first tendency may be described either as 'transformative purism', since it emphasized change, or as 'separatism', since one aim of the purists was to set themselves apart from other people. The second tendency may be described as 'defensive' purism because it attempted to preserve a status quo that the purists considered to be under threat.

STANDARDIZATION AS PURIFICATION

The first form of purism is none other than the standardization discussed in chapter 4. The point to be made here is that some leading standardizers viewed their task as one of purifying the language.

In Italy, Bembo declared that his stylistic ideal was always to follow 'the purest, cleanest and clearest' (*le più pure, le più monde, le più chiare*). He thought that writers should avoid low subjects so as not to 'stain' (*macchiar*)

[19] Bembo, *Prose della vulgar lingua* (1525: repr. Bembo, *Prose e rime*, ed. Carlo Dionisotti, Turin, 1960, pp. 71–309).
[20] Claudio Tolomei, *Il Cesano* (1546: ed. M. R. Franco Subri, Rome, 1975, p. 37).
[21] Johann Reuchlin, *De rudimentis hebraicis* (Pforzheim, 1506).

the text. His choice of an archaic standard, that of the fourteenth century, followed a recurrent strategy of purists.[22] The Crusca, a Florentine language academy founded to support Bembo's ideals, took its name from a metaphor of purification, since its aim was to separate the wheat from the 'chaff' (*crusca*). The ideal spread to other cities in the seventeenth century. The English virtuoso John Evelyn noted in the course of his travels in Italy that 'the purity of the Italian tongue' was 'daily improved' by the efforts of the Roman academy of the Umoristi.[23]

In seventeenth-century France, the poet François de Malherbe carried on the tradition of Bembo with the motto 'aimez la pureté'. Even on his deathbed he was supposed to have declared that his aim was 'maintenir la pureté de la langue française'. Malherbe's successor as arbiter of French, Claude de Vaugelas, also stressed the need both to speak and to write *purement*. The Académie Française followed the Florentine model and its function was described as 'to clean the tongue from dirt' (*nettoyer la langue des ordures*). The preface to its famous *Dictionary* (1694) stated its aim as to give the French language the opportunity 'to maintain its purity' (*conserver sa pureté*).[24] To view standardization in terms of purity makes it easier to understand the role in the movement of ladies, especially the so-called *précieuses* (above, p. 35).

In England, attempts to purify the language in this way came later and the movement was weaker than in France. Daniel Defoe's project for a language academy was intended to help 'establish purity and propriety of style'.[25] Samuel Johnson's famous *Dictionary* was part of a larger enterprise to preserve the 'purity' of English, which Johnson considered to have been under threat since the Restoration of Charles II in 1660.[26] In arguing in favour of the Copenhagen standard for Danish, Henrik Gerner described it as 'the best form of speech, purified from all dialects' (*det beste Sprock, rensed fra alle Dialecten*).[27]

DEFENSIVE PURISM, RENAISSANCE AND REFORMATION

In a famous book, the British anthropologist Mary Douglas studied ideas of purity and dirt as parts of symbolic systems, and purification as a response

---

[22] Bembo, *Prose della vulgar lingua*, pp. 71–309.
[23] John Evelyn, *Diary*, ed. Esmond S. De Beer, 6 vols. (Oxford, 1955), vol. II, p. 364.
[24] Alexis François, *La grammaire du purisme et l'Académie Française au 18e siècle* (Paris, 1905).
[25] Daniel Defoe, *An Essay upon Projects* (1697: repr. Menston, 1969), pp. 227–59.
[26] Samuel Johnson, *Plan of a Dictionary* (London, 1747), p. 32.
[27] Quoted in Skautrup, *Danske sprog*, vol. II, p. 316.

to perceived danger, especially the danger to the cultural order posed by crossing its boundaries.[28] Although she did not have much to say about language, her ideas are extremely relevant to defensive purism in that domain, explaining the violence of some contemporary reactions to what was perceived as the invasion of the culture by foreign words, words that came from the other side of the frontier.

In the case of early modern Europe, there is much evidence for an 'anxiety of contamination', the complementary opposite to the 'anxiety of deficit' discussed earlier (p. 17). Indeed, the strength of the reaction makes it appropriate to borrow a term from contemporary sociology and speak of a 'moral panic', or at least a cultural one. In the age of the Renaissance, it was Italian words that seemed to pose the greatest threat. The reaction of the purists may be illustrated from the work of the French scholar-printer Henri Estienne. The positive side of Estienne's interest in the vernacular, his praise of the French language and his comparison between modern French and ancient Greek, has already been discussed (above, p. 68).

The negative side, Estienne's critique of what he called the 'italianization' of French, emerges in the two dialogues he published in 1578, *Deux dialogues du nouveau langage françois, italianizé et autrement desguisé, principalement entre les courtisans de ce temps*. The speakers in these dialogues comment on and condemn a number of linguistic 'novelties' or *courtisanismes*. Instead of *se promener*, for instance, the courtiers say *spaceger*, in imitation of the Italian *passeggiare*. The route they take is not the normal *chemin* but the *strade*, derived from the Italian *strada*. The conversations they have as they walk are described not as *converser* but as *ragionner*, following the Italian *ragionare*, and so on. These attempts to be elegant (*leggiadres*, from the Italian *leggiadro*) are condemned by the speakers in the dialogue as *barbarismes*, *barragouinage* (pidgin), *langage farragineux* (a confused mixture or farrago), or, in verse this time, as 'ce jergon si sauvage/appelé courtisan langage'.[29]

So far as the facts were concerned, Estienne may have exaggerated for dramatic effect, since some of his examples are recorded for the first or only time in the dialogue itself. So is the term *italianizé* in his title, as if this enemy of neologisms was irritated into perpetrating some of his own. All the same, Estienne was essentially correct in the sense that however the courtiers spoke, a considerable number of Italian words were entering French at this time, just as they were entering English, German and other

[28] Mary Douglas, *Purity and Danger* (London, 1966).
[29] Henri Estienne, *Deux dialogues* (1578: ed. Pauline M. Smith, Geneva, 1980). In the original Latin *farrago* meant a mixed fodder given to cattle.

European languages, especially in the military domain (above, p. 129), and in that of art and architecture.

What some contemporaries considered to be an enrichment of the language was viewed by Estienne as corruption. Like some German writers of the seventeenth century, what worried him was not so much the rise of new technical terms in specific domains as the invasion of ordinary language by words from abroad. If new words there had to be, according to Estienne, it was best to coin what he called *mots composez*, in other words compounds of existing terms, a technique well-known in the Germanic languages but less often advocated for French.[30]

Defensive purism was not confined to France at this time, even if Estienne's highly articulate presentation of the case was exceptional. Some writers went further than he did – for it may be useful to distinguish a mild purism, opposed to recent neologisms, from a more radical variety that aimed at rooting out even old words with a foreign origin.

A certain Jan van de Werve, for instance, condemned the corruption of Dutch by romance words in his *Tresoor der Duitsche Tale* (1553). At that point he seems not to have noticed that the word *tresoor* was itself derived from the French *trésor*, an omission he put right in the second edition of his book, when the title was changed to the Germanic *Schat*. Hendrik Spiegel argued against the use of French expressions such as *bon jour* in Dutch and against words of Latin origin such as *conscientie*, *disputatie* or *inventie*, and suggested that if borrowing had to take place at all, it should be from Germanic languages such as Danish, Frisian or English.[31] Again, the mathematician Simon Stevin, in his coinages of mathematical and other technical terms, preferred native compounds to borrowing from abroad; his word for 'triangle', for instance, was *driehoek* and for 'logic', *bewysconst*, 'the art of proof'. In similar fashion, Spieghel described his dialogue as a 'speaking between two people' (*twee-spraak*). The word 'philosophy' was rendered into Dutch, following the literal Greek meaning of the term, as 'desire for wisdom' (*wijsbegeerte*).[32]

German translations of Vitruvius resisted Latin architectural terms in a way that the French and English, for instance, did not. One sixteenth-century physician, Laurentius Fries, advocated the 'germanization' of medical terms, while the schoolmaster and pastor Valentin Ickelsamer opposed

---

[30] Henri Estienne, *La précellence du langage françois* (1579: ed. Edmond Huguet, Paris, 1896), p. 165.

[31] Hendrik L. Spieghel, *Twee-spraak* (1584: repr. Groningen, 1913), pp. xiv–xv, lxxxii.

[32] Lode van den Branden, *Het streven naar verheerlijking, zuivering en opbouw van het Nederlands in de 16de eeuw* (Ghent, 1956), pp. 20–5, 72–4, 188–209.

the introduction of foreign words for police (*Policey*), for example, gout (*Podagra*), recipe (*Recept*) and mayor (*Syndicus*). The translator Johann Fischart, whose contribution to the mixing of languages has already been discussed (above, p. 121) may seem out of place in a discussion of purity. All the same, among his many neologisms are some compounds that seem designed to avoid the introduction of foreign-sounding words: *Allein-herrschung* for 'monarchy', for instance, or *Bilderschrift* for 'hieroglyphics'.[33]

In Scandinavia, there was a similar movement, linked to the Reformation. In Denmark, Christiern III's Bible (above, p. 103) avoided both Latinisms and Germanisms. In Sweden, the translators of the Gustav Vasa Bible also avoided Germanisms, while Johan III told his son and successor to take action 'so that foreign words would not be mixed into Swedish, but the language preserved in a pure and incorrupt form' (*ne peregrinae voces misceretur Sveticae linguae, sed ut ea pura et incorrupta servaretur*).[34] However, it was the Icelanders who placed most emphasis on the purity of their language – understandably enough, since it is the closest of the Scandinavian languages to Old Norse.[35]

In England too there were purists, though not many. The Cambridge professor John Cheke, a Fellow of St John's College, argued for what he called a 'clean and pure' English, 'unmixed and unmangled with other tongues'. In his translation of the Gospels, for instance, Cheke wrote 'crossed' not 'crucified' and he replaced the traditional term 'centurion' by 'hundreder'. Thomas Hoby, who studied at St John's, was a disciple of Cheke, whose influence underlies Hoby's translation of Castiglione's *Courtier* (1566), for example his notorious rendering of the key term *sprezzatura* by the Germanic 'recklessness' rather than – as might have been expected – by the Latinate 'negligence'.[36]

The influence of Cheke on Thomas Wilson, a student at King's College and the author of the *Art of Rhetoric* (1553), may also be suspected, especially in Wilson's attack on 'inkhorn terms', in other words latinate English such as 'to fatigate your intelligence' or 'obtestate your confidence'. Wilson also criticized what he called 'outlandish English' or 'English italianated'. In similar fashion the Anglican divine Ralph Lever, the author of *The Art of Reason* (1573), and a former St John's man like Cheke and Hoby, created what he called 'compounded terms' in the Dutch or German manner as

---

[33] Walter E. Spengler, *Johann Fischart* (Göppingen, 1969), p. 171.
[34] Quoted in Johan Loccenius, *Historiae Suecanae* (Stockholm, 1676), p. 68.
[35] Pierre Halleux, 'Le purisme islandais', *Etudes Germaniques* 20 (1965), pp. 417–27.
[36] Peter Burke, *The Fortunes of the Courtier* (Cambridge, 1995), pp. 70–71.

an alternative to borrowing words from abroad. Among his coinages were 'forespeech' for preface and 'witcraft' for logic.[37]

Incidentally, English purists did not agree about the role of Chaucer in their story, hero or villain. For Peter Betham, a Cambridge don writing in 1543, the poet's English revealed his 'endeavour to bring again to his own cleanness our English tongue', but for Richard Verstegan in 1605, Chaucer was 'a great mingler of English with French'.[38]

In the Slavonic languages too there were attempts at purification, beginning with Czech. In the fifteenth century, the reformer Jan Hus already felt the need to resist German influences and in his *Exposition of the Ten Commandments* he coined the term *radnice*, for instance, for 'town hall' to replace the obviously Germanic *ratusa* (from *Rathaus*, 'council house'), and advised his readers to call a towel an *ubrusec* rather than a *hantuch*.

THE SEVENTEENTH AND EIGHTEENTH CENTURIES

In Germany the seventeenth century was a time of intense discussion of this problem. Societies were founded with the purity of the language as one of their main ideals. The Fruchtbringende Gesellschaft, for instance, modelled on the Crusca, was founded in 1617.[39]

The critique of the invasion of German by French words, especially in the domain of good behaviour (*compliment, galant, mode*, etc.), was particularly intense in the middle decades of the century.[40] The linguistic campaign was part of a more general reaction against foreign and especially French cultural models, from clothes to cuisine, the 'imitation of the French' (*Nachahmung der Französen*) denounced by the philosopher Christian Thomasius.[41]

Christian Gueintz, a superintendent of schools in Halle and a member of the Fruchtbringende Gesellschaft, compared the German language to 'a pure maiden embraced by foreign tongues' (*eine reine Jungfrau von fremden Sprachen enthalten*).[42] The poet Georg Weckherlin criticized what he called 'Welsch-vermischten Sprach', in other words German larded with Italian.[43] Another poet, Johann Rist, published a book on the 'rescue of the noble German language' from fashionable corruptions. Like Estienne

---

[37] Quoted in Richard F. Jones, *Triumph of the English Language* (Stanford, 1953), p. 124.

[38] Derek Brewer (ed.) *Chaucer: the Critical Heritage*, vol. 1 (London, 1978), pp. 98–9, 145.

[39] Hans Martin Schultz, *Die Bestrebungen der Sprachgesellschaften des xvii Jhts für Reinigung der deutschen Sprache* (1888: repr. Leipzig, 1975); Martin Bircher (ed.), *Sprachgesellschaften* (Hamburg, 1978).

[40] Hans Wolff, *Der Purismus in der deutschen Literatur des siebzehnten Jhts* (1888: repr. Leipzig, 1975).

[41] Christian Thomasius, *Von Nachahmung der Franzosen* (1687: repr. Stuttgart, 1894).

[42] Quoted in Strassner, *Sprachkultur*, p. 66.

[43] Quoted in Leonard Forster, *The Poet's Tongues* (Cambridge, 1970), p. 37.

before him, Rist was irritated into coining neologisms such as *alamode-sirende* ('fashionable') as well as into parodying the mixed German of his time. Rist's spokesman, Teutschherz ('German heart') recommends native equivalents for some German words, including technical terms, for example *Obrist* instead of *Colonel*.[44]

In similar fashion, the writer Philipp von Zesen coined compound terms in order to replace foreign imports – in some cases, ironically enough, following Dutch models. Although he was not opposed to the entry of every foreign word into the language, Justus Georg Schottel, another member of the Fruchtbringende Gesellschaft, also created new words out of combinations of old ones, for example *Beweiskunst* ('the art of proof') for 'logic'. Leibniz agreed with the principle, though he preferred to render 'logic' as *Vernunftkunst*, 'the art of reason'.[45]

In the eighteenth century, the German campaign against foreign words was still in progress, a sure sign that it had not been successful. The first historian of the German language, Egenolff, complained about the entry into German of 'a horde of foreign and barbarous words' (*eine Menge fremder und barbarischer Wörter*).[46] The Hamburg weekly *Der Patriot* made fun of the continuing use of French words and phrase such as *maison de campagne*, *saison* or *séjour*. Gottsched criticized the 'language mixers' (*Sprachen-Mischer*), comparing Frenchified German with the language of beggars or Hottentots.[47] Like the translators of architectural treatises in the Renaissance, German chemists rejected international scientific terms of Greek derivation, such as 'hydrogen' and 'oxygen', preferring native compounds, such as 'water-stuff' or 'sour-stuff' (*Wasserstoff, Sauerstoff*).[48]

In the case of other Germanic languages there were similar movements in a milder form. In his Dutch translation of Descartes, for instance, following the model of Stevin and others, Jan Glazemaker devised native or native-sounding equivalents for the new philosophical terms. A campaign to purify Danish was mounted by the writer Frederik Horn, author of a 'defence of

[44] Johann Rist, *Rettung der edlen Teutschen Hauptsprache* (Hamburg, 1642); cf. Richard J. Brunt, 'The Reaction against Foreign Borrowings', in *The Influence of the French Language on the German Vocabulary, 1649–1735* (Berlin 1983), pp. 48–58.

[45] L. Seiffel, 'J. G. Schottelius and the Traditions of German Linguistic Purism', in Werner Hüllen (ed.), *Historiography of Linguistics* (Münster, 1990), pp. 241–61; Manfred Faust, 'Schottelius' Concept of Word Formation' in Horst Geckeler, et al. (eds.), *Logos Semantikos* (Berlin, 1981), pp. 359–70.

[46] Johan Augustin Egenolff, *Historie der Teutschen Sprache* (2 vols., Leipzig, 1716–20), preface to vol. II.

[47] Quoted in Eric A. Blackall, *The Emergence of German as a Literary Language, 1700–75* (Cambridge, 1959), pp. 85, 94, 95n, 118.

[48] Jan Golinski, 'The Chemical Revolution and the Politics of Language', *Eighteenth Century* 33 (1992), pp. 238–51; Bernadette Bensaud-Vincent and Marco Abbri (eds.), *Lavoisier in European Context: Negotiating a New Language for Chemistry* (Canton, MA, 1995).

the Danish language against the Danes' (*Apologie for det danske Sprog imod Danske*, 1731). There were other critics of French influence on the language, including the dramatist Holberg.

Some Swedes were also concerned with this issue in the seventeenth century, the age in which Sweden was a great power and in which much was made of the supposed descent of the Swedes from the warlike Goths. The poet Georg Stiernhielm, for instance, recommended archaism, in this case the borrowing of terms from Old Norse, or from what he called the 'Swedo-Gothic' language, 'pure and undefiled' (*pura et intaminata*). However, it was only in 1786 that Gustav III founded the Swedish Academy in order to promote the 'purity, strength and sublimity' of Swedish. The purity of Icelandic was defended by Arngrímur Jónsson in the seventeenth century and in the eighteenth by the Icelandic Literary Society (founded 1779), whose members bound themselves to reject new words of foreign origin.[49]

In England, a few radicals denounced the linguistic aspect of the domination of the Anglo-Saxons by the Norman invaders, the 'Norman Yoke', as they called it, arguing for a return to Saxon words. In a pamphlet published in 1647 under the dramatic title of *St Edwards Ghost*, a certain John Hare proposed 'that our language be cleared of the Norman and French invasion upon it, by purging it of all words and terms of that descent, supplying it from the old Saxon and the learned tongues'. Hare argued that 'our language was a dialect of the Teutonic' and that it was 'most fruitful and copious in significance and well-sounding roots and primitives', roots which allow 'a Greek-like ramosity of derivations and compositions, beyond the power of the Latin and her offspring dialects'.[50]

There was more anxiety about recent foreign invasions and what the architect John Webb called the 'Latinizing, Italianizing, Frenchizing' of English. Dryden, for instance, expressed his opposition to those who 'corrupt our English idiom by mixing it too much with French'. Thomas Sprat, giving a new turn to the old topos linking language to empire, declared that 'the purity of speech and greatness of empire have in all countries still met together'.[51] Xenophobia contributed to the campaign against foreign words. The Laudable Association of Anti-Gallicans, founded by London

---

[49] Halleux, 'purisme', pp. 418–9.
[50] John Hare, *St Edwards Ghost: or, Anti-Normanisme* (London, 1647), p. 10; cf. Jones, *Triumph*, pp. 221–2, 228, 249.
[51] John Webb, *An Historical Essay Endeavouring a Probability that the Language of the Empire of China is the Primitive Language* (London, 1669); Dryden quoted in Manfred Görlach, *Introduction to Early Modern English* (1978: English translation, Cambridge, 1991), p. 253; Sprat quoted in Hermann M. Flasdieck, *Der Gedanke einer englischen Sprachakademie* (Jena, 1928), p. 37.

tradesmen in 1745, included in its remit a campaign against the use of French phrases in English.[52]

By the later seventeenth century, Italians too were worried about the Frenchification of their language. The Neapolitan scholar Gianvicenzo Gravina, for example, used the term 'pollute' (*inquinari*) to refer to the entry into Italian of foreign words, especially French ones.[53] Among the French words and phrases that arrived in the last thirty years of the seventeenth century were *bello spirito* ('bel esprit'), *bel mondo* ('beau monde'), *buon senso* ('bon sens'), and *civilizzare* ('civiliser').[54] In the eighteenth century, the invasion continued and the Venetian writer Carlo Gozzi condemned French for spoiling Italian, deforming it and turning it upside down (he called it the *maggior guastatore, rovesciatore e difformatore dell'eccellente idioma nostro*).[55]

Italian, English, German, Danish and Dutch comedies and satires all mocked the use of French phrases in everyday speech, like the imitation of French fashions. However, although Quevedo had spoken in favour of the purity of Spanish in the seventeenth century, it was not until 1713 that a Spanish academy was founded on the French model. Paradoxically, the occasion of this foundation was the need to defend the language against the invasion of French words.[56] In other words, the academy formed part of the strategy of the Spanish Bourbons, using French methods to defend themselves against France.

In Bohemia, it was in the later seventeenth century that the grammarian Václav Rosa coined new Czech abstract nouns to replace borrowings from German. In Polish, Jan Malecki was already complaining in the middle of the sixteenth century about the excessive use of words from Latin and German. Of the two, it was the former that posed the main threat, and satirists such as Krzysztof Opaliński mocked fellow-nobles for speaking 'macaronically' (*macaronice*) and mixing Latin into Polish 'stupidly and poorly and inopportunely'. In his Polish dictionary, Gregorz Knapski condemned what he called 'mixed language' (*mowa mieszona*), while a textbook on rhetoric used in a Jesuit school in Lwów (now L'viv) in 1699 advised

---

[52] Linda Colley, *Britons* (London, 1995), p. 90.

[53] Quoted in Andrea Dardi, *Dalla provincia all'Europa: l'influsso del francese sull'italiano tra il 1650 e il 1715* (Florence, 1992), p. 40n.

[54] Dardi, *Provincia*; Maurizio Vitale, *L'oro nella lingua. Contributi per una storia del tradizionalismo e del purismo italiano* (Milan-Naples, 1986).

[55] Mario Puppo (ed.), *Discussioni linguistiche del '700* (Turin, 1957), p. 509.

[56] Werner Mulertt, 'Aus der Geschichte der Spanische Sprachreinigungsbestrebungen', *Estudios Adolfo Bonilla* (Madrid, 1927), vol. I, pp. 583–603; Dagmar Fries, *Limpia, fija y da esplendor: la Real Academia Española ante el uso de la lengua* (Madrid, 1989).

readers against the use of foreign words in Polish. The examples against which pupils were warned included *bagatela* and *sentinela*, suggesting that the greatest threat to the language was now from French.[57]

In Russian, on the other hand, despite massive borrowing from foreign languages, there are few signs of purism until the middle of the eighteenth century. Alexander Sumarokov claimed that 'the acceptance of foreign words is not an enrichment but a corruption of the language', and recommended 'the expulsion of foreign words' from Russian, while Mikhaylo Lomonosov criticized Latinisms, Germanisms and Gallicisms and planned to write on purity of style.[58] As readers of *War and Peace* will be well aware, these recommendations had little effect.[59]

The Ottoman Empire followed similar trends, in its own time. In the sixteenth century, official documents were written in Persian and Arabic. In the seventeenth century, in a movement like that of the European Renaissance, the documents were drawn up in a Turkish mixed with Persian and Arabic words. In the eighteenth century, purists eliminated these foreign expressions in favour of Turkish ones.[60]

ANTI-PURISM

It would be misleading to give the impression either that the purists won without a struggle or that resistance was purely passive or unconscious. There is also evidence of anti-purist reactions.

Erasmus, for instance, made fun of Ciceronians such as Bembo in his dialogue the *Ciceronianus* (1528). In Italy, too, Bembo was often disobeyed and sometimes mocked. For example, the writer Pietro Aretino was surely making fun of Bembo and his chaste language when he presented a discussion of the best words to use for 'door', 'window' and so on, in the setting of a Roman brothel, with purism represented by a whore named after her catch-phrase 'Mummy doesn't like it' (*Matremma non vuole*).

[57] Maria Renata Mayenowa, 'Aspects of the Language Question in Poland', in Picchio and Goldblatt, *Aspects*, vol. I, pp. 337–76, at pp. 343, 349, 353; Martel, *La langue polonaise*, p. 46n.

[58] Antoine Martel, *Michel Lomonosov et la langue littéraire russe* (Paris, 1933), pp. 41–4; Sumarokov quoted in Hans Rogger, *National Consciousness in Eighteenth-Century Russia* (Cambridge, MA, 1960), p. 106.

[59] Robert Auty, 'The Role of Purism in the Development of the Slavonic Literary Languages', *Slavic and East European Review* 51 (1973), pp. 335–43; Auty, 'Czech', in Alexander M. Schenker and Edward Stankiewicz (eds.), *The Slavic Literary Languages: Formation and Development* (New Haven, 1980), pp. 163–82, at p. 173; Gerta Hüttl-Worth, *Foreign Words in Russian: A Historical Sketch, 1550–1800* (Berkeley, 1963), p. 25.

[60] I should like to thank Professor Metin Kunt of Sabanc University for information about Ottoman Turkish.

Like Aretino's dialogue, the lyrics in Venetian dialect by the patrician Matteo Venier, which name directly what we still euphemistically call our 'private parts', express a rebellion against the linguistic standards of Bembo as well as against the poetry of Petrarch. Again, the publication of the dictionary of the Crusca was immediately followed by Paolo Beni's *Anticrusca*, a critique of the fourteenth-century Tuscan standard.[61]

In France, the campaign of Vaugelas and his followers provoked a reaction on the part of some writers. Among them was the elderly historian Scipion Dupleix, who attacked 'the refiners of our language' and their 'oracle' Vaugelas for 'an affected elegance' and defended linguistic liberty against what he called 'an over-scrupulous purity of style and language'.[62] The drama was also used to mock the purists. Before Molière ridiculed the *précieuses*, St-Evremond's *Comédie des académistes* (1638) was already making fun of the newly-founded Académie Française. In the next century, Voltaire joined the ranks of the anti-purists, describing the French language as 'a poor beggarwoman who is afraid of charity' (*une indigente orgueilleuse qui craint qu'on ne lui fasse l'aumône*).[63]

Another sign of the anti-purist reaction is the rise of the term 'purist' itself in different European languages. In France, for instance, the writer and churchman Jean-Pierre Camus was making critical remarks about the 'académie des puristes' even before the French Academy was founded. The dictionary-maker Furetière also denounced the *puristes*. In the case of German, it was Leibniz who criticized the linguistic 'Puritans' as he called them, with their 'superstitious fear' of foreign words that they avoided as if they were 'mortal sins'. Leibniz's views on language were linked to his interest in science and technology, since he criticized both the Crusca and the French Academy for their omission of technical terms from their dictionaries.[64] In the case of Danish, the playwright Ludwig Holberg aimed at what he called a 'middle way' between mixers and 'purists' (*purister*).[65]

In England, it was only in the eighteenth century that the term 'purist' was coined, to refer to 'one that affects to speak or write neatly and properly'.[66] In Italy, too, references to the *puristi della lingua* date from the eighteenth century, from the circle of Milanese intellectuals centred on the

[61] W. Theodor Elwert, *Studi di letteratura veneziana* (Venice-Rome, 1958), pp. 163–4; P. B. Diffley, *Paolo Beni: a biographical and critical study* (Oxford, 1988), pp. 139–41.

[62] Scipion Dupleix, *Liberté de la langue françoise en sa pureté* (1651: repr. Geneva, 1973), pp. 5, 15.

[63] Voltaire to Beauzée, 15 January 1768.

[64] Strassner, *Sprachkultur*, p. 105.   [65] Skautrup, *Danske sprog*, vol. III, p. 50.

[66] Phillips (1706), quoted in the *Oxford English Dictionary*, sub voce 'purist'.

journal *Il Caffè*.[67] It might be argued that the term was scarcely needed in Italian, where it was traditional to mock a style that was *bembesco* or *cruscaio* – in other words, one that followed the manner recommended by the Academia della Crusca (above, p. 146). All the same, the Paduan writer Melchiorre Cesarotti's critique of purism deserves to be noted, because it posed the problem in general terms. Cesarotti denounced the idea 'that all languages are closed to encounters, that their greatest quality is purity, and that any tincture of the foreign makes them bastards and corrupts them' (*che tutte le lingue siano reciprocamente insociabili, che il loro massimo pregio sia la purità, che qualunque tintura di peregrinità le imbastardisca e corrompa*).[68]

PURITY AND DANGER

At this point, it may be useful to stand back from the material and try to explain why there should have been an acute concern with the purity of language in certain places and at certain times in early modern Europe, in contrast to the Middle Ages, when the purity of language was not an issue. Possible explanations are either internal to the history of language or external to it.

The obvious internal explanation is the one already offered by speaking of a defensive reaction to language change, especially to the invasion of certain languages by large numbers of foreign words. What we see is the defence of linguistic territory. After all, language is one of the principal markers of community. As the anthropologist Mary Douglas, cited above, has suggested, a concern with purity expresses a sense of danger, a perceived threat to the cohesiveness of the community.[69]

If this is the case, there should be more concern with purity whenever there is more borrowing and mixing. The earliest example of a movement of linguistic purification – at least, the earliest known to me – confirms this hypothesis, since it comes from the Roman Empire in the Hellenistic period, when words from Latin and other languages were invading Greek. This was the time that Herodian the Grammarian described those who objected to words of foreign origin as *hoi kathareuontes*, 'the purists'.[70]

---

[67] Ferdinando Neri, 'Purista', in his *Letteratura e legende* (Milan, 1951), pp. 118–22; Maurizio Vitale, 'Purista e purismo', *Acme* 17 (1964), pp. 187–211; Vitale, 'Discussioni linguistiche del '700', in Lia Formigari (ed.), *Teorie e pratiche linguistiche nell'Italia del '700* (Bologna, 1984), pp. 11–36.

[68] Melchiorre Cesarotti, *Saggio sopra la lingua italiana* (1785: repr. in Emilio Bigi (ed.), *Dal Muratori al Cesarotti*, Milan and Naples, 1960), pp. 304–468, at p. 306.

[69] Douglas, *Purity.*   [70] Quoted in Swain, *Hellenism and Empire.*

On the edge between internal and external factors, the role of the printing-press in the creation of linguistic standards has already been noted (above, p. 106). The increasing number of printed texts available in the vernacular after 1500 made impurities more dangerous than before, since the infection could easily spread. It is unlikely to be a coincidence that one of the leading purists discussed above, Pietro Bembo, worked in close collaboration with the Venetian printer Aldus Manutius, while Henri Estienne, a printer himself, had also worked with Aldus. Language purifiers reject forms that do not meet a certain standard and so assume the prior existence of that standard. The lack of standard forms of language explains the absence of movements for linguistic purification in the Middle Ages.

In the case of external explanations, this chapter has already hinted at possible connections between movements of linguistic purification and other kinds of purification: religious, political, social and so on. It is time to investigate these connections a little further.

There is something to say about the politics of language purification at this time, though less than in the case of the nineteenth and twentieth centuries (below, p. 163). In the case of Italy, Grand Duke Cosimo de'Medici of Tuscany, a new ruler who needed legitimation, was shrewd enough to see that he could associate the Tuscan standard with his regime by founding an academy concerned with language (above, p. 98). To employ the terminology of Pierre Bourdieu, Cosimo had learned how to transform cultural capital into political capital.[71] In the case of England, the idea of the 'Norman Yoke' in language (above, p. 152), gave the story of language purification a political twist.

In the case of French, Richelieu's interest in the Académie Française had political as well as cultural roots, although the political motive for the reform of language surely derived from foreign rather than domestic policy. Linguistic reform was less an aspect of state-building than an extension of France's rivalry with Spain into the speech domain.[72] The parallel between the centralization of government and the rise of formal control over language is of course a tempting one, especially when it is contrasted with British resistance both to absolute monarchy and a language academy. However, to attribute language planning to Richelieu – or to any seventeenth-century statesman – is surely anachronistic. The shift to an official 'politique de la langue' came with the French Revolution (below, p. 165).[73]

---

[71] Bourdieu, *Distinction*; Sergio Bertelli, 'L'egemonia linguistica come egemonia culturale', *Bibliothèque d'Humanisme et Renaissance* 38 (1976), pp. 249–81.

[72] Claude-Gilbert Dubois, *Mythe et langage au 16e siècle* (Bordeaux, 1970), p. 90.

[73] Henri Peyre, *La royauté et les langues provinciales* (Paris, 1933).

At this time, religious motives were more important than political ones in the purification of language, a point that may be illustrated from the examples of two purists already discussed, Henri Estienne and John Cheke. Both were strong Protestants. Their hostility to Italian and Latin words was surely linked to their hatred and fear of the Church of Rome, so often described by reformers in terms of impurity. In the case of the translation of the Gospels, Cheke's preference for traditional English equivalents of Greek words, such as 'overseer' for *episkopos*, expressed his awareness of the way in which earlier translations, in this case 'bishop', had helped legitimate a form of Church organisation which he rejected. In short, there were links between purism and Puritanism.

Whether purists belong to a particular psychological type is a fascinating question. It is tempting to speculate on this topic, to suggest, for example, that their obsession with purity locates them in the group that Freud classified as 'anal-retentive'.[74] Unfortunately, so far as the early period is concerned, there is no way of verifying or falsifying the hypothesis. We are on firmer ground if we offer social explanations for linguistic purification, beginning from the point already made (above, p. 32), about linguistic separation as a sign of social separation. Social factors may also be important in the emergence of defensive purism. In the search for these factors, it may be illuminating to pay attention to the metaphors used by contemporaries when discussing linguistic issues. Two are particularly noteworthy: nobility and citizenship.

An eighteenth-century Spanish writer once described his criteria for accepting a new word. If it was 'of known origin and expressive' (*castiza y expressiva*), then two or three classic authors would be sufficient 'testimonies to prove its nobility' (*testigos fidedignos para probar sua nobleza*). Thanks to the frequent use of the term *castiza* (derived from *casta*, 'family'), the language debate in eighteenth-century Spain was described as a battle between *casticistas* and *afrancescados*, 'the Frenchified'.[75]

In other words, the legitimation of words is compared to the legitimation of claims to status, more especially to practices for making claims to nobility at this time, by investigating the family of the claimant and calling witnesses. New words are compared to the new rich, outsiders who have to wait to be accepted by the established. This point leads to the second revealing metaphor, that of citizenship. As we have seen (above, pp. 19, 140), new or

---

[74] Cf. André Mirambel, 'Les aspects psychologiques du purisme dans la Grèce moderne', *Journal de Psychologie* (1964), pp. 405–36.
[75] Quoted in Mulertt, 'Sprachreinigung', p. 587; on *casticistas*, Amado Alonso, *Castellano, español, idioma nacional: historia spiritual de tres nombres* (Buenos Aires, 1938), pp. 121–3.

foreign words were perceived as immigrants, outsiders to the community and so objects of suspicion, but capable of being 'naturalized'.

In short, attitudes to language were coloured by social attitudes, not to say prejudices. Whose prejudices in particular it is not easy to say. As we have seen, purists ranged from patricians, such as Bembo, to professors, such as Cheke, merchants, such as Werve, and printers, such as Estienne. If we may trust the testimony of literature, female purists, from 'Matremma non vuole' to the *précieuses ridicules*, were also prominent in the movement.

The Renaissance may have been a great moment of heteroglossia, as Bakhtin has suggested, but this chapter has suggested that mixing was not to everyone's taste at the time. There is a good deal of evidence for what might be called linguistic xenophobia, though not – so it has been argued – for linguistic nationalism in the modern sense. The idea that members of a given nation ought to speak alike was first voiced during the French Revolution as part of its universalizing policies.[76] The international movement for language purification discussed in this chapter was a movement by minorities on behalf of minorities.

[76] Michel de Certeau, Jacques Revel and Dominique Julia, *Une Politique de la langue: la Révolution Française et les patois* (Paris, 1975).

Epilogue: languages and nations

This book has presented a few central themes in the story of European languages from the late-fifteenth to the late-eighteenth century. The choice of the French Revolution as the moment to end the story implies that in language, as in government, an old regime was replaced by a new one after 1789.

Roughly speaking, this view is correct. From 1789 onwards, governments in Europe and elsewhere have become increasingly concerned with the everyday language of ordinary people. The point is that language both expresses and helps to create national communities. We might say that language was 'nationalized' at this time, or that it became an instrument of the 'cult of the nation'. From this time onward, it becomes appropriate to speak of conscious 'language policies'.[1]

To be more precise, though, this view requires a few qualifications. As so often in history, it is more illuminating to view change in relative terms than in absolute ones, to speak of more or less rather than of presence or absence. Cultural regimes are not transformed overnight, or even in a decade. Changes in the linguistic regime and the idea of the nation were becoming visible before the Revolution and continuities remained apparent long after that date. This is the reason for the following epilogue. It does not aspire to be a general survey of European languages in the last two centuries. It is simply intended to offer a few explicit comparisons and contrasts between European languages and their communities before and after 1789.

LANGUAGES AND NATIONS BEFORE 1750

At first sight, the links between language and nation appear to be very old. Indeed, they seem to go back to the Middle Ages. It was said that 'the language makes the people' (*gentem lingua facit*). In the later Middle

---

[1] David A. Bell, *The Cult of the Nation* (Cambridge, MA, 2001), p. 171; cf. Daniel Baggioni, *Langues et nations en Europe* (Paris, 1997), and Anne-Marie Thiesse, *La création des identités nationales: Europe xviii–xx siècle* (Paris, 1999), esp. pp. 67–82.

Ages, the same word was often used to refer both to language and to the people who spoke it: *lingua* in Latin, *langue* in French, *Zung* in German, *jazyk* in Czech. The recurrent statements that rulers were planning the destruction of subordinate 'languages' (quoted above, p. 16) may express fears of genocide.[2]

The Latin word *natio* was in use in the Middle Ages, meaning much the same as *gens* or *populus*, in other words, 'people'.[3] On occasion, it was employed in what seems at first sight to be a modern way. Take the case of the Council of Constance, for example, a council of the Church held between 1414 and 1418. At the Council, an Englishman argued that languages are 'the greatest and most authentic mark of a nation' (*maximam et verissimam probant nationem et ipsius essentiam*). He sounds about four hundred years ahead of his time, but his argument needs to be replaced in its context. The point was that voting in the Council was not by individuals but by nations (French, German, Italian, Spanish and English). These were not nations in the modern sense, for the so-called 'German' nation included the Hungarians, Czechs, Poles, Danes and Swedes. When the French denied the English claim to be a separate nation, the point about language was made in its support. It did not refer to the use of English alone, but to the five languages spoken in the realm, which made the English as worthy as the Germans to be classified as a nation.[4]

All the same, the association between a people and its language expressed by the term *lingua* is a revealing one. In the later Middle Ages, as some vernaculars entered the domains of literature and administration, language was becoming a source of pride, identity and consequently of conflict. If a people that had previously been independent became part of an empire, it might be allowed to retain its official language. Hence, in 1527, Ferdinand of Austria promised those Hungarians who lived in the Habsburg Empire – the rest were now under the rule of the Turks – that he would preserve 'your nation and language' (*nationem et linguam vestrum*).[5]

On the other side, as we have seen, rulers and their advisers might view a uniform language, at least a uniform administrative language, as a valuable

[2] Robert Bartlett, *The Making of Europe* (1993: second ed., Harmondsworth, 1994), pp. 198–203; cf. Rees R. Davies, 'The Peoples of Britain and Ireland 1100–1400: Language and Historical Mythology', *Transactions of the Royal Historical Society* 7 (1997), pp. 1–24, at p. 2.

[3] Johan Huizinga, 'Patriotism and Nationalism in European History' (1940; English translation in *Men and Ideas*, New York, 1959), pp. 97–155, at pp. 106–7.

[4] Louise R. Loomis, 'Nationality at the Council of Constance', *American Historical Review* 44 (1940), pp. 508–27.

[5] Quoted in Leon Dominian, *The Frontiers of Language and Nationality in Europe* (New York, 1917), p. 154.

support for the state, an encouragement to loyalty. In the words of Irenius, a character in a dialogue by Edmund Spenser – who was engaged at the time in imposing English rule in Ireland – 'the speech being Irish the heart must needs be Irish, for out of the abundance of the heart the tongue speaketh'.[6] 'Speak that I may see thee'.

In the early seventeenth century, the traveller Fynes Moryson expressed the view that 'all nations have thought nothing more powerful to unite minds than the community of language'. As in the case of the Council of Constance, Moryson's observation looks extremely modern. Once again, this apparent modernity is an illusion. The reference is almost certainly to language as a bond of realms or empires, rather than of nations in our sense of the term.[7]

THE CASE OF SKÅNE

Another case of apparent modernity, practical rather than theoretical this time, comes from Sweden. It concerns the policy of the Swedish government in the later seventeenth century, when several provinces which had formerly been Danish, notably Scania or Skåne, were incorporated into Sweden. The island of Gotland became Swedish in 1645, and Skåne in 1658. At first, cultural traditions were not disrupted. The Danish bishop of Lund remained in office, apparently feeling that the change, however unwelcome, was tolerable because the new ruler, like his predecessor, was a Lutheran. For twenty years, Danish remained the language of the churches and the schools.[8] However, the so-called 'Ljungby rescript' of 1678 issued by King Karl XI ordered that the language of the liturgy in Skåne be changed to Swedish, while schoolchildren would henceforth learn to read from Swedish Bibles and psalm-books.[9]

What was the significance of this change of mind on the part of the government? In the 1690s, the new policy was applied by a governor-general

[6] Edmund Spenser, *A View of the Present State of Ireland*, ed. William L. Renwick (Oxford, 1970), p. 67.
[7] Quoted in Blank, *Broken English*, p. 126.
[8] Skautrup, *Danske sprogs*, vol. II, pp. 293–7; Stig Ohlsson, *Skånes språkliga försvenskning* (Lund, 1978); Lars S. Vikør, 'Northern Europe: Languages as Prime Markers of Ethnic and National Identity', in Stephen Barbour and Cathy Carmichael (eds.), *Language and Nationalism in Europe* (Oxford, 2000), pp. 105–29; Hanne Sanders, 'Religiøst eller nationalt verdensbillede? Skåne efter overgangen til Sverige i 1658', in Sanders (ed.), *Mellem Gud og Djaevalen: Religiøse og magiske verdensbillede i Norden 1500–1800* (Copenhagen, 2001), pp. 231–52.
[9] Harald Gustafsson, 'Att göra svenskar av danskar? Den svenska integrationspolitikens föreställningsvärld 1658–93', in his *Da Østdanmark blev Sydsverige* (forthcoming). I should like to thank Prof. Gustafsson for sending me his chapter before publication. Cf. Jens Lerbom, *Mellan två riken: Integration, Politisk kultur och förnationella identiteter på Gotland 1500–1700* (Lund, 2003), pp. 130, 235.

who saw himself as 'civilizing' the people of Skåne by making them Swedish. All the same, it is likely that the government's intentions were more pragmatic. Political rather than cultural integration was the aim, following the old principle, quoted more than once in this study, that conquered peoples should adopt the language of their conquerors (above, pp. 22, 82).[10] As a French official declared in 1744, 'it is inappropriate to use a foreign language in preference to that of the prince under whose domination one finds oneself' (*il est indecent que l'on s'applique plutôt à une langue étrangère qu'à celle du prince sous la domination duquel on se trouve*).[11]

In the case of Skåne, the government was for once concerned with the language of the people and not only with the language of administration. In similar fashion, the French government was concerned to spread French in Roussillon (at the expense of Catalan) and Alsace (at the expense of German) when these provinces became French in the later seventeenth century. All the same, these policies – rare instances of a conscious language policy from the period before 1789 – were not examples of nationalism in the modern sense. A number of scholars working on different parts of Europe have made this point in the last few years, using a variety of substitutes for the N-word: 'proto-nationalism', for instance, 'linguistic nationalism', or 'regnalism'. My own preference is for 'statism', suggesting that a strong state, rather than a unified nation, was the aim of rulers and their advisers.

During the old regime, according to the French historian Lucien Febvre, 'the concepts of language and nationality were not linked at all'.[12] This statement, like many of Febvre's, is a little too strong. However, it is safe to say that before the year 1750 or thereabouts, the connections between languages and states were closer than those between languages and nations.

THE LATER EIGHTEENTH CENTURY

From the middle of the eighteenth century onwards, the links between language and nation become increasingly close and we find more and more examples of the idea that 'one language' should join the traditional trinity of 'one king, one faith, one law' (*une roi, une foi, une loi*). In 1768, King Carlos III of Spain decreed that there should be one language and one currency in his kingdom. In this respect, the history of European languages confirms the suggestion of the German historian Reinhart Koselleck that

---

[10] Gustafsson, 'Svenskar'.

[11] Argenson quoted in Ignasi Iglésias, *La llengua del Rosselló, 1659–1789* (Vic, 1998), p. 9.

[12] Lucien Febvre, 'Politique royale ou civilisation française? Remarques sur un problème d'histoire linguistique', *Revue de Synthèse Historique* 38 (1924), pp. 37–53, at p. 31.

in the history of European ideas, the late eighteenth century was a turning-point or *Sattelzeit*.[13] We might even speak of a second 'discovery of language', focused this time not on variety, as in the sixteenth and seventeenth centuries, but on unity, and linked to the discovery, or, as some scholars prefer to say, the 'invention' of the nation.[14]

Johann Gottfried Herder's description of a nation as a community held together by language, especially a spoken language, has become famous, like his argument that dominant nations have ruled not so much by the sword as by 'the use of a more cultivated language'.[15] Johann Gottlieb Fichte went further in his equally famous assertion that 'Wherever a separate language can be found, there is also a separate nation which has the right to manage its affairs and rule itself', while Friedrich Schlegel declared that 'a nation which allows herself to be deprived of her language . . . ceases to exist'. Napoleon spoke in the same vein when he told the Hungarians that 'you have a national language . . . take up then once again your existence as a nation'.[16]

In France, Antoine Rivarol's discussion of the genius of a specific language reformulated the humanist discourse on empire and language (above, p. 20) to declare that 'languages are like nations', rising and falling with them.[17] It was in this context that intellectuals discussed the teaching of the vernacular in French schools.[18]

In Italy, Melchiorre Cesarotti declared that 'the language belongs to the nation' (*La lingua appartiene alla nazione*), while Gianfrancesco Galeani Napione claimed that 'Language is one of the strongest ties binding us to our native country' (*La lingua è uno dei più forti vincoli che stringe alla patria*). In the case of the Italian peninsula, however, the term *patria* was still ambiguous. Ferdinando Galiani claimed to have written his essay on the Neapolitan dialect out of what he called 'our love of the fatherland' (*nostro amore alla patria*). He was referring to Naples, not to Italy.[19]

[13] Reinhart Koselleck, *Futures Past* (1979: English translation, Cambridge, MA, 1985).
[14] Hervé Le Bras and Emmanuel Todd, *L'invention de la France* (Paris, 1981); Murray G. H. Pittock, *The Invention of Scotland* (London, 1991); Inman Fox, *La invención de España* (Madrid, 1997).
[15] Johann Gottfried Herder, 'Abhandlung über den Ursprung der Sprache', in *Sämtliche Werke*, ed. Bernard Suphan (Hildesheim, 1877–1913); Michael Townson, *Mother-Tongue and Fatherland* (Manchester, 1992), pp. 80–102.
[16] Napoleon quoted in Joshua Fishman, *Language in Sociocultural Change* (New York, 1972), p. 9.
[17] Antoine Rivarol, *De l'universalité de la langue française* (1784: ed. T. Suran, Paris, 1930), p. 255.
[18] Louis Trenard, 'L'enseignement de la langue nationale: une réforme pédagogique, 1750–1790', *Réflexions Historiques* 7 (1990), pp. 95–114.
[19] Cesarotti, *Saggio sopra la lingua italiana*, pp. 304–468, at p. 314; Gianfrancesco Galeani Napione, *Dell'uso e dei pregi della lingua italiana* (Turin, 1791); Ferdinando Galiani, *Del dialetto napoletano* (Naples, 1779).

In linguistic practice as well as in theory, the later eighteenth century appears to have been a turning-point. In Denmark, for instance, it seems that the link between language and national consciousness was forged around the year 1770 in the course of a reaction against a regime in which a German, Count Struensee, had exercised power. Before this time, the coexistence of German and Danish appears to have been politically 'unproblematic'.[20]

In the course of the French Revolution, the 'politics of language' came to the fore, especially in 1793, when fear of counter-revolution was widespread.[21] Bertrand Barère, a member of the Committee for Public Safety, called for a revolution in language, in order to combat 'federalism and superstition' in Brittany and Languedoc, while Henri Grégoire, a priest who had rallied to the Revolution, was commissioned by the government to investigate the state of the French language. In his report, presented to the National Convention in 1794, Grégoire declared the need to destroy *patois* and 'universalize' the use of French, precisely in order 'to melt the citizens into a national mass' (above, p. 10). This vivid example of the revolutionaries' concern with unanimity was also an early instance of language planning, furnishing a model that many governments would follow in the nineteenth century.[22]

There was a similar trend in the New World. In the United States, ten years after the outbreak of the American Revolution, the dictionary-maker Noah Webster wrote that 'a national language is a national tie, and what country wants it more than America?'[23] In Peru, after the defeat of the revolt of Thupa Amaru, the chair in Quechua, founded at the University of Lima in the sixteenth century, was abolished, while the governor of Arequipa

---

[20] Vibeke Winge, *Dänische Deutsche – deutsche Dänen. Geschichte der deutschen Sprache in Dänemark 1300–1800* (Heidelberg, 1992), pp. 9, 312–4.

[21] 'Une politique de la langue' is the title of chapter 2 of Ferdinand Brunot's *Histoire de la langue française*, vol. IX (Paris, 1927), as well as of the book by Certeau cited in the following note.

[22] Michel de Certeau, Jacques Revel and Dominique Julia, *Une politique de la langue* (Paris, 1975); Jean-Yves Lartichaux, 'Linguistic Politics during the French Revolution', *Diogenes* 97 (1977), pp. 65–84; Patrice Higonnet, 'The Politics of Linguistic Terrorism', *Social History* 5 (1980), pp. 41–69; Martyn Lyons, 'Politics and Patois: the Linguistic Policy of the French Revolution', *Australian Journal of French Studies* (1981), pp. 264–81; Lorenzo Renzi, *La politica linguistica della rivoluzione francese* (Naples, 1981); Lynn Hunt, *Politics, Culture and Class in the French Revolution* (Berkeley, 1984), pp. 19–51; Henri Boyer and Philippe Gardy (eds.), *La question linguistique au sud au moment de la Révolution Française* (Montpellier, 1985) [special issue, no. 17, of *Lengas*]; Peter Flaherty, 'The Politics of Linguistic Uniformity during the French Revolution', *Historical Reflections* 14 (1987), pp. 311–28; David A. Bell, '*Lingua Populi, Lingua Dei*: Language, Religion and the Origins of French Revolutionary Nationalism', *American Historical Review* 100 (1995), pp. 1403–37.

[23] Allen W. Read, 'American Projects for an Academy to Regulate Speech', *Publications of the Modern Language Association* 51 (1936), pp. 1141–79, at p. 1146.

advocated the extirpation of indigenous languages, which he viewed as an obstacle to centralization.[24] In the Portugal of the Marquis of Pombal, a decree of 1757 made Portuguese the official language of Brazil and ordered the Indians to be taught it. There were also attempts to extirpate indigenous languages at this time.[25]

IMAGINED COMMUNITIES

The intense discussions of the culture of nationalism that have taken place in the last generation help us to place the nationalization of language in a wider context. After 1789, we see the increasing importance of the centralized state, of the national army, of universal education, and of new media of communication, especially the railway and the newspaper, followed by the radio, the cinema and the television.

Taken together, these institutions encouraged the creation of what Benedict Anderson has called the 'imagined communities' of the nations. Anderson sees national languages, spread by what he calls 'print-capitalism', as central to this process of imagining. He has been criticized for 'Whorfianism', that is for assuming, like the linguist Benjamin Whorf, that thought is determined by language, and also for failing to note that 'homogeneous language is as much imagined as is community'. A moderate or qualified version of Anderson's argument is proof against the first objection, while the problem of homogeneity will be addressed below.[26]

National armies raised by conscription, from the French revolutionary *levée en masse* onwards, contributed to the process of standardizing of national languages just as international armies of mercenaries had contributed to the process of language mixing during the Thirty Years' War. The new armies brought together in the barracks recruits from different regions. The standard vernacular was used for orders and perhaps as a lingua franca as well.

Grégoire had dreamed of a primary school in each French commune. Universal compulsory elementary education was introduced into a number

[24] Bruce Mannheim, *The Language of the Inka since the European Invasion* (Austin, 1991), pp. 74–5.
[25] David Brading, *The First Americans* (Cambridge, 1991), pp. 491–4.
[26] Benedict Anderson, *Imagined Communities: Reflections on the Origin and Spread of Nationalism* (1983: second ed., London, 1991). For criticisms, see Judith Irvine and Susan Gal, 'Language Ideology and Linguistic Differentiation' and Michael Silverstein, 'Whorfianism and the Linguistic Imagination of Nationality', in Paul V. Kroskrity (ed.), *Regimes of Language: ideologies, polities and identities* (Santa Fe and Oxford, 2000), pp. 35–84 and 85–138. Cf. Ernest Gellner, *Nations and Nationalism* (London, 1983) and Eric Hobsbawm, *Nations and Nationalism since 1780: Progress, Myth, Reality* (Cambridge, 1990).

of European countries in the course of the nineteenth century. Unlike the Latinophone colleges for elites in the early modern period, the language of the classroom was the vernacular. Thanks to the schools, the majority of the population in many parts of Europe became literate for the first time, although the literacy rate was still only about 25 per cent in Italy and Spain in 1850, and 10 per cent or less in the Russian Empire – there was no compulsory primary education before the Bolshevik Revolution.[27]

Elementary schools also furthered attempts to extend official linguistic standards ('the King's English', and its equivalents) to everyone. The school curriculum often included the study of the national literature, Shakespeare, Racine, Goethe, Manzoni and so on. In short, the schools encouraged national languages and national communities at the expense of local languages and local communities.

Railways encouraged the unification of national languages by making internal migration easier, and they also delivered the metropolitan newspapers to the provinces. National newspapers presented the news in the same form of language to all readers within the national borders. Radio and television brought the standard language, 'BBC English', for example, to a still wider audience. Gradually, the majority of French people came – for the first time – to speak French, the Germans German and the Italians Italian.

An exemplary study of the history of Italian after the country was politically united in 1860 gives due weight to all the factors mentioned above. Beginning from the estimate that in 1860, less than 3 per cent of the population used Italian for everyday purposes, Tullio De Mauro discusses the role of the school, the army, the media of communication and, not least, the part played in the unification of the language by the new capital city, Rome, and by its bureaucracy, recruited as it was from different parts of the peninsula and thus unable to communicate in anything but the standard language.[28]

As in the case of the so-called 'rise of the vernaculars', however, the temptations of Whig or triumphalist history must be avoided. Once again, an emphasis on competition is in order. The simple model of 'one nation, one language' did not fit many parts of Europe. What looked from the centre like unification was viewed from the periphery as cultural invasion, an attack on alternative languages such as Czech, Occitan, Flemish or Welsh.

Languages became symbols of political autonomy and weapons in political conflicts, even in schools. In Brittany in the nineteenth and early

---

[27] Carlo Cipolla, *Literacy and Development in the West* (Harmondsworth, 1969), p. 115; Jeffrey Brooks, *When Russia Learned To Read* (Princeton, 1985).

[28] De Mauro, *Storia linguistica*.

twentieth centuries, children were punished if they did not speak French in the playground, just as boys in earlier centuries had been punished for not speaking Latin. In Finland, the journalist-poet Adolf Arwidsson urged the use of Finnish in schools in order to make Finland a 'united whole', but for ethnic Swedes, Finnish was a foreign language.[29]

The linguistic diversity of the Habsburg Empire became a liability, since speakers of its different languages demanded first linguistic autonomy and then political autonomy as well. The early nineteenth century was a crucial period in the standardization of a number of these languages, thanks to the efforts of scholars and writers such as Jernej Kopitar for Slovene, Ján Kollár and L'udovít Štúr for Slovak, Vuk Stefanović Karadžić and Milovan Vidaković for Serbian and Ljudevit Gaj for Croat. Kopitar, for example, wanted to purify Serbian from Russian, while Vidaković was more concerned to eliminate words coming from Turkish, Hungarian and German.[30] In 1850, a formal treaty was signed between Serb and Croat writers (on the neutral ground of Vienna), accepting a common standard of 'Serbo-Croat'.[31]

Despite these attempts at homogenization, varieties of language proved impossible to suppress. In Belgium, we need to speak of 'triglossia' rather than diglossia, a situation of competition and conflict not only between French (the language of administration, the upper classes, and the Walloons) and Flemish (the language of the majority of the population), but also between Flemish and Dutch, a more standardized variety of the same language.[32]

Norway offers another illustration of the competition between varieties of language and also of their politicization. When Norway became independent from Denmark in 1814, the intellectuals tried to make the language independent as well, and there was a movement in favour of *landsmål* (a term which means both the rural and the national language). In the late nineteenth century, there was a reaction against this rural, popular and Western norm in favour of *bokmål* ('book language') or *riksmål* ('state language'), a variety which was at once closer to Danish, to the language of the upper classes and to the speech of eastern Norway. Since that time, ministers and members of parliament have been involved in attempts to

[29] John H. Wuorinen, *Nationalism in Modern Finland* (New York, 1931).
[30] On Kollár, Peter Brock, *The Slovak National Awakening* (Toronto, 1976); on Vuk, Duncan Wilson, *The Life and Times of Vuk Stefanović Karadžić* (Oxford, 1970); cf. Thomas Butler, 'The War for a Serbian Language and Orthography', *Harvard Slavic Studies* 5 (1970), pp. 1–75.
[31] Wilson, *Life*, pp. 312–3.
[32] Roland Willemyns, 'Religious Fundamentalism and Language Planning in Nineteenth-Century Flanders', *IJGLSA* 2 (1997), pp. 281–302; Wim Vandenbussche, 'Triglossia and Pragmatic Variety Choice in Nineteenth-Century Bruges', *Journal of Historical Pragmatics* 3 (2002).

fuse the two forms of Norwegian, now known as *riksmål* and *nynorsk* ('new Norwegian'), but they remain distinct.[33]

Even alphabets became a cause of contention. Despite their linguistic union, Serbs and Croats used two different alphabets. The Serbs, who were Orthodox Christians and looked eastwards to Russia, wrote in Cyrillic, while the Croats, who were Catholics and looked westwards, preferred the Latin alphabet for this very reason. The Romanians changed alphabets in the nineteenth century, abandoning Cyrillic because it symbolized the Orthodox tradition, while the Latin alphabet signified secularism, taking Paris as a cultural model. In Turkey in the 1920s, Kemal Atatürk ordered his people to give up writing in the Arabic script and adopt a slightly modified version of the Latin alphabet, to symbolize the break with the Ottoman past and the rapprochement with the West. In similar fashion, Peter the Great had taken a personal interest in the reform of the Cyrillic alphabet in 1708, because the break with conventions derived from Church Slavonic signified secularism and Westernization.

These and other 'alphabet wars' are reminiscent of what Freud famously called 'the narcissism of minor differences', exaggerating the distance between self and other.[34] The same point might be made about the increasing importance of purism.

NATIONALISM AND PURITY

The nineteenth century was a time of a number of strong movements of linguistic purification, associated with nationalism.[35] As we have seen, purity and standardization had often been discussed in early modern Europe with reference to the language of elites. These debates were now extended to include the language of everyone. What is more, the language of peasants was often taken as a standard. One reason for choosing this standard was that rustic language was freer from contamination by foreign words because peasants met fewer foreigners, a point that had already been made in the sixteenth century (above, p. 23). In the nineteenth century, however, the peasants and their language were often idealized as symbols of national values. The linguists participated in the general 'discovery of the people' and their culture by European folklorists and other intellectuals in the early nineteenth century.[36]

---

[33] Einar Haugen, *Language Conflict and Language Planning* (Cambridge, MA, 1966).

[34] Anton Blok, 'The Narcissism of Minor Differences' (1998: repr. *Honour and Violence*, Cambridge, 2001, pp. 115–31).

[35] Björn Jernudd and Michael Shapiro (eds.), *The Politics of Language Purism* (Berlin, 1989); George Thomas, *Linguistic Purism* (London, 1991).

[36] Peter Burke, *Popular Culture in Early Modern Europe* (1978: revised ed., Aldershot, 1995), chapter 1.

Writers were becoming increasingly uncomfortable with high or formal language and took popular speech as a model instead. William Wordsworth, for instance, declared his intention 'to adapt to the uses of poetry, the ordinary language of conversation among the middling and lower orders of the people'.[37] Achim von Arnim, a Prussian poet, argued that the folksongs he collected 'united their dispersed people' (*sammelte sein zerstreutes Volk*) in a German-speaking area that was divided into a number of states.

In Finland, the language of the 'unspoiled' peasant was the model for a pure national language.[38] In Norway, the supporters of *landsmål* had similar ideals. Again, Vuk Stefanović Karadžić followed the popular usage of Bosnia and Hercegovina in his standardization of Serbian.[39] The campaign for purity also involved the elimination of foreign words.

The movement for Greek independence included attempts to eliminate foreign, especially Turkish, words and thus create a pure language, *katharevousa*. Adamantios Korais, for instance, one of the nationalist leaders, like Henri Estienne in sixteenth-century France (above, p. 147) denounced 'borrowing from strangers . . . words and phrases amply available in one's own language'. These words were to be rooted out. The gaps left by the disappearance of foreign words were to be filled with ancient Greek terms, including compounds. Thus potato, for example, would no longer be *patata* but *gêomêlon*, 'earth-apple' (on the model, ironically enough, of the French *pomme de terre*). In 1830, the new Greek state officially adopted *katharevousa*.[40]

Katharevousa had anti-democratic implications. For this reason, in the late nineteenth century, there was a campaign for a 'people's language', *demotike*, which eventually succeeded. For the same reason, the right-wing government of the colonels (1967–74) brought back *katharevousa*, while in 1976 *demotike* became once again the language of the state and of education.[41]

In Bulgaria, too, some purists wanted to exclude from the language the Turkish words that had entered it while the country had been part of the Ottoman Empire, replacing these words with terms from Church Slavonic or Russian because these Slav languages were more prestigious (other purists attacked the Russian expressions as foreign innovations and defended the

[37] William Wordsworth, *Lyrical Ballads* (London, 1798), preface.
[38] Wuorinen, *Nationalism.*   [39] Wilson, *Karadžić.*
[40] Michael Jeffreys, 'Adamantios Korais: Language and Revolution', in Roland Sussex and J. Christopher Eade (eds.), *Culture and Nationalism in Nineteenth-Century Eastern Europe* (Columbus, Ohio, 1983), pp. 42–55.
[41] Robert Browning, 'Greek Diglossia Yesterday and Today', *International Journal of the Sociology of Language* 35 (1982), pp. 49–68; Kostas Kazazis, 'Dismantling Modern Greek Diglossia: the Aftermath', *Lingua e Stile* 36 (2001), pp. 291–8.

Turkish ones as traditional).[42] As for the Turks, they were also concerned with purifying their language, particularly after the Ottoman Empire had been replaced after the First World War by a nation-state, and the Turkish Language Association (*Türk Dil Kurumu*) did its best to eliminate Arabic and Persian words.[43]

In Germany, the preoccupation with linguistic purity was an old one, as we have seen (above, p. 150). The career of Joachim Campe suggests that this concern was being taken more seriously, or taken seriously by more people, at the end of the eighteenth century.[44] Throughout the nineteenth century, there were regular attempts to purify the language from foreign words. In 1885, the movement took institutional form with the foundation of the German Language Association (*Allgemein Deutsche Sprachverein*), with its journal *Muttersprache*.[45] The association was particularly concerned with the invasion of French and English words. The 1930s were the high point of the so-called *Fremdwortjagd*, the hunt for and replacement of foreign terms which had concealed themselves in the German language. Thus, *Perron*, 'platform', became *Bahnsteig*; *Universität* turned into *Althochschule*, and so on. This programme fitted in quite well with Nazi ideals of *Deutschtum* and cultural purification. The Nazis supported the *Sprachverein* at first, although they ended the hunt in 1940 after a linguist had been rash enough to criticize the language of the *Führer*.[46]

In England, too, there was a similar movement, even if its scale was comparatively small. Take the case of William Barnes, for instance.[47] Barnes was a Dorset dialect poet, a contemporary and a friend of Thomas Hardy, an enthusiast for Anglo-Saxon and for English as a 'Teutonic tongue', free from what Barnes described as 'Latin and Greek mingled-speech'. Barnes's book on rhetoric (which, in order to avoid a word of French origin, he called 'speechcraft') was an essay (which he called a 'trial') in support (which he called 'upholding') of 'our fine old Anglo-Saxon tongue'.[48]

---

[42] Giuseppe Dell'Agata, 'The Bulgarian Language Question from the Sixteenth to the Nineteenth Century', in Picchio and Goldblatt, *Aspects*, vol. 1, pp. 157–88.

[43] Uriel Heyd, *Language Reform in Modern Turkey* (Jerusalem, 1954); Kemal H. Karpat, 'A Language in Search of a Nation: Turkish in the Nation-State', in Scaglione, *Emergence*, pp. 175–208, at p. 200.

[44] Jürgen Schiewe, *Sprachpurismus und Emanzipation: J. H. Campes Verdeutschungsprogramm* (Hildesheim, 1988).

[45] Townson, *Mother-Tongue*, pp. 98–107.

[46] Peter von Polenz, 'Sprachpurismus und Nationalsozialismus', in Eberhard Lämmert (ed.), *Germanistik* (Frankfurt, 1967), pp. 113–65; Alan Kirkness, *Zur Sprachreinigung in Deutschen: eine historische Dokumentation 1789–1871* (Tübingen, 1975); Kirkness, 'Das Phänomen des Purismus in der Geschichte des Deutschen', in Werner Besch et al. (eds.), *Sprachgeschichte* (Berlin, 1984), pp. 290–9.

[47] Willis D. Jacobs, *William Barnes, Linguist* (Albuquerque, 1952).

[48] William Barnes, *Outline of English Speechcraft* (London, 1878).

Since the term 'purist' has a Latin origin, it seems more appropriate to describe Barnes as a 'cleanser' of the English tongue, along the lines of John Cheke and Ralph Lever (above, p. 149). According to Barnes, there was no need to borrow: English vocabulary (or as he called it, 'word-stock') could be increased by creating compounds, such as 'speech-craft' or 'word-stock' itself. Barnes was a populist, or, as he would have said, 'folkish'. He was not, it should be added, a proto-fascist. On the contrary, one of the reasons for his opposition to Latinized English was that it was undemocratic, because it was difficult for ordinary people to understand.

Barnes was relatively isolated (not to say eccentric) in his time, although a Society for Pure English was founded in 1913 with the poet Robert Bridges as its president. The purity movement was, and indeed still is, taken more seriously in other countries, among them France. The concern with the purity of language, relatively muted in the nineteenth and early twentieth centuries, became more acute in France after the Second World War. It should perhaps be interpreted as a reaction to and against the linguistic aspect of what the French used to call *le défi américain*.

In 1964, the intellectual René Etiemble launched his attack, in the book *Parlez-vous franglais?* General de Gaulle found time between the Algerian crisis and the events of 1968 to set up a committee for defence of the French language. The Bas-Lauriol law (1975) and the Toubon law (1994) prohibited the use of a foreign word by government departments, 'le shuttle', for instance, when an approved native word (in this case, *la navette*) already conveyed the meaning, while a *délégation générale à la langue française* still meets to coin more terms of this kind. The issue remains a live one in France.[49]

The current 'language question' illustrates both the continuities between the periods separated by the events of 1789 and some of the contrasts as well. The preoccupation with linguistic purity has a long history, as we have seen. What is distinctively modern is the attempt to legislate for languages, the direct intervention of the government in a domain that was once regulated, if at all, by academies of scholars and writers. It was at this time, in the nineteenth century, that scholars and writers turned to writing histories of the organic growth of their national languages. This is precisely the kind of national, or even nationalist, history that this book – together with other studies in the social history of language, with their stress on multiple communities and identities – has been trying to undermine.

---

[49] Philip Thody, *Franglais: Forbidden English, Forbidden American* (London, 1995).

Languages in Europe 1450–1789

'Cf.' signals the problem of deciding whether a given variety of language should be classified – for the period 1450–1789 – as a language or a dialect.

1. Albanian
2. Arabic (spoken in early modern Spain)
3. Aragonese (cf. Catalan)
4. Basque
5. Belorussian (cf. Ruthenian)
6. Breton
7. Bulgarian
8. Catalan
9. Church Slavonic
10. Cornish
11. Croat (cf. Serbian)
12. Curonian
13. Czech (cf. Slovak)
14. Dalmatian (a romance language, not a dialect of Croat)
15. Danish
16. Dutch
17. English
18. Estonian
19. Faroese (cf. Danish)
20. Finnish
21. Flemish (cf. Dutch)
22. French
23. Frisian
24. Galician (cf. Portuguese)
25. Gascon (cf. Occitan)
26. German

27. Gothic
28. Greek (demotic)
29. Hebrew
30. Hungarian
31. Icelandic
32. Irish
33. Italian
34. Karelian (cf. Finnish)
35. Kashubian (cf. Polish)
36. Ladino (cf. Spanish)
37. Lallans (cf. English)
38. Latin
39. Latvian
40. Lithuanian
41. Livonian
42. Luxembourgian (cf. German)
43. Macedonian (cf. Croat)
44. Maltese
45. Manx
46. Moldavian (cf. Romanian)
47. Norwegian (cf. Danish)
48. Occitan
49. Polabian
50. Polish
51. Portuguese
52. Provençal (cf. Occitan)
53. Romanian
54. Romansh
55. Romany
56. Russian
57. Ruthenian (cf. Belorusian, Ukrainian)
58. Sami
59. Sardinian
60. Scottish Gaelic
61. Serbian (cf. Croat)
62. Slovak (cf. Czech)
63. Slovene
64. Sorbian (Upper and Lower, cf. Czech)
65. Spanish

66. Swedish
67. Turkish
68. Ukrainian (cf. Ruthenian)
69. Vlach
70. Welsh
71. Yiddish

Bibliography

This list is confined to works cited in the notes.

Aarsleff, Hans, *The Study of Language in England, 1780–1860* (Princeton, 1967).
Aarsleff, Hans, 'The Rise and Decline of Adam and his *Ursprache* in Seventeenth-Century Thought', in Allison P. Coudert (ed.), *The Language of Adam* (Wiesbaden, 1999), pp. 277–95.
Aehle, Wilhelm, *Die Anfänge des Unterrichts in der englischen Sprache, besonders auf den Ritterakademien* (Hamburg, 1938).
Ahnlund, Nils, *Svenskt och Nordiskt* (Stockholm, 1943).
Aldrete, Bernardo de, *Del origen, y principio de la lengua castellana*, (1604: facsimile ed., Madrid, 1972).
Alonso, Amado, *Castellano, español, idioma nacional: historia spiritual de tres nombres* (Buenos Aires, 1938).
Amelang, James, *Honoured Citizens of Barcelona* (Princeton, 1986).
Anchieta, José de, *Lírica portuguesa e tupí*, ed. Armando Cardoso (São Paulo, 1984).
Anderson, Benedict, *Imagined Communities: Reflections on the Origin and Spread of Nationalism* (1983: revised ed., London, 1991).
Aretino, Pietro, *Sei Giornate*, ed. Giovanni Aquilecchia (Bari, 1975).
Armstrong, Charles A. J., 'The Language Question in the Low Countries', in John R. Hale, Roger Highfield and Beryl Smalley (eds.), *Europe in the Late Middle Ages* (London, 1965), pp. 386–409.
Arndt, Erwin and Brandt, G., *Luther und die deutsche Sprache* (Leipzig, 1983).
Auerbach, Erich, 'La cour et la ville' (1951: English translation in his *Scenes from the Drama of European Literature*, New York, 1959), pp. 133–79.
Auerbach, Erich, *Literary Language and its Public* (1958: English translation, London, 1965).
Auroux, Sylvain, *Histoire des idées linguistiques*, 2 vols (Liège, 1989–92).
Auty, Robert, 'The Role of Purism in the Development of the Slavonic Literary Languages', *Slavic and East European Review* 51 (1973), pp. 335–43.
Auty, Robert, 'Czech', in Schenker and Stankiewicz, *Slavic Literary Languages*, pp. 163–82.
Axtell, James, 'Babel of Tongues: Communicating with the Indians in Eastern North America', in Gray and Fiering, *Language Encounter*, pp. 15–60.

Christmann, Hans Helmut, 'Italienische Sprache in Deutschland', in Schröder, *Fremdsprachenunterricht*, pp. 43–56.

Churchill, Awnsley and John (eds.), *A Collection of Voyages*, 6 vols. (London, 1732).

Cifoletti, Guido, *La lingua franca mediterranea* (Padua, 1989).

Cipolla, Carlo, *Literacy and Development in the West* (Harmondsworth, 1969).

Cipolla, Carlo, *Fighting the Plague in Seventeenth-Century Italy* (Madison, 1981).

Cittadini, Celso, *Formazione della lingua Toscana* (Florence, 1600).

Coates, William A., 'The German Pidgin-Italian of the Sixteenth-Century *Lanzichenecchi*', *Papers from the Fourth Annual Kansas Linguistics Conference* (1969), pp. 66–74.

Cole, Richard, 'Reformation Printers: Unsung Heroes', *Sixteenth-Century Journal* 15 (1984), pp. 327–39.

Cole, William, *The Blecheley Diary* (London, 1931).

Coletti, Vittorio, *Parole del pulpito: chiesa e movimenti religiosi tra latino e volgare* (Casale, 1983).

Colie, Rosalie L., *Some Thankfulness to Constantine: a Study of English Influence upon the Early Works of Constantijn Huygens* (The Hague, 1956).

Collet Sedola, Sabina, 'L'étude de l'espagnol en France à l'époque d'Anne d'Autriche', in Charles Mazouet (ed.), *L'âge d'or de l'influence espagnole: la France et l'Espagne à l'époque d'Anne d'Autriche* (Mont-de-Marsan, 1991).

Colley, Linda, *Britons* (London, 1995).

Cornish, Vaughan, *Borderlands of Language in Europe and their Relation to the Historic Frontiers of Christendom* (London, 1936).

Cortelazzo, Manlio, 'Lingua franca', in Hans Georg Beck, Manoussos Manoussacas and Agostino Pertusi (eds.), *Venezia centro di mediazione tra Oriente e Occidente* (Florence, 1977), pp. 523–35.

Corvisier, André, *Arts et sociétés dans l'Europe du 18e siècle* (Paris, 1978).

Coulton, George G., *Europe's Apprenticeship: a Survey of Medieval Latin with Examples* (London, 1940).

Crane, Susan, 'Social Aspects of Bilingualism in the Thirteenth Century', in Michael Prestwich, R. H. Britnell and Robin Frame (eds.), *Thirteenth-Century England* (Woodbridge, 1989).

Croce, Benedetto, *Uomini e cose della vecchia Italia*, vol. 1 (Bari, 1926).

Croll, Morris W., *Style, Rhetoric and Rhythm* (Princeton, 1966).

Crosby, Alfred W., *The Columbian Exchange: Biological and Cultural Consequences of 1492* (Newport, CT, 1972).

Crouzet, Denis, *Les guerriers de Dieu*, 2 vols. (Paris, 1990).

Crystal, David, *Language Death* (Cambridge, 2000).

Cuervo, Rufino J., 'El Castellano en América', *Bulletin Hispanique* 3 (1901), pp. 35–62.

Curtis, Mark H., *Oxford and Cambridge in Transition, 1558–1642* (Oxford, 1959).

Curto, Diogo Ramada, 'A língua e o império', in Francisco Bethencourt and Kirti N. Chaudhuri (eds.), *História da expansão portuguesa*, vol. 1 (Lisbon, 1998), pp. 414–33.

D' Agostino, Mari, *La Piazza e l'altare: momenti della politica linguistica della chiesa siciliana* (Palermo, 1988).

Danckert, Werner, *Unehrlich Leute* (Munich, 1963).

Dardi, Andrea, *Dalla provincia all'Europa: l'influsso del francese sull'italiano tra il 1650 e il 1715* (Florence, 1992).

Daube, Anna, *Der Aufstieg der Muttersprache im deutschen Denken des 15 und 16 Jahrhunderts* (Frankfurt, 1949).

Davies, Norman, *God's Playground: a History of Poland*, vol. 1 (Oxford, 1981).

Davies, Rees R., 'The Peoples of Britain and Ireland 1100–1400: Language and Historical Mythology', *Transactions of the Royal Historical Society* 7 (1997), pp. 1–24.

Davis, Natalie Z., *Society and Culture in Early Modern France* (Stanford, 1975).

Defoe, Daniel, *An Essay upon Projects* (1697: repr., Menston, 1969).

Delepierre, Octave, *Macaronéana*, 2 vols. (London, 1862–3).

Dell'Agata, Giuseppe, 'The Bulgarian Language Question from the Sixteenth to the Nineteenth Century', in Picchio and Goldblatt, *Aspects*, vol. 1, pp. 157–88.

De Mauro, Tullio, *Storia linguistica dell'Italia unita* (1963: revised ed., Rome, 1991).

Demonet, Marie-Lucie, *Les voix du signe. Nature et origine du langage à la Renaissance (1480–1580)* (Paris, 1992).

Derrida, Jacques, *Dissemination* (1972: English translation, Chicago, 1982).

Devyver, André, *Le sang épuré* (Brussels, 1973).

Deyon, Solange, and Alain Lottin, *Les casseurs de l'été 1566* (Paris, 1981).

Diffley, Paul B., *Paolo Beni: a Biographical and Critical Study* (Oxford, 1988).

Dillard, Joey L., *Black English: its History and Use in the United States* (New York, 1972).

Dillard, Joey L., *Toward a Social History of American English* (Berlin, 1985).

Dimnik, Martin, 'Gutenberg, Humanism, the Reformation and the Emergence of the Slovene Literary Language 1550–1584', *Canadian Slavonic Papers* 26 (1984), pp. 141–59.

Dimnik, Martin, 'Primoz Trubar and the Mission to the South Slavs (1555–64)', *Slavonic and East European Review* 66 (1988), pp. 380–99.

Dionisotti, Carlo, 'Introduzione' to Pietro Bembo, *Prose e rime* (Turin, 1960), pp. 9–56.

Dionisotti, Carlo, *Gli umanisti e il volgare fra quattro- e cinquecento* (Florence, 1968).

Dolet, Etienne, *La manière de bien traduire* (1540: repr. Paris, 1830).

Dominian, Leon, *The Frontiers of Language and Nationality in Europe* (New York, 1917).

Douglas, Mary, *Purity and Danger* (London, 1966).

Droixhe, Daniel, *La linguistique et l'appel de l'histoire* (1600–1800) (Geneva and Paris, 1978).

Droixhe, Daniel, 'Leibniz et le finno-ougrien', in Tullio De Mauro and Lia Formigari (eds.), *Leibniz, Humboldt and the Origins of Comparativism* (Amsterdam and Philadelphia, 1990), pp. 3–29.

Du Bellay, Joachim, *Deffense et illustration de la langue françoyse* (1549: ed. Jean-Charles Monferras, Geneva, 2001).

Dubois, Claude Gilbert, *Mythe et langage au 16e siècle* (Bordeaux, 1970).

Dupleix, Scipion, *Liberté de la langue françoise en sa pureté* (1651: repr. Geneva, 1973).

Durkacz, Victor, *The Decline of the Celtic Languages* (Edinburgh, 1983).

Eco, Umberto, *The Search for the Perfect Language* (1993: English translation, Oxford, 1995).

Egenolff, Johan Augustin, *Historie der Teutschen Sprache*, 2 vols. (Leipzig, 1716–20).

Eisenstein, Elizabeth, *The Printing Press as an Agent of Change*, 2 vols. (Cambridge, 1979).

Elias, Norbert, *The Civilizing Process* (1939: English translation, 2 vols., Oxford, 1981–2).

Elwert, W. Theodor, *Studi di letteratura veneziana* (Venice–Rome, 1958).

Elwert, W. Theodor, *Aufsätze zur italienischen Lyrik* (Wiesbaden, 1967).

Erasmus, 'On Pronunciation' (1528: English translation in *Collected Works* 26, Toronto, 1985), pp. 347–475.

Erasmus, *Ciceronianus* (1528: English translation in *Collected Works* 28, Toronto, 1986), pp. 323–68.

Errington, J. Joseph, *Language Shift* (Cambridge, 1998).

Esparza Torres, Miguel Angel, *Las ideas linguísticas de Antonio de Nebrija* (Münster, 1995).

Estèbe, Janine, *Tocsin pour un massacre* (Paris, 1968).

Estienne, Henri, *Deux dialogues du nouveau langage françois* (1578: ed. Pauline M. Smith, Geneva, 1980).

Estienne, Henri, *La precellence du langage françois* (1579: ed. Edmond Huguet, Paris, 1896).

Evans, Robert J. W., *The Making of the Habsburg Monarchy, 1550–1700: an Interpretation* (Oxford, 1979).

Evans, Robert J. W., *The Language of History and the History of Language* (Oxford, 1998).

Evelyn, John, *Diary*, ed. Esmond S. De Beer, 6 vols. (Oxford, 1955).

Fabian, Bernhard, 'Englisch als neue Fremdsprache des 18. Jahrhunderts', in Dieter Kimpel (ed.), *Mehrsprachigkeit in der deutschen Aufklärung* (Hamburg, 1985), pp. 178–96.

Fabian, Johannes, *Language and Colonial Power* (Cambridge, 1986).

Fauchet, Claude, *Origine de la langue française* (Paris, 1581).

Faust, Manfred, 'Schottelius' Concept of Word Formation' in Geckeler, *Logos*, pp. 359–70.

Febvre, Lucien, 'Politique royale ou civilisation française? Remarques sur un problème d'histoire linguistique', *Revue de synthèse historique* 38 (1924), pp. 37–53.

Febvre, Lucien, 'Langue et nationalité en France au 18e siècle', *Revue de synthèse historique* 42 (1926), pp. 19–40.

Febvre, Lucien, *The Problem of Unbelief in the Sixteenth Century: the Religion of Rabelais* (1942: English translation, Cambridge, MA, 1982).

Febvre, Lucien, and Henri-Jean Martin, *The Coming of the Book* (1958: English translation, London, 1976).

Ferguson, Charles, 'Diglossia', *Word* 15 (1959), pp. 325–40.

Finkenstaedt, Thomas, 'John Tompson', in Schröder, *Fremdsprachenunterricht*, pp. 57–74.

Fiorelli, Piero, 'Pour l'interprétation de l'ordonnance de Villers-Cotterêts', *Le français moderne* 18 (1950), pp. 277–88.

Firmin-Didot, Ambroise, *Alde Manuce et l'Hellénisme à Venise* (Paris, 1875).

Fish, Stanley, *Is There a Text in This Class? The Authority of Interpretive Communities* (Cambridge, MA, 1980).

Fisher, John H., *The Emergence of Standard English* (Lexington, 1996).

Fishman, Joshua A., *Sociolinguistics* (Rowley, MA, 1970).

Fishman, Joshua A., *Language in Sociocultural Change* (New York, 1972).

Flaherty, Peter, 'The Politics of Linguistic Uniformity during the French Revolution', *Historical Reflections* 14 (1987), pp. 311–28.

Flasdieck, Hermann M., *Der Gedanke einer englischen Sprachakademie* (Jena, 1928).

Flecknoe, Richard, *A Relation of Ten Years' Travels* (London, no date but c. 1650).

Florio, John, *First Fruits* (London, 1578).

Fodor, István, and Claude Hagège (eds.), *Language Reform*, vol. III (Hamburg, 1984).

Folena, Gianfranco, *L'italiano in Europa: Esperienze linguistiche del Settecento* (Turin, 1983).

Folena, Gianfranco, *Il linguaggio del caos: studi sul plurilinguismo rinascimentale* (Turin, 1991).

Fonvisin, Denis I., *Dramatic Works* (Bern, 1974).

Formigari, Lia (ed.), *Teorie e pratiche linguistiche nell'Italia del '700* (Bologna, 1984).

Forster, Leonard W., *The Poet's Tongues: Multilingualism in Literature* (Cambridge, 1970).

Fox, Adam, *Oral and Literate Culture in England, 1500–1700* (Oxford, 2000).

Fox, Inman, *La invención de España* (Madrid, 1997).

François, Alexis, *La grammaire du purisme et l'Académie Française au 18e siècle* (Paris, 1905).

Fraso Gracia, Juan Antonio, *Historia del español de América* (Madrid, 1999).

Freyre, Gilberto, *The Masters and the Slaves* (1933: English translation, New York, 1946).

Fries, Dagmar, *Limpia, fija y da esplendor: la Real Academia Española ante el uso de la lengua* (Madrid, 1989).

Fumaroli, Marc, *L'âge de l'éloquence* (Geneva, 1980).

Fumerton, Patricia, 'Homely Accents: Ben Jonson Speaking Low', in Fumerton and Simon Hunt (eds.), *Renaissance Culture and the Everyday* (Philadelphia, 1999), pp. 92–111.

Furetière, Antoine, *Le roman bourgeois* (1666: repr. in Antoine Adam (ed.), *Romanciers du 17e siècle*, Paris, 1968).

Galbraith, Vivian H., 'Language and Nationality in Medieval England', *Transactions of the Royal Historical Society* 23 (1941), pp. 113–28.

Galeani Napione, Gianfrancesco, *Dell'uso e dei pregi della lingua italiana* (Turin, 1791).

Galiani, Ferdinando, *Del dialetto napoletano* (Naples, 1779).

Garavini, Fausta, and Lucia Lazzerini (eds.), *Macaronee provenzali* (Milan–Naples, 1984).

García, Carlos, *La oposición y conjunction de los dos grandes luminares de la tierra, o la antipatia de franceses y españoles* (1617: ed. Michel Bareau, Edmonton, 1979).

García Carcel, Ricardo, *Historia de Cataluña: siglos xvi–xvii* (Barcelona, 1985).

Gardy, Philippe, *La leçon de Nérac* (Bordeaux, 1999).

Garner, Bryan A., 'Shakespeare's Latinate Neologisms', *Shakespeare Studies* 15 (1982), pp. 149–70.

Geckeler, Horst, et al. (eds.), *Logos Semantikos* (Berlin, 1981).

Gelli, Giambattista, *Capricci del bottaio* (Florence, 1546).

Gellner, Ernest, *Nations and Nationalism* (London, 1983).

Gesner, Conrad, *Mithridates* (Zurich, 1555).

Giesecke, Michael, *Der Buchdruck in der frühen Neuzeit* (Frankfurt, 1991).

Giles, Peter, 'Dialect in Literature', in *The Scottish Tongue* (London, 1924), pp. 91–123.

Gill, Alexander, *Logonomia anglica* (1619: ed. and trans. Bror Danielsson and Arvid Gabrielson, Stockholm, 1972).

Ginzburg, Carlo, *Cheese and Worms* (1976: English translation, London, 1980).

Gneuss, Helmut, 'The Origin of Standard Old English', *Anglo-Saxon England* 1 (1972), pp. 63–83.

Golinski, Jan, 'The Chemical Revolution and the Politics of Language', *Eighteenth Century* 33 (1992), pp. 238–51.

Görlach, Manfred, *Introduction to Early Modern English* (1978: English translation, Cambridge, 1991).

Gray, Edward G., *New World Babel: Languages and Nations in Early America* (Princeton, 1999).

Gray, Edward G., and Norman Fiering (eds.), *The Language Encounter in the Americas, 1492–1800* (New York, 2000).

Grayson, Cecil, *A Renaissance Controversy, Latin or Italian* (Oxford, 1959).

Green, Janet M., 'Queen Elizabeth I's Latin reply to the Polish Ambassador', *Sixteenth-Century Journal* 31 (2000), pp. 987–1006.

Grillo, Ralph, *Dominant Languages: Language and Hierarchy in Britain and France* (Cambridge, 1989).

Groeneboer, Kees, *Gateway to the West: the Dutch Language in Colonial Indonesia, 1600–1950: a History of Language Policy* (1993: English translation, Amsterdam, 1998).

Guiraud, Pierre, *Les mots étrangers* (Paris, 1965).

Guitarte, Guillermo L., 'La dimension imperial del español en la obra de Aldrete', in Antonio Quilis and Hans-Juergen Niederehe (eds.), *The History of Linguistics in Spain* (Amsterdam and Philadelphia, 1986), pp. 129–81.

Gustafsson, Harald, 'Att göra svenskar av danskar? Den svenska integrationspolitikens föreställningsvärld 1658–93', in his *Da Østdanmark blev Sydsverige* (forthcoming).

Gutierrez, Asensio, *La France et les français dans la literature espagnole: un aspect de la xénophobie en Espagne 1598–1665* (St-Etienne, 1977).

Hall, Robert A., Jr, *The Italian Questione della Lingua* (Chapel Hill, 1942).

Hall, Robert A., Jr, 'Thorstein Veblen and Linguistic Theory', *American Speech* 35 (1960), pp. 124–30.

Halleux, Pierre, 'Le purisme islandais', *Etudes Germaniques* 20 (1965), pp. 417–27.

Hammar, Elisabet, *L'enseignement du français en Suède jusqu'en 1807* (Stockholm, 1980).

Hanssens, Giovanni Michele, 'Lingua liturgica', in *Enciclopedia Cattolica* (Vatican City, 1951), vol. VII, columns 1377–82.

Hare, John, *St Edwards Ghost: or, Anti-Normanisme* (London, 1647).

Harris-Northall, Ray, 'Printed Books and Linguistic Standardization in Spain', *Romance Philology* 50 (1996), pp. 123–46.

Haugen, Einar, *Language Conflict and Language Planning* (Cambridge, MA, 1966).

Haugen, Einar, *The Ecology of Language* (Stanford, 1972).

Haugen, Einar, *The Scandinavian Languages: an Introduction to their History* (London, 1976).

Hausmann, Frank-Rutger, *Bibliographie der deutschen Übersetzungen aus dem italienischen bis 1730*, 2 vols. (Tübingen, 1992).

Hay, Denys, *The Church in Italy in the Fifteenth Century* (Cambridge, 1977).

Hazard, Paul, *The European Mind, 1680–1715* (1935: English translation, London, 1953).

Head, Randolph C., 'A Plurilingual Family in the Sixteenth Century', *Sixteenth-Century Journal* 26 (1995), pp. 577–93.

Heath, Shirley, *Telling Tongues: Language Policy in Mexico, Colony to Nation* (New York, 1972).

Heere, Lucas de, *Beschrijving der Britsche Eilanden* (Antwerp, 1937).

Herder, Johann Gottfried, *Sämtliche Werke*, ed. Bernard Suphan, 33 vols. (Hildesheim, 1877–1913).

Herskovits, Melville J., and Frances S. Herskovits, *Suriname Folklore* (New York, 1936).

Hexter, Jack, *Reappraisals in History* (London, 1961).

Heyd, Uriel, *Language Reform in Modern Turkey* (Jerusalem, 1954).

Higonnet, Patrice, 'The Politics of Linguistic Terrorism', *Social History* 5 (1980), pp. 41–69.

Hill, Christopher, *Puritanism and Revolution* (London, 1958).

Hill, Christopher, *Intellectual Origins of the English Revolution* (Oxford, 1965).

Hill, Christopher, *The World Turned Upside Down* (London, 1972).

Hobsbawm, Eric, *Nations and Nationalism since 1780: Progress, Myth, Reality* (Cambridge, 1990).

Hodermann, Richard, *Universitätsvorlesungen in deutscher Sprache um die Wende des 17. Jahrhunderts* (Jena, 1891).

Holberg, Ludvig, *Memoirs*, ed. and trans. Stewart E. Fraser (Leiden, 1970).

Holm, John A., *Pidgins and Creoles*, 2 vols. (Cambridge, 1988).

Holmes, Janet, *Women, Men and Politeness* (London, 1995).

Hope, Thomas E., *Lexical Borrowing in the Romance Languages*, 2 vols. (Oxford, 1971).

Howell, James, *Ecclesiastical Affairs*, vol. III (London, 1685).

Howell, Robert B., 'The Low Countries', in Barbour and Carmichael, *Language and Nationalism*, pp. 130–50.

Huffines, Marion L., 'Sixteenth-Century Printers and the Standardization of New High German', *Journal of English and Germanic Philology* 73 (1974), pp. 60–72.

Huizinga, Johan, *Men and Ideas* (New York, 1959).

Hull, Geoffrey, 'Maltese, from Arabic Dialect to European Language', in Fodor and Hagège, *Language Reform*, vol. VI, pp. 331–46.

Hunt, Lynn, *Politics, Culture and Class in the French Revolution* (Berkeley, 1984).

Hüttl-Worth, Gerta, *Foreign Words in Russian: A Historical Sketch, 1550–1800* (Berkeley, 1963).

Iglésias, Ignasi, *La llengua del Rosselló, 1659–1789* (Vic, 1998).

Ijsewijn, Jozef, 'Neolatin: a Historical Survey', *Helios* 14 no. 2 (1987), pp. 93–107.

Innis, Harold, *The Bias of Communications* (Toronto, 1951).

Irvine, Judith, and Susan Gal, 'Language Ideology and Linguistic Differentiation', in Kroskrity, *Regimes*, pp. 35–84.

Jacobs, Willis D., *William Barnes, Linguist* (Albuquerque, 1952).

Jahr, Ernst H. (ed.), *Language Change: Advances in Historical Sociolinguistics* (Berlin, 1999).

Jeanneret, Michel, *A Feast of Words: Banquets and Table Talk in the Renaissance* (1987: English translation, Cambridge, 1991).

Jeffreys, Michael, 'Adamantios Korais: Language and Revolution', in Roland Sussex and J. Christopher Eade (eds.), *Culture and Nationalism in Nineteenth-Century Eastern Europe* (Columbus, Ohio, 1983), pp. 42–55.

Jenkins, Geraint H. (ed.), *The Welsh Language before the Industrial Revolution* (Cardiff, 1997).

Jernudd, Björn, and Michael Shapiro (eds.), *The Politics of Language Purism* (Berlin, 1989).

Jespersen, Otto, *Growth and Structure of the English Language* (Leipzig, 1905).

Johnson, Samuel, *Plan of a Dictionary* (London, 1747).

Johnson, Samuel, *A Dictionary of the English Language* (London, 1755).

Jones, Colin, 'Plague and its Metaphors in Early Modern France', *Representations* 53 (1996), pp. 97–127.

Jones, R. Brinley, *The Old British Tongue: the Vernacular in Wales, 1540–1640* (Cardiff, 1970).

Jones, Richard F., *Triumph of the English Language* (Stanford, 1953).

Jones, William J., *A Lexicon of French Borrowings in the German Vocabulary 1575–1648* (Berlin, 1976).

Jonson, Ben, *Timber or Discoveries* (1641: ed. Ralph S. Walker, Syracuse, 1953).

Jörder, Otto, *Die Forme des Sonetts bei Lope de Vega* (Halle, 1936).

Joseph, John E., *Eloquence and Power: the Rise of Language Standards and Standard Languages* (Oxford, 1987).

Joseph, John E., and Talbot J. Taylor (eds.), *Ideologies of Language* (London, 1990).

Jouanna, Arlette, *L'idée de race en France, 1498–1614* (Paris, 1976).

Juste, Théodore, *La Révolution des Pays-Bas sous Philippe II* (Paris, 1860–3).

Kajanto, Iiro, 'The Position of Latin in Eighteenth-Century Finland', in Pierre Tuynman et al. (eds.), *Acta Conventus Neo-Latini Amstelodamensis* (Munich, 1979), pp. 93–106.

Karpat, Kemal H., 'A Language in Search of a Nation: Turkish in the Nation-State', in Scaglione, *Emergence*, pp. 175–208.

Kazazis, Kostas, 'Dismantling Modern Greek Diglossia: the Aftermath', *Lingua e Stile* 36 (2001), pp. 291–8.

Kelley, Donald, *Foundations of Modern Historical Thought* (New York, 1970).

Kelly, John N. D., *Jerome: His Life, Writings and Controversies* (London, 1975).

Kettmann, Gerhard, *Die kursächische Kanzleisprache zwischen 1486 und 1546* (Berlin, 1967).

Key, Mary R., *Catherine the Great's Linguistic Contribution* (Carbondale and Edmonton, 1980).

Kiernan, Victor, 'Languages and Conquerors', in Burke and Porter, *Language, Self*, pp. 191–210.

Kirkness, Alan, *Zur Sprachreinigung in Deutschen: eine historische Dokumentation 1789–1871* (Tübingen, 1975).

Kirkness, Alan, 'Das Phänomen des Purismus in der Geschichte des Deutschen', in Besch, *Sprachgeschichte*, pp. 290–9.

Klein, Lawrence E., *Shaftesbury and the Culture of Politeness* (Cambridge, 1994).

Knowlson, James, *Universal Language Schemes in England and France, 1600–1800* (Toronto, 1975).

Koselleck, Reinhart, *Futures Past* (1979: English translation, Cambridge, MA, 1985).

Kristeller, Paul, 'The Origin and Development of the Language of Italian Prose', in his *Renaissance Thought*, vol. II (New York, 1965), pp. 119–41.

Kroskrity, Paul V. (ed.), *Regimes of Language: Ideologies, Polities and Identities* (Santa Fe and Oxford), 2000.

Kullberg, N. A. (ed.), *Svenska Riksrådets Protokoll* (Stockholm, 1878).

Lafont, Robert, *Renaissance du Sud, essai sur la littérature occitane au temps de Henri IV* (Paris, 1970).

Lambley, Kathleen, *The Teaching and Cultivation of the French Language in England during Tudor and Stuart Times* (Manchester and London), 1920.

Langeli, Attilio Bartoli, *La scrittura dell'italiano* (Bologna, 2000).

Langer, August, *Der Wortschatz des deutschen Pietismus* (Tübingen, 1954).

Lartichaux, Jean-Yves, 'Linguistic Politics during the French Revolution', *Diogenes* 97 (1977), pp. 65–84.

Lass, Roger (ed.), *The Cambridge History of the English Language*, vol. III, *1476–1776* (Cambridge, 1999).

Lasso, Orlando di, *Briefe*, ed. Horst Leuchtmann (Wiesbaden, 1977).

Lathuillère, Roger, *La préciosité* (Geneva, 1966).

Laven, Mary, *Virgins of Venice* (2002: second ed., London, 2003).

Lazzerini, Lucia, 'Per latinos grossos: studio sui sermoni mescidati', *Studi di Filologia Italiana* 29 (1971), pp. 219–339.

Lazzerini, Lucia, 'Aux origines du macaronique', *Revue des langues romanes* 86 (1982), pp. 11–33.

Le Bras, Hervé, and Emmanuel Todd, *L'invention de la France* (Paris, 1981).

Lehmann, Paul, 'Mittelalter und Küchenlatein' (1928: repr. in his *Erforschung des Mittelalters*, 5 vols., Leipzig, 1941), vol. I, pp. 46–61.

Leith, David, *A Social History of English* (1983: second ed., London, 1997).

Lentner, Leopold, *Volksprache und Sakralsprache: Geschichte einer Lebensfrage bis zum Ende des Konzil von Trient* (Vienna, 1964).

Leopold I, *Korrespondence*, ed. Zdeněk Kalista (Prague, 1936).

Le Page, Robert, and Andrée Tabouret-Keller, *Acts of Identity* (Cambridge, 1985).

Lerbom, Jens, *Mellan två riken: Integration, Politisk kultur och förnationella identiteter på Gotland 1500–1700* (Lund, 2003).

Le Roy, Louis, *Vicissitudes* (Paris, 1575).

Le Roy Ladurie, Emmanuel, *Les paysans de Languedoc* (Paris, 1966).

Lévy, Paul, *La langue allemande en France*, vol. I, *Des origines à 1830* (Lyon, 1950).

Lewicka, Halina, 'Le mélange des langues dans l'ancien théâtre du Midi de la France', *Mélanges Jean Boutière*, 2 vols. (Liège, 1971), vol. I, pp. 347–59.

Lindberg, Bo, *De lärdes modersmål* (Göteborg, 1984).

Lindberg, Bo, *Europa och Latinet* (Stockholm, 1993).

Llwyd, Edward, *Archaeologia Britannica* (London, 1707).

Loccenius, Johan, *Historiae Suecanae* (Stockholm, 1676).

Lockhart, James, *The Nahua after the Conquest* (Stanford, 1992).

Lockwood, William B., *A Panorama of the Indo-European Languages* (London, 1972).

Loomis, Louise R., 'Nationality at the Council of Constance', *American Historical Review* 44 (1940), pp. 508–27.

Loonen, Petrus L. M., *For to Learne to Buye and Sell: Learning English in the Low Dutch Area between 1500 and 1800* (Amsterdam-Maarssen, 1991).

Lusignan, Serge, *Parler vulgairement: les intellectuels et la langue française aux 13e et 14e siècles* (Montreal and Paris, 1986).

Luther, Martin, *Tisch-Reden*, 5 vols. (Weimar, 1912).

Lyons, Martyn, 'Politics and *Patois*: the Linguistic Policy of the French Revolution', *Australian Journal of French Studies* (1981), pp. 264–81.

McArthur, Tom, *The English Languages* (Cambridge, 1998).

McClure, J. Derrick, 'English in Scotland', *Cambridge History of the English Language*, vol. V (Cambridge, 1994), pp. 23–93.

MacDonald, Robert H. (ed.), *William Drummond: Poems and Prose*, Edinburgh, 1976.

Malkiel, Yakov, 'A Linguist's View of the Standardization of a Dialect', in Scaglione, *Emergence*, pp. 51–73.

Mamcarz, Irena, 'Alcuni aspetti della questione della lingua in Polonia nel '500', in Riccardo Picchio (ed.), *Studi sulla questione della lingua presso gli slavi* (Rome, 1972), pp. 279–326.

Mannheim, Bruce, *The Language of the Inka since the European Invasion* (Austin, 1991).

Marazzini, Claudio, *Storia e coscienza della lingua in Italia dall'umanesimo al romanticismo* (Turin, 1989).

Marfany, Joan-Lluís, *La llengua maltractada: El castellà i el català a Catalunya del segle xvi al segle xix* (Barcelona, 2001).

Marnef, Guido, *Antwerp in the Age of Reformation: Underground Protestantism in a Commercial Metropolis 1550–77* (Baltimore, 1996).

Martel, Antoine, *Michel Lomonosov et la langue littéraire russe* (Paris, 1933).

Martel, Antoine, *La langue polonaise dans les pays ruthènes, Ukraine et Russie Blanche, 1569–1667* (Lille, 1938).

Martin, Henri-Jean, *Print, Power and People in 17th-Century France* (1969: English translation, Metuchen, NJ, and London, 1993).

Martinell Gifre, Emma and Mar Cruz Piñol (eds.), *La consciencia lingüística en Europa* (Barcelona, 1996).

Mattheier, Klaus J., 'Nationalsprachentwicklung, Sprachenstandardisierung und historische Soziolinguistik', *Sociolinguistica* 2 (1988), pp. 1–9.

Mattingly, Garrett, *Renaissance Diplomacy* (London, 1955).

Mauro, Tullio De, *Storia linguistica dell'Italia unita* (1963: revised ed., Rome, 1991).

Mayenowa, Maria R., 'Aspects of the Language Question in Poland', in Picchio and Goldblatt, *Aspects*, pp. 337–76.

Megged, Amos, *Exporting the Catholic Reformation: Local Religion in Early Colonial Mexico* (Leiden, 1996).

Meillet, P. J. Antoine, *Linguistique historique et linguistique générale*, 2 vols. (Paris, 1921–38).

Menéndez Pidal, Ramón, 'La lengua en tiempo de los Reyes Católicos', *Cuadernos Hispanoamericanos* 13 (1950), pp. 9–24.

Metcalf, George J., 'Abraham Mylius on Historical Linguistics', *Publications of the Modern Language Association* 68 (1953), pp. 535–54.

Metcalf, George J., 'The Indo-European Hypothesis in the Sixteenth and Seventeenth Centuries', in Dell Hymes (ed.), *Studies in the History of Linguistics* (Bloomington, 1974), pp. 233–57.

Mietzsche, Alfred ['Frido Mětšk'], 'Der Entstehung der obersorbischen Schriftsprache (1668–1728), *Zeitschrift für Slavische Philologie* 28 (1960), pp. 122–48.

Migliorini, Bruno, *Saggi linguistici* (Florence, 1956).

Mignolo, Walter D., 'On the Colonization of Amerindian Languages and Memories', *Comparative Studies in Society and History* 34 (1992), pp. 301–30.

Milhou, Alain, 'Les politiques de la langue à l'époque moderne de l'Europe et l'Amérique', in Bénassy-Berling, Clément and Milhou, *Langues et cultures*, pp. 15–40.

Miller, Peter, *Peiresc's Europe* (New Haven, 2000).

Milo, Daniel, 'La bourse mondiale de la traduction: un baromètre culturel?' *Annales: économies, sociétés, civilisations* 39 (1984), pp. 93–115.

Milroy, James, *Linguistic Variation and Change* (London, 1992).

Milroy, James, 'Toward a Speaker-Based Account of Language Change', in Jahr, *Language Change*, pp. 21–36.

Mirambel, André, 'Les aspects psychologiques du purisme dans la Grèce moderne', *Journal de Psychologie* (1964), pp. 405–36.

Mitchell, Linda C., *Grammar Wars: Language as Cultural Battlefield in 17th- and 18th-Century England* (Aldershot, 2001).

Mohrmann, Christine, *Die altchristliche Sondersprache in den Sermones des hl. Augustin* (Nijmegen, 1932).

Mohrmann, Christine, *Latin vulgaire, Latin des chrétiens, Latin médiéval* (Paris, 1955).

Molière, Jean-Baptiste, *Les Précieuses Ridicules*, ed. Micheline Cuénin (Geneva, 1973).

Mongin, Edme, *Oraison funèbre de Louis le Grand* (Paris, 1715).

Morson, Gary S., and Caryl Emerson, *Mikhail Bakhtin: Creation of a Prosaics* (Stanford, 1990).

Moryson, Fynes, *Shakespeare's Europe* (London, 1903).

Mossé, Fernand, *Esquisse d'une histoire de la langue anglaise* (Lyon, 1947).

Mugglestone, Lynda, *'Talking Proper': The Rise of Accent as Social Symbol* (Oxford, 1995).

Mulcaster, Richard, *The First Part of the Elementarie* (1582: facsimile repr., Menston, 1970).

Mulertt, Werner, 'Aus der Geschichte der Spanische Sprachreinigungsbestrebungen', *Estudios Adolfo Bonilla* (Madrid, 1927), vol. 1, pp. 583–603.

Nadal, Josep M., 'El català en els segles xvi i xvii', *L'Avenç* 100 (1987), pp. 24–31.

Naro, Anthony J., 'A Study on the Origins of Pidginisation', *Language* 54 (1978), pp. 314–47.

Nebrija, Antonio, *Gramática de la lengua castellana* (1492: ed. Antonio Quilis, Madrid, 1989).

Neri, Ferdinando, *Letteratura e legende* (Milan, 1951).

Nettle, Daniel, and Suzanne Romaine, *Vanishing Voices* (London, 2000).

Nevaainen, Terttu, 'Lexis and Semantics', in Lass, *Cambridge History*, pp. 332–458.

Niederehe, Hans-Josef, *Die Sprachauffassung Alfons des Weisen* (Tübingen, 1975).

Nordström, Johan, *De Yverborenes Ö* (Stockholm, 1934).

Notestein, Wallace (ed.), *Commons Debates 1621*, vol. 2 (New Haven, 1935).

Nunes de Leão, Duarte, *Ortografia* (1576) and *Origem de língua portuguesa* (1606), in Maria Leonor Carvalhão Buescu (ed.), *Ortografia e origem da língua portuguesa* (Lisbon, 1983).

Ohlsson, Stig, *Skånes språkliga försvenskning*, 2 vols. (Lund, 1978).

Oksaar, Els, 'Social Networks, Communicative Acts and the Multilingual Individual', in Jahr, *Language Change*, pp. 3–19.

Opitz, Martin, *Gesammelte Werke* (Stuttgart, 1968).

Ormsby-Lennon, Hugh, 'From Shibboleth to Apocalypse: Quaker Speechways during the Puritan Revolution', in Burke and Porter, *Language, Self*, pp. 72–112.

Ortiz, Fernando, *Cuban Counterpoint* (1940: English translation, New York, 1947).

Paccagnella, Ivano, 'Mescidanza e macaronismo', *Giornale Storico della Letteratura Italiana* 150 (1973), pp. 363–81.

Paccagnella, Ivano, *Il fasto delle lingue: plurilinguismo letterario nel '500* (Rome, 1984).

Padley, G. Arthur, *Grammatical Theory in Western Europe 1500–1700*, vol. II (Cambridge, 1988).

Padoan, Giorgio, *La commedia rinascimentale veneta* (Vicenza, 1982).

Palmer, Patricia, *Language and Conquest in Early Modern Ireland* (Cambridge, 2001).

Paoli, Ugo E., *Il latino maccheronico* (Florence, 1959).

Parker, Geoffrey, *The Spanish Road* (Cambridge, 1972).

Parkes, Malcolm B., *Pause and Effect: an Introduction to the History of Punctuation in the West* (Aldershot, 1992).

Pasek, Jan, *Pamiętnik* (Cracow, 1929).

Pasquier, Etienne, *Recherches de la France* (Paris, 1566).

Pastor, José Francisco (ed.), *Las apologías de la lengua castellana en el siglo de oro* (Madrid, 1929).

Peiresc, Nicholas-Claude Fabri de, *Lettres*, ed. Philippe Tamizey de Larroque, 7 vols. (Paris 1888–98).

Peletier du Mans, Jacques, *L'art poétique* (1555: ed. André Boulanger, Paris, 1930).

Percival, W. Keith, 'La connaissance des langues du monde', in Auroux, *idées linguistiques*, vol. II, pp. 226–38.

Perion, Joachim, *De linguae gallicae origine* (Paris, 1554).

Pettegree, Andrew, *Emden and the Dutch Revolt* (Oxford, 1992).

Peyre, Henri, *La royauté et les langues provinciales* (Paris, 1933).

Pfeiffer, Rudolf, 'Küchenlatein' (1931: repr. his *Ausgewählte Schriften*, Munich, 1960), pp. 183–7.

Phillipps, Kenneth C., *Language and Class in Victorian England* (London, 1984).

Picchio, Luciana Stegagno, 'La questione della lingua in Portogallo', in João Barros, *Diálogo* (1540: new ed., Modena, 1959), pp. 5–54.

Picchio, Riccardo (ed.), *Studi sulla questione della lingua presso gli slavi* (Rome, 1972).

Picchio, Riccardo, and Harvey Goldblatt (eds.), *Aspects of the Slavic Language Question*, 2 vols. (New Haven, 1984).

Pimentel Pinto, Edith, 'O português no Brasil: época colonial', in Ana Pizarro (ed.), *América Latina: Palavra, Literatura, Cultura* (São Paulo, 1993), pp. 515–26.

Pittock, Murray G. H., *The Invention of Scotland* (London, 1991).

Polenz, Peter von, 'Sprachpurismus und Nationalsozialismus', in Eberhard Lämmert (ed.), *Germanistik* (Frankfurt, 1967), pp. 113–65.

Pontano, Giovanni, *De sermone*, ed. Alessandra Mantovani (Rome, 2002).

Postel, Guillaume, *Origines hebraicae linguae* (Paris, 1538).

Poullet, Edmond (ed.), *Correspondance du cardinal de Granvelle* (Brussels, 1877).

Pozzi, Mario, 'Il pensiero linguistico di Vincenzo Borghini', *Giornale Storico della Letteratura Italiana* 88 (1971), pp. 216–94.

Prestwich, Michael, R. H. Britnell and Robin Frame (eds.), *Thirteenth-Century England* (Woodbridge, 1989).

Price, Glanville (ed.), *Encyclopaedia of the Languages of Europe* (Oxford, 1998).

Price, Mary B., and Lawrence M. Price, *The Publication of English Literature in Germany in the Eighteenth Century* (Berkeley, 1934).

Prosperi, Adriano, *Tribunali di Coscienza* (Turin, 1996).

Puppo, Mario (ed.), *Discussioni linguistiche del '700* (Turin, 1957).

Puttenham, George, *The Arte of English Poesie* (1588: ed. Gladys D. Willcock and Alice Walker, Cambridge, 1936).

Quevedo, Francisco de, *Obras en Prosa* (Madrid, 1941).

Quilis, Antonio, 'Le sort de l'espagnol au Philippines: un problème de langues en contact', *Revue Linguistique Romane* 44 (1980), pp. 82–107.

Quintilian, *De Oratore* (Cambridge, MA, 2001).

Raes, Alphonsus, *Introductio in liturgiam orientalem* (Rome, 1947).

Ramson, William S. (ed.), *English Transported* (Canberra, 1970).

Read, Allen W., 'American Projects for an Academy to Regulate Speech', *Publications of the Modern Language Association* 51 (1936), pp. 1141–79.

Read, Allen W., 'The Assimilation of the Speech of British Immigrants in Colonial America', *Journal of English and Germanic Philology* 37 (1938), pp. 70–9.

Renzi, Lorenzo, *La politica linguistica della rivoluzione francese* (Naples, 1981).

Reuchlin, Johann, *De rudimentis hebraicis* (Pforzheim, 1506).

Ribeiro Chiado, António, *Auto das regateiras*, ed. Giulia Lanciani (Rome, 1970).

Richardson, Brian, 'Gli italiani e il toscano parlato nel '500', *Lingua Nostra* 48 (1987), pp. 97–107.

Richardson, Brian, *Print Culture in Renaissance Italy: the Editor and the Vernacular Text, 1470–1600* (Cambridge, 1994).

Richardson, Brian, 'La riforma ortografica dal 1501 al 1533', in Mirko Tavoni (ed.), *Italia e Europa* (Ferrara, 1996), pp. 257–66.

Richardson, Malcolm, 'Henry V, the English Chancery and Chancery English', *Speculum* 55 (1980), pp. 726–50.

Richter, Michael, *Studies in Medieval Language and Culture* (Dublin, 1995).

Rico, Francisco, *Nebrija frente a los barbaros* (Salamanca, 1978).

Ridder-Symoens, Hilde de (ed.), *A History of the University in Europe*, vol. 1 (Cambridge, 1992).

Riemens, Kornelis J., *Esquisse historique de l'enseignement du français en Hollande du 16e au 19e siècle* (Leiden, 1919).

Rist, Johann, *Rettung der edlen Teutschen Hauptsprache* (Hamburg, 1642).

Rivarol, Antoine, *De l'universalité de la langue française* (1786: ed. T. Suran, Paris, 1930).

Roberts, Michael, *Gustavus Adolphus*, vol. II, *1626–32* (London, 1958).

Roberts, Michael, *The Early Vasas: a History of Sweden, 1523–1611* (Cambridge, 1968).

Roberts, Michael, *The Swedish Imperial Experience, 1560–1718* (Cambridge, 1979).

Roberts, Peter R., 'The Welsh Language, English Law and Tudor Legislation', *Transactions Cymmrodorion* (1989), pp. 19–75.

Robinson, Philip, 'The Scots Language in Seventeenth-Century Ulster', *Ulster Folklife* 35 (1989), pp. 86–99.

Rodrigues, José Honorio, 'The Victory of the Portuguese Language in Colonial Brazil', in Alfred Hower and Richard A. Preto-Rodas (eds.), *Empire in Transition* (Gainsville, 1985), pp. 32–64.

Rössing-Hager, Monika, 'Küchenlatein und Sprachpurismus im frühen 16. Jht', in Nikolaus Henkel and Nigel F. Palmer (eds.), *Latein und Volksprache im deutschen Mittelalter, 1100–1500* (Tübingen, 1992), pp. 360–86.

Rogger, Hans, *National Consciousness in Eighteenth-Century Russia* (Cambridge, MA, 1960).

Romaine, Suzanne, *Socio-historical Linguistics* (Cambridge, 1982).

Rosenblat, Angel, *Los conquistadores y su lengua* (Caracas, 1977).

Rosetti, Alexandru, 'Langue mixte et mélange de langues', *Acta Linguistica* 5 (1945), pp. 73–9.

Rousseau, André, *Sur les traces de Busbecq et le Gothique* (Lille, 1991).

Rowe, John H., 'Sixteenth- and Seventeenth-Century Grammars', in Dell Hymes (ed.), *Studies in the History of Linguistics* (Bloomington, 1974), pp. 361–79.

Russell, Joycelyne G., *Diplomats at Work: Three Renaissance Studies* (Stroud, 1992).

Rydberg, Sven, *Svenska Studieresor till England under Frihetstiden* (Uppsala, 1951).

Sahlins, Peter, *Boundaries: the Making of France and Spain in the Pyrenees* (Berkeley, 1989).

Saint-Simon, Louis de, *Mémoires*, ed. Yves Coirault, 8 vols. (Paris, 1983–8).

Salmon, Vivian, *The Works of Francis Lodwick* (London, 1972).

Salmon, Vivian, 'Orthography and Punctuation', in Lass, *Cambridge History of the English Language*, vol. III, pp. 13–55.

Sanders, Hanne, 'Religiøst eller nationalt verdensbillede? Skåne efter overgangen til Sverige i 1658', in Sanders (ed.), *Mellem Gud og Djaevalen: Religiøse og magiske verdensbillede i Norden 1500–1800* (Copenhagen, 2001), pp. 231–52.

Sanders, Willy, *Sachsensprache, Hansesprache, Plattdeutsch: Sprachgeschichtliche Grundzüge des Niederdeutschen* (Göttingen, 1982).

Santesson, Lillemor, 'Ecclesiastical History III: Luther's Reformation', in Bandle, *Nordic Languages*, pp. 412–24.

Saumaise, Claude de, *Hellenistica* (Leiden, 1643).

Sauvageot, Aurélien, *L'élaboration de la langue finnoise* (Paris, 1973).

Sauvageot, Aurélien, 'Le finnois de Finlande', in Fodor and Hagège, *Language Reform*, vol. III, pp. 173–90.

Scaglione, Aldo (ed.), *The Emergence of National Languages* (Ravenna, 1984).

Schama, Simon, *The Embarrassment of Riches* (London, 1987).

Schenker, Alexander M., and Edward Stankiewicz (eds.), *The Slavic Literary Languages: Formation and Development* (New Haven, 1980).

Schiewe, Jürgen, *Sprachpurismus und Emanzipation: J. H. Campes Verdeutschungsprogramm* (Hildesheim, 1988).

Schiewe, Jürgen, *Die Macht der Sprache: Eine Geschichte der Sprachlichkeit von der Antike bis zur Gegenwart* (Munich, 1998).

Schmalstieg, William R., *An Old Prussian Grammar* (University Park, MD, 1974).

Schmidt, Herman, *Liturgie et langue vulgaire: Le problème de la langue liturgique chez les premiers Réformateurs et au Concile de Trente* (Rome, 1950).

Schottenloher, Karl, *Die Buchdruckertätigkeit Georg Erlingers in Bamberg* (Leipzig, 1907).

Schrijnen, Josef, *Charakteristik des altchristlichen Latein* (Nijmegen, 1932).

Schröder, Konrad (ed.), *Fremdsprachenunterricht 1500–1800* (Wiesbaden, 1992).

Schulenberg, Sigrid von der, 'Leibnizens Gedanken zur Erforschung der deutschen Mundarten', *Abhandlungen des Preussischen Akademie der Wissenschaften* (1937), pp. 3–37.

Schulenberg, Sigrid von der, *Leibniz als Sprachforscher* (Frankfurt, 1973).

Schultz, Hans Martin, *Die Bestrebungen der Sprachgesellschaften des xvii Jhts für Reinigung der deutschen Sprache* (1888: repr. Leipzig, 1975).

Scott, Mary Augusta, *Elizabethan Translations from the Italian* (Boston, 1916).

Seiffel, L., 'J. G. Schottelius and the Traditions of German Linguistic Purism', in Werner Hüllen (ed.), *Historiography of Linguistics* (Münster, 1990), pp. 241–61.

Seip, Didrik A., *Dansk og Norsk i Norge i eldre tider* (Oslo, 1932).

Seip, Didrik A., *Norwegische Sprachgeschichte* (Berlin, 1971).

Serianni, Luca, 'La lingua del Seicento: espansione del modello unitario, resistenze ed esperimenti centrifughi', in Enrico Malato (ed.), *Storia della letteratura italiana*, vol. v (Rome, 1997), pp. 561–96.

Sgard, Jean (ed.), *Dictionnaire des journaux*, 1600–1789, 2 vols. (Paris, 1976).

Sheridan, Thomas, *A Course of Lectures on Elocution* (London, 1762).

Sicroff, Albert A., *Les controverses des statuts de 'pureté de sang' en Espagne aux 16e et 17e siècles* (Paris, 1960).

Silverstein, Michael, 'Whorfianism and the Linguistic Imagination of Nationality', in Kroskrity, *Regimes*, pp. 85–138.

Skautrup, Peter, *Det danske sprogs historie*, 5 vols. (Copenhagen, 1944–70).

Skippon, Philip 'An Account of a Journey', in Awnsley and John Churchill (eds.), *A Collection of Voyages*, 6 vols. (London, 1732), vol. vi.

Slaughter, Mary M., *Universal Languages and Scientific Taxonomy in the Seventeenth Century* (Cambridge, 1982).

Solomon, Howard M., *Public Welfare, Science and Propaganda in Seventeenth-Century France* (Princeton, 1972).

Somaize, Antoine Baudeau de, *Le procez des pretieuses*, ed. Elisa Biancardi (Rome, 1980).

Sommervogel, Carlos, et al., *Bibliothèque de la Compagnie de Jésus*, 12 vols. (Brussels, 1890–1932).

Sori, Ercole, *La città e i rifiuti* (Bologna, 2001).

Spengler, Walter E., *Johann Fischart* (Göppingen, 1969).

Spenser, Edmund, *A View of the Present State of Ireland*, ed. William L. Renwick (Oxford, 1970).

Speroni, Sperone, *Dialogo della lingua* (1542: ed. Helene Harth, Munich, 1975).

Spieghel, Hendrik L., *Tweespraak* (1584: Groningen, 1913).

Stang, Christian S., *Die west-russische Kanzleisprache des Grossfürstentums Litauen* (Oslo, 1935).

Stankiewicz, Edward, 'The "Genius" of Language in Sixteenth-Century Linguistics', in Geckeler, *Logos*, vol. 1, pp. 177–89.

Stearns, Macdonald, *Crimean Gothic: Analysis and Etymology of the Corpus* (Saratoga, CA, 1978).

Stein, Gabriele, *John Palsgrave as Renaissance Linguist* (Oxford, 1997).

Steinberg, Sigfrid H., *Five Hundred Years of Printing* (1955: revised ed., Harmondsworth, 1961).

Steiner, George, *After Babel* (Oxford, 1975).

Stevenson, Jane, 'Women and Latin in Renaissance Europe', *Bulletin of the Society for Renaissance Studies* 19, no. 2 (2002), pp. 10–16.

Stevin, Simon, *Works*, vol. 1, ed. Eduard J. Dijksterhuis (Amsterdam, 1955).

Stiernhielm, Georg (ed.), *Evangelia ab Ulfila*, Stockholm, 1671.

Stock, Brian, *The Implications of Literacy: Written Language and Models of Interpretation in the Eleventh and Twelfth Centuries* (Princeton, 1983).

Stolt, Birgit, *Die Sprachmischung in Luthers Tischreden* (Stockholm, 1964).

Strassner, Erich, *Deutsche Sprachkultur* (Tübingen, 1995).

Strumins'kyi, Bohdan, 'The Language Question in the Ukrainian Lands before the Nineteenth Century', in Picchio and Goldblatt, *Aspects*, vol. II, pp. 9–47.

Suggett, Helen, 'The Use of French in England in the Later Middle Ages', *Transactions of the Royal Historical Society* 28 (1946), pp. 61–84.

Swain, Simon, *Hellenism and Empire: Language, Classicism and Power in the Greek World, AD 50–250* (Oxford, 1996).

Symcox, Geoffrey, 'The Savoyard State: a Negative Case-Study in the Politics of Linguistic Unification', in Chiappelli, *Fairest Flower*, pp. 185–91.

Taszycki, Witold, *Obrońcy języka polskiego* (Wrocław, 1953).

Tavoni, Mirko, *Latino, grammatica, volgare* (Padua, 1984).

Ternes, Elmar, 'The Breton Language', in Donald Macaulay (ed.), *The Celtic Languages* (Cambridge, 1992), pp. 371–452.

Teyssier, Paul, *La langue de Gil Vicente* (Paris, 1959).

Thiesse, Anne-Marie, *La création des identités nationales: Europe xviii–xx siècle* (Paris, 1999).

Thody, Philip, *Franglais: Forbidden English, Forbidden American* (London, 1995).

Thomas, George, *Linguistic Purism* (London, 1991).

Thomasius, Christian, *Von Nachahmung der Franzosen* (1687: repr. Stuttgart, 1894).

Tolomei, Claudio, *De corruptis verbis* (Siena, c. 1516).

Tolomei, Claudio, *Il Cesano* (1546: ed. Maria Rosa Franco Subri, Rome, 1975).

Toorians, Lauran, 'Wizo Flandrensis and the Flemish Settlement in Pembrokeshire', *Cambridge Medieval Celtic Studies* 20 (1990), pp. 99–118.

Torres-Alcalà, Antonio, *Verbigratia: los escritores macarronicos de España* (Madrid, 1984).

Torres Naharro, Bartolomé de, *Obra Completa* (Madrid, 1994).

Tóth, István G., *Literacy and Written Culture in Early Modern Europe* (1996: English translation, Budapest, 2000).

Townson, Michael, *Mother-Tongue and Fatherland* (Manchester, 1992).

Trenard, Louis, 'L'enseignement de la langue nationale: une réforme pédagogique, 1750–1790', *Réflexions historiques* 7 (1990), pp. 95–114.

Trifone, Pietro, 'La lingua e la stampa nel '500', *Storia della lingua Italiana*, vol. 1 (Turin, 1993), pp. 425–46.

Trovato, Paolo, *Con ogni diligenza corretto: la stampa e le revisioni editoriali dei testi letterari italiani, 1470–1570* (Bologna, 1991).

Trudeau, Danielle, 'L'ordonnance de Villers-Cotterêts et la langue française: histoire ou interpretation?' *Bibliothèque d'Humanisme et Renaissance* 45 (1983), pp. 461–72.

Trudgill, Peter, 'Third-Person Singular Zero' (1997: repr. Jacek Fisiak and Peter Trudgill (eds.), *East Anglian English*, Cambridge, 2001), pp. 179–86.

Turtas, Raimondo, 'La questione linguistica nei collegi gesuitici nella Sardegna nella seconda metà del Cinquecento', *Quaderni sardi di storia* 2 (1981), pp. 55–86.

Twaddell, William F., 'Standard German', *Anthropological Linguistics* 1, no. 3 (1959), pp. 1–7.

Underdown, David, *Pride's Purge: Politics in the Puritan Revolution* (Oxford, 1971).

Valdés, Juan de, *Diálogo de la lengua* (written c. 1536, published 1737: ed. Juan M. Lope Blanch, Madrid, 1969).

Vandenbussche, Wim, 'Triglossia and Pragmatic Variety Choice in Nineteenth-Century Bruges', *Journal of Historical Pragmatics* 3 (2002).

Varchi, Benedetto, *L'Ercolano* (Venice, 1570).

Vaugelas, Claude de, *Remarques sur la langue française* (Paris, 1647).

Veblen, Thorstein, *The Theory of the Leisure Class* (New York, 1899).

Verdenius, Andries A., *Bredero's Dialectkunst als Hollandse Reaktie tegen zuidnederlandse taalhegemonie* (Groningen, 1933).

Verdonk, Robert A., *La lengua española en Flandes en el siglo xvii* (Madrid, 1980).

Verstegan, Richard, *Restitution of Decayed Intelligence* (*sine loco*, 1605).

Vicente, Gil, *Obras*, 3 vols. (Coimbra, 1912–14).

Vigarello, Georges, *Concepts of Cleanliness* (1985: English translation, Cambridge, 1988).

Vikør, Lars S., 'Northern Europe: Languages as Prime Markers of Ethnic and National Identity', in Barbour and Carmichael, *Language and Nationalism*, pp. 105–29.

Vinogradov, Vladimir V., *The History of the Russian Literary Language from the Seventeenth Century to the Nineteenth* (1949: condensed adaptation, Madison, 1969).

Vitale, Maurizio, *La lingua volgare della cancelleria viscontea-sforzesca nel '400* (Varese-Milan, 1953).

Vitale, Maurizio, *La questione della lingua* (1960: revised ed., Palermo, 1984).

Vitale, Maurizio, 'Purista e purismo', *Acme* 17 (1964), pp. 187–211.

Vitale, Maurizio, 'Discussioni linguistiche del '700', in Formigari, *Teorie*, pp. 11–36

Vitale, Maurizio, *L'oro nella lingua. Contributi per una storia del tradizionalismo e del purismo italiano* (Milan-Naples, 1986).

Viziana, Martin, *Libro de alabanças de las lenguas castellana y valenciana* (Valencia, 1574).

Voloshinov, *see* Bakhtin.

Vooys, Cornelis G. N. de, *Geschiedenis van de Nederlandse taal* (1931: 5th ed., Antwerp and Groningen, 1952).

Voss, Gerard Jan, *De vitiis sermonis* (Amsterdam, 1645).

Vossler, Karl, *Sprachgemeinschaft und Interessengemeinschaft* (Munich, 1924).

Walker, L., 'A Note on Historical Linguistics and Marc Bloch's Comparative Method', *History and Theory* 19 (1980), pp. 154–64.

Wallenstein, Albrecht von, *Briefe*, ed. Ferdinand Tadra (Vienna, 1879).

Wallenstein, Albrecht von, *Briefe*, ed. Hermann Hallwich (Vienna, 1912).

Walsh, Paul, 'The Irish Language and the Reformation', *Irish Theological Quarterly* 15 (1920), pp. 239–50.

Waquet, Françoise, *Latin: the Empire of a Sign* (1998: English translation, London, 2001).

Waquet, Françoise, *Parler comme un livre* (Paris, 2003).

Wardhaugh, Ronald, *Languages in Competition* (Oxford, 1987).

Waterman, John, *A History of the German Language with Special Reference to the Cultural and Social Forces that Shaped the Standard Literary Language* (Seattle, 1966).

Webb, John, *An Historical Essay Endeavouring a Probability that the Language of the Empire of China is the Primitive Language* (London, 1669).

Weinberg, Maria Beatriz Fontanella de, 'La lengua española in América durante el periódo colonial', in Ana Pizarro (ed.), *América Latina: palavra, literatura, cultura* (São Paulo, 1993), pp. 493–500.

Weinreich, Max, *History of the Yiddish Language* (1973: English translation, Chicago, 1980).

Weinrich, Harald, *Wege der Sprachkultur* (Stuttgart, 1985).

Weithase, Irmgard, *Zur Geschichte der gesprochenen deutschen Sprache*, vol. 1 (Tübingen, 1961).

Wenzel, Siegfried, *Macaronic Sermons: Bilingualism and Preaching in Late Medieval England* (Ann Arbor, 1994).

Wermser, Richard, *Statistische Studien zur Entwicklung des englischen Wortschatzes* (Bern, 1976).

Wessén, Elias, 'Studier over språket i Gustav Vasas Bibel', *Nysvenska studier* 7 (1927), pp. 251–63.

Westrin, T., 'Några iakttagelser angående franskan såsom diplomatiens språk', *Historisk Tidskrift* 20 (1900), pp. 329–40.

Whinnom, Keith, 'Lingua Franca: Historical Problems', in Albert Valdman (ed.), *Pidgin and Creole Linguistics* (Bloomington, 1977), pp. 295–310.

Whitelocke, Bulstrode, *A Journal of the Swedish Embassy*, 2 vols. (London, 1855).

Wieruszowski, Helene, *Politics and Culture in Medieval Spain and Italy* (Rome, 1971).

Wilkins, John, *Essay toward a Real Character and a Philosophical Language* (London, 1668).

Willemyns, Roland, 'Religious Fundamentalism and Language Planning in Nineteenth-Century Flanders', *IJGLSA* 2 (1997), pp. 281–302.

Williams, Glyn, *Sociolinguistics: a Sociological Critique* (London, 1992).

Wilson, Duncan, *The Life and Times of Vuk Stefanović Karadžić* (Oxford, 1970).

Wind, Bartina H., *Les mots italiens introduits en français au 16e siècle* (Deventer, 1926).

Winge, Vibeke, *Dänische Deutsche – deutsche Dänen. Geschichte der deutschen Sprache in Dänemark 1300–1800* (Heidelberg, 1992).

Wis, Marjatta, *Ricerche sopra gli italianismi nella lingua tedesca* (Helsinki, 1955).

Withers, Charles W. J., *Gaelic in Scotland, 1698–1981: the Geographical History of a Language* (Edinburgh, 1984).

Wolff, Hans, *Der Purismus in der deutschen Literatur des siebzehnten Jhts* (1888: repr. Leipzig, 1975).

Wolff, Philippe, *Western Languages AD 100–1500* (London, 1971).

Wood, Michael T., 'Bernardo Aldrete and Celso Cittadini', *Hispanic Review* 61 (1993), pp. 65–85.

Woodbine, George. E., 'The Language of English Law', *Speculum* 18 (1943), pp. 395–436.

Woolard, Kathryn A., 'Bernardo de Aldrete and the Morisco Problem', *Comparative Studies in Society and History* 44 (2002), pp. 446–80.

Wordsworth, William, *Lyrical Ballads* (London, 1798).

Wright, Roger, 'Linguistic Standardization in the Middle Ages in the Iberian Peninsula: Advantages and Disadvantages', in Stewart Gregory and David A. Trotter (eds.), *De mot en mot* (Cardiff, 1997), pp. 261–75.

Wrigley, E. Anthony, 'A Simple Model of London's Importance, 1650–1750', *Past and Present* 37 (1967), pp. 44–70.

Wuorinen, John H., *Nationalism in Modern Finland* (New York, 1931).

Zsirai, Miklós, 'Sámuel Gyarmathi, Hungarian Pioneer of Comparative Linguistics' (1951: repr. Thomas Sebeok (ed.), *Portraits of Linguists*, 2 vols., Bloomington, 1966), vol. 1, pp. 58–70.

Index

References to English, French, German, Italian and Spanish are omitted as they occur virtually *passim*.